OBERBRECHEN

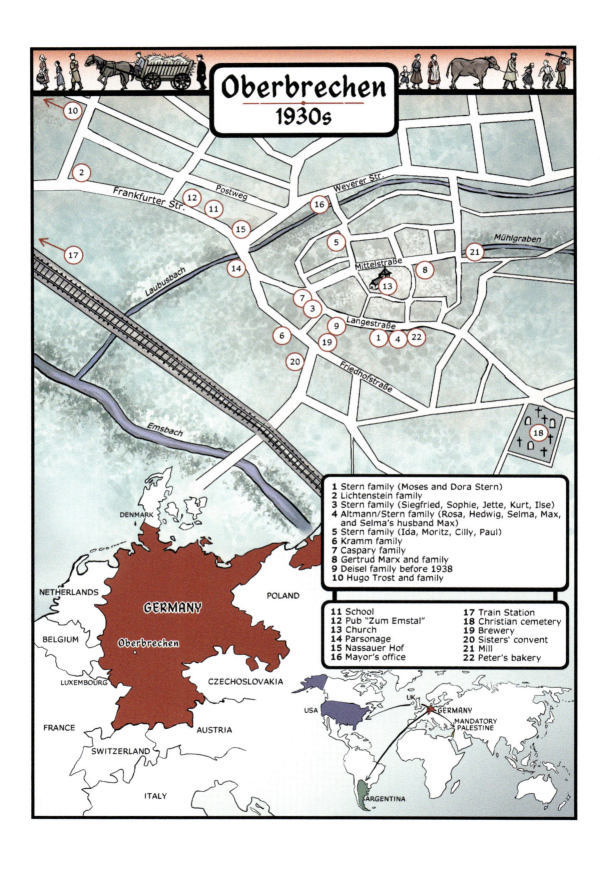

OBERBRECHEN
A GERMAN VILLAGE CONFRONTS ITS NAZI PAST
A GRAPHIC HISTORY

STEFANIE FISCHER

KIM WÜNSCHMANN

LIZ CLARKE

Oxford University Press is a department of the University of Oxford.
It furthers the University's objective of excellence in research, scholarship,
and education by publishing worldwide. Oxford is a registered trade mark
of Oxford University Press in the UK and in certain other countries.

Published in the United States of America by Oxford University Press
198 Madison Avenue, New York, NY 10016, United States of America.

© 2025 by Oxford University Press

For titles covered by Section 112 of the US Higher Education Opportunity
Act, please visit www.oup.com/us/he for the latest information about
pricing and alternate formats.

All rights reserved. No part of this publication may be reproduced,
stored in a retrieval system, or transmitted, in any form or by any means,
without the prior permission in writing of Oxford University Press,
or as expressly permitted by law, by license or under terms agreed with
the appropriate reprographics rights organization. Inquiries concerning
reproduction outside the scope of the above should be sent to the Rights
Department, Oxford University Press, at the address above.

You must not circulate this work in any other form
and you must impose this same condition on any acquirer

Library of Congress Cataloging-in-Publication Data

Names: Fischer, Stefanie (Researcher in Jewish studies), author. |
  Wünschmann, Kim (Researcher in Jewish studies), author. | Clarke, Liz,
  1982- illustrator.
Title: Oberbrechen : a German village confronts its Nazi past / Stefanie
  Fischer, Kim Wünschmann ; [illustrated by] Liz Clarke.
Description: New York, NY : Oxford University Press, [2024] | Series: A
  graphic history | Includes bibliographical references. | Summary:
  "Oberbrechen offers a moving portrayal of how Jews and non-Jews from a
  village in rural Germany experienced the devastating Nazi years and
  attempts at reconciliation in the postwar period. It includes a rich
  collection of primary sources, an essay that situates the stories of the
  villagers in their wider historical context, and an incisive reflection
  on the writing of this graphic history"— Provided by publisher.
Identifiers: LCCN 2024017249 (print) | LCCN 2024017250 (ebook) | ISBN
  9780197566039 (paperback) | ISBN 9780197566060 (ebook) | ISBN
  9780197566053 (epub) | ISBN 9780197566084
Subjects: LCSH: Oberbrechen (Germany)—History—Comic books, strips, etc. |
  World War, 1939–1945—Social aspects—Germany—Oberbrechen—Comic books,
  strips, etc. | Collective memory—Germany—Oberbrechen—Comic books,
  strips, etc. | Jews—Germany—Oberbrechen—History—Comic books, strips,
  etc. | National socialism—Psychological aspects—Comic books, strips,
  etc. | Stern, Herman, 1887–1980—Family—Comic books, strips, etc. |
  Graphic novels.
Classification: LCC DD901.O2135 F57 2024 (print) | LCC DD901.O2135
  (ebook) | DDC 943/.41—dc23/eng/20240523
LC record available at https://lccn.loc.gov/2024017249
LC ebook record available at https://lccn.loc.gov/2024017250

Printed by Integrated Books International, United States of America

CONTENTS

List of Maps, Tables, and Figures IX
Preface XI
Acknowledgments XV
About the Authors and the Illustrator XIX

PART I
THE GRAPHIC HISTORY 1

Chapter 1: Oberbrechen 3
Chapter 2: Nazi Persecution 17
Chapter 3: War, Holocaust, and Rescue 35
Chapter 4: Justice? 51
Chapter 5: The Orange Book 71
Chapter 6: Epilogue 93

PART II
THE PRIMARY SOURCES 99

Document 1: Letter from an Unknown Relative, Venlo, The Netherlands, to Herman Stern in Valley City, North Dakota, July 24, 1933 101

Document 2: Letter from Dora and Moses Stern, Oberbrechen, to Herman Stern in Valley City, North Dakota, December 31, 1933 104

Document 3: Letter from Ilse Stern, [New York], to Herman Stern in Valley City, North Dakota, March 15, 1939 105

Document 4: Letter from Herman Stern, Valley City, North Dakota, to James S. Milloy in Washington, D.C., January 15, 1941 107

v

Document 5: Letter from Herman Stern, Valley City, North Dakota, to Ruth Harrison, Office of James S. Milloy, in Washington, D.C., March 19, 1941 — 108

Document 6: Letter from Herman Stern, Valley City, North Dakota, to U.S. Secretary of State Cordell Hull in Washington, D.C., August 27, 1941 — 110

Document 7: Eugen Caspary, Diary Entry, November 16, 1944 — 111

Document 8: Carl Reifert, Entry in the Oberbrechen School Chronicle Detailing Events in 1945, undated — 111

Document 9: Father Alois Kunz, Statement in the Denazification Case of Former Oberbrechen Mayor Hugo Trost, April 29, 1948 — 115

Document 10: Letter from Franz Pabst, Flörsheim am Main, to the Denazification Board in Limburg an der Lahn, May 22, 1948 — 116

Document 11: Letter from Kurt Stern, New York, to the Denazification Board in Limburg an der Lahn, July 12, 1948 — 117

Document 12: Letter from Albert Schmidt, Oberbrechen, to Herman Stern in Valley City, North Dakota, July 20, 1948 — 119

Document 13: Minutes of the Public Session of the Appeals Court in Wiesbaden, Reviewing the Decision of the Denazification Board in Limburg an der Lahn, December 13, 1949 — 120

Document 14: Irene Lenkiewicz, née Lichtenstein, Account of Her Life under Nazi Persecution and in Exile, Composed in Córdoba, Argentina, November 25, 1958 — 122

Document 15: Letter from Carl Reifert, Oberbrechen, to the Compensation Office in Wiesbaden, April 30, 1960 — 123

Document 16: Letter from the Compensation Office, Wiesbaden, to Gertrud Marx in Oberbrechen, June 16, 1961 — 125

Document 17: Letter from Gertrud Marx, Oberbrechen, to the Compensation Office in Wiesbaden, July 1, 1961 — 126

Document 18: Letter from Mayor Josef Keuler, Oberbrechen, to the District Administrator in Wiesbaden, June 26, 1961 — 126

Document 19: Medical Opinion from Neurology Specialists for Selma Altman, The Hacker Clinic, Beverly Hills, California, March 1966 — 127

Document 20: Letter from Selma Altman, Los Angeles, California, to Mayor Josef Kramm in Oberbrechen, November 26, 1973 — 134

Document 21: Letter from Eugen Caspary, Niederselters, to Herman Stern in Valley City, North Dakota, July 7, 1974 — 135

Document 22: Letter from Gustave and Gertrude Stern, Seattle, Washington, to Eugen Caspary in Niederselters, July 11, 1974 — 137

Document 23: Letter from Gustave Stern, Seattle, Washington, to Mayor Josef Kramm in Oberbrechen, August 1, 1974 — 140

Document 24: Letter from Gustave Stern, Seattle, Washington, to Eugen Caspary in Niederselters, September 28, 1974 — 141

Document 25: Eugen Caspary, "Jewish Citizens in Oberbrechen, 1711–1942: A Survey," 1975 — 142

Document 26: *Nassauische Landeszeitung*, Report on Kurt Lichtenstein's First Postwar Visit to Oberbrechen, April 24, 1978 — 147

Document 27: Christmas Greetings from Selma Altman, Los Angeles, California, to Josef Kramm in Oberbrechen, December 1980 — 149

Document 28: Provisional Minutes of a Meeting on "Catholic Resistance against the Hitler Youth and the Repercussions of the National Socialist Seizure of Power in Oberbrechen," July 30, 1984 — 152

Document 29: *Nassauische Neue Presse*, Report on Kurt Lichtenstein's Visit to Oberbrechen, November 29, 1986 — 155

Document 30: Letter from Eugen Caspary, Camberg-Erbach, to Kim Wünschmann in Jerusalem, July 3, 2013 — 158

PART III
THE HISTORICAL CONTEXT — 163

Oberbrechen — 166

Nazi Persecution — 177

War, Holocaust, and Rescue — 190

Justice? — 200

The "Orange Book," or Local Attempts at *Wiedergutmachung* — 211

PART IV
THE MAKING OF OBERBRECHEN — 223

    A Conversation between Stefanie Fischer and
    Kim Wünschmann with Jay H. Geller and Deborah
    Pomeranz — 225
    The Research Process — 226
    Reflections on Methodology — 239
    Using the Graphic History Medium — 247
    Contributors — 258

Essay Questions — 259
Timeline — 263
Further Reading — 269
Family Trees — 273

LIST OF MAPS, TABLES, AND FIGURES

MAPS
Map 1.	German Lands, 1815–1866 (with Duchy of Nassau, 1806–1866)	167
Map 2.	The German Empire, 1871–1918	167
Map 3.	Percentage of Catholics in Population of Germany, 1925	183
Map 4.	Jews as a Percentage of the Overall Population of Germany, 1933	184
Map 5.	The Pogrom of November 9, 1938	191
Map 6.	The Federal Republic of Germany, 1949–1990	207
Map 7.	The Federal Republic of Germany since 1990	221

TABLES
Table 1.	NSDAP Results at Reichstag Elections, 1928–1933	179
Table 2.	Reichstag Election Results for the Nazi Party (NSDAP) and the Center Party (Z)	180

FIGURES
Figure 1.	Gustave Stern, Josef Kramm, Marcia Smith (Gustave's partner), and Eugen Caspary during Gustave's last visit to Oberbrechen in September 1989	227
Figure 2.	Josef Kramm, Eugen Caspary, and Kurt Lichtenstein during a visit in Oberbrechen, Kramm family home, early 1980s	228
Figure 3.	Gertrude Stern at the Jewish Cemetery in Weyer during a visit to Oberbrechen in the 1970s	230
Figure 4.	Scene from the theater performance *Dorfgeschichte(n)—Fragmente aus 1250 Jahren Niederbrechen und Oberbrechen* (Village History/ies: Fragments from 1250 Years of Niederbrechen and Oberbrechen), directed by Cara Basquitt, showing Selma and Max Altmann with Gertrud Marx (standing), Oberbrechen, July 2022	240

Figure 5. An early draft shows Father Alois Kunz wearing a chasuble while collecting money for a new church building, Oberbrechen, 1933 — 248

Figure 6. After Professor Matthias Theodor Kloft from the museum of the Limburg diocese explained that priests do not wear a chasuble when collecting money, we asked Liz Clarke to remove it from the picture — 249

Figure 7. Students attending the *Volkschule* Oberbrechen, the village's local school, shown in a photograph taken by Chaplain Franz Pabst between 1936 and 1939 — 251

Figure 8. Drawing by Liz Clarke showing Kurt Lichtenstein as an adult at *Volksschule* Oberbrechen, 1930s — 252

PREFACE

In this book, we examine a single place in Germany: the village of Oberbrechen in Hesse. There is nothing particularly important about Oberbrechen. But this village of just a few hundred inhabitants opens a window onto a rich history of Jewish–non-Jewish relations in twentieth-century Germany. Oberbrechen is a predominantly Catholic village in west-central Germany that was home to a small Jewish community before the Nazi takeover of power in 1933. Through the lens of this village, we tell an intimate history of Jews and non-Jews, and address painful questions about how the horrific events of the twentieth century shaped the lives of its residents, ultimately ending Jewish life in the village. However, the book does not end there. It continues into the postwar period and asks how processes of denazification, restitution, and compensation impacted the lives of Jews and non-Jews in the aftermath of the Holocaust. It shifts the focus away from Germany's postwar political and intellectual elite, shining a spotlight on the grassroots level, such as local politicians, the clergy, public historians, and schoolteachers. This microhistory reveals how these "ordinary people" actively participated in the process of how Germany dealt with its Nazi past and performed what they understood as *Wiedergutmachung* ("making good again"). It also shows how Jews from Oberbrechen, who found themselves scattered all over the globe, passively and actively engaged in the German process of *Vergangenheitsbewältigung* (coming to terms with the past). By considering these different perspectives, *Oberbrechen: A German Village Confronts Its Nazi Past* brings to light the many inconsistencies and flaws that have accompanied a process that continues to this day.

When we began working on this project, we had many questions, some of which are voiced in the opening sequences of the Graphic History (Part I). These panels depict the start of our intellectual journey into a troubled past. As life under Nazism deeply affected social bonds in the village microcosm— just as it did everywhere else in Germany—we asked ourselves: How did Christians and Jews live together in the village, what did their daily lives look like, and how did the Nazi dictatorship impact their lives, individually and collectively? How did Jews experience persecution and their displacement from the Hessian village? How could they rebuild their lives in exile? What was the fate of those who did not survive the Holocaust?

On the basis of a rich collection of so far unknown private letters, photographs, and documents, we draw a nuanced picture of Jewish and Catholic life in the village before Nazism and how it gradually changed after Hitler's takeover of power in 1933. Oberbrechen's Catholic population, which predominately voted for the Christian democratic Center Party in pre-1933 free elections, experienced a dramatic disruption of religious and communal life through the anticlerical policy of the Nazi state. We also discuss how Nazism's struggle against the Catholic Church affected the Christian villagers. How did they react to Nazi oppression? To what extent did they take part in and benefit from the dispossession and expulsion of their Jewish neighbors? The results of this research, which brought us in contact with researchers and survivors from Argentina, Germany, Israel, and the United States, are presented in this book.

In line with wider historiographical trends, this study aims to contribute to the "social turn" in Holocaust Studies, taking into account the experiences and agencies of the persecuted and the behavior of their non-Jewish contemporaries to analyze how Nazi policies played out in everyday life. Scholars increasingly explore and reevaluate the role of ordinary people, and how their attitudes and reactions changed depending on circumstances. *Oberbrechen* sheds light on different reactions to the Nazi regime's all-embracing effort to mobilize so-called "national comrades" in a racialized "people's community" while defining political opponents, social outsiders, Jews, and other racially targeted "community aliens" as "enemies of the people." In researching these reactions, we seek to dispel the still widely held claims that those who lived through the dictatorship could have been uninvolved "bystanders."

Our study also contributes to the field of Aftermath Studies that explores how experiences of Nazi violence continue to shape the history of the postwar years. Apart from the ever-growing research on German-Jewish history before and during the Holocaust, scholars are increasingly investigating the years and decades after the Second World War not just as an epilogue to catastrophe, but as a period in its own right. While the overall atmosphere in postwar Germany was still antisemitic after 1945, a growing interest in Jews and all things Jewish in the Federal Republic began to become discernible in the early 1970s. In a country in which the Jewish community amounted to, at best, a tenth of the pre-Nazi era population of about half a million, the younger generation of non-Jewish Germans (many of them raised and educated during the 1930s and 1940s) gradually started researching the history of German Jews. These research projects conducted by public historians set in motion a genuine, but also fraught, social process of coming to terms with the past that continued after the German reunification of 1989–1990, as the example of Oberbrechen shows. Similarly complex issues of identity and belonging occupied Jews of German origin in the diaspora. Those Jews from Oberbrechen who managed to escape Nazism rebuilt their lives under extremely harsh conditions in Argentina, Palestine (later Israel), or the United States. Their ambiguous relationship to German language and culture, but also to their places of origin, is also addressed in this book.

In all this scholarship, we argue, the countryside has been neglected as a space for Jewish–non-Jewish relations. Individuals from rural communities are too often relegated to the margins of historiography, despite the fact that rural areas had been a center of interactions between Jews and non-Jews for centuries. As late as 1933, up to one-fifth of all German Jews were still living in rural settings where they engaged with non-Jews in the economic and social sphere on a daily basis.[1] In these villages and small towns, an often repressed history of anti-Jewish discrimination held particular immediacy after the Holocaust. Here, reconnections were highly personal affairs that forced ordinary people to face the acutely painful legacies of violence and collaboration perpetrated within their own communities. An appreciation of the everyday-life experiences of people living in small towns and villages is key to understanding the multilayered historical processes of rupture and rapprochement that characterize the history of Jews and non-Jews in twentieth-century Germany.

Together with artist Liz Clarke, we study events in Oberbrechen in the form of a graphic history. We feel that the graphic history format strikes a unique link between more popular representations of the past and the rigor of historical scholarship. The combination of image and text that characterizes the genre of graphic history suits our approach of exploring ambiguities in Jewish–non-Jewish relations and the many things that have remained unspoken in this history. Moreover, the actor-centered approach taken by the genre allows us, the authors of this book, to connect the past with the present and to insert alter egos of ourselves into the narrative. While many scholarly texts on genocides and their aftermaths are written in a distant and neutral tone, our study stresses the personal dimension and vulnerability of history writing. By bringing in the personal, we aim to explore the long-term legacies of the German past—overt and hidden—and reflect on the impact

---

1 Monika Richarz, "Ländliches Judentum als Problem der Forschung," in *Jüdisches Leben auf dem Lande: Studien zur deutsch-jüdischen Geschichte*, ed. Monika Richarz and Reinhard Rürup, Schriftenreihe wissenschaftlicher Abhandlungen des Leo-Baeck-Instituts 56 (Tübingen: Mohr Siebeck, 1997), 1–8, here 1.

the Holocaust had not only on the lives of our historical subjects, but also on our own. We invite you to follow our research process as it unfolds.

While graphic histories and historiographies like ours may challenge constructions of historical narratives and push the boundaries of representation, it is important to stress that they are works of history rather than fiction. All characters, events, and places depicted in the graphic section are real. In interpreting the past as historians, we adhere to the standards of our profession and build our argument on the evidence in front of us. The book allows you, the reader, to go back to the sources and understand how we use them. True to the discursive nature of our discipline, you may pose your own questions to them and extract new meaning from them. In this way, historical studies hold relevance for our present and future.

Oberbrechen is divided into four parts, each with its own purpose. Part I, The Graphic History, tells the story of Jews and Catholics in the village of Oberbrechen. It uses the genre-specific combination of text and image to analyze the constructed and contested nature of historical narratives. It is structured into five chapters and an epilogue, roughly covering the period from before the First World War, through the Nazi years and the postwar era up to the present. Part II, The Primary Sources, contains reproductions and excerpts of key original documents from the period and place under consideration. Many of these sources are made available to an English-speaking audience for the first time. These sources provide access to an intimate world of personal stories and perspectives that shaped the history of Oberbrechen and its Jewish diaspora during the twentieth century. By reproducing some of the sources we worked with in our research, we encourage readers to undertake their own historical analysis. To make connections easy, we introduce each source by relating it to the moments in the Graphic History that were informed or inspired by it. Part III, The Historical Context, provides the background for placing the events that occurred in Oberbrechen into a larger history of Jewish–non-Jewish relations before, during, and after the Holocaust. The structure of the text with its five sections echoes the structure of the chapters in the Graphic History. Part IV, The Making of *Oberbrechen*, takes the form of a conversation with our colleagues Jay H. Geller and Deborah Pomeranz. It offers insights into how this book was created. We discuss the various challenges we encountered during the course of writing, and we reflect on the choice of the graphic history medium, our own relationship to the topic of our study, and ethical considerations in representing traumatic personal histories.

It is our hope that *Oberbrechen: A German Village Confronts Its Nazi Past* will provide not only a deeper understanding of German-Jewish history in the twentieth century, but also a deeper understanding of how history writing works and how it relates to us and our experience of the world today.

ACKNOWLEDGMENTS

One of the great pleasures of finishing a book is that it gives authors the opportunity to thank those who helped bring the project to life. We embarked on this journey shortly after finishing our first monographs. Over the span of several years, *Oberbrechen* brought together many people: historians, artists, archivists, editors, and other dedicated individuals across the globe. Their enthusiasm and support turned the graphic history into a unique collegial and professional, and a rewarding scholarly experience. It is our privilege to thank all of them.

A book of this kind, focusing as it does on the women and men, both Jews and non-Jews, from a single village in western Germany, could not have been written without the trust of those who shared their family histories with us. During the course of our research, we entered into the most fruitful and moving exchanges with the children and grandchildren of members of Oberbrechen's Jewish community, who live today in Argentina, Israel, and the United States. We owe an outstanding debt of gratitude to them for generously entrusting us with their recollections, including extremely painful parts of their family history. We learned more from listening to them than from reading any written document. Our special thanks go to the descendants of the Lichtenstein and Stern families, including Doris and Ronnie Frank, Evelyn Lichtenstein, Haydee and Beatrice Lenkiewicz, Susan and Scott Mayerowitz, Elyse Novello, Cheryl Seltzer, Yossi and Rivka Shachar, Margot Stern, Rick Stern, Walter Straus, Yehudit Turnheim, and Alan Ullman. We are indebted to Christof Caspary and Yvonne Habermehl, who helped us in so many ways and continued to give us access to Eugen Caspary's private collection after he had passed away. The Wünschmann and Kramm-Abendroth family was equally supportive. They contributed their own family history to this project, patiently answered our countless questions, initiated valuable reflections, and thereby taught us more about Oberbrechen than we could ever have hoped to uncover through archival research. We thank them for their time, curiosity, and the great care they devoted to this enterprise.

We could not have written this book without the support of many locals from Oberbrechen and its surroundings. Invaluable was the help of the Gemeindearchiv and the Arbeitskreis Historisches Brechen. We are particularly grateful to Doris Hecker, Gregor Beinrucker, Paul Dillmann, Ursula Königstein, and Jürgen Scherer. They also put us into contact with Philomena and Heinz Höhler, Ria Schneider, Mathilde Roth, Inge Stautz, and Thea Trost, whom we wish to thank for providing us with precious memories and materials. Huge thanks are also due to Cara Basquitt, Christa Pullmann, and the late Lydia Aumüller for discussing with us their work on Jewish–Christian relations in the region, past and present. We owe an immense debt to Markus Streb, who has accompanied this project from the very beginning until the day of publication, continuously offering advice and critical feedback. We were fortunate to benefit not only from his vast knowledge of regional Jewish history but also from his profound expertise in comic studies.

Apart from the Brechen Gemeindearchiv, many other archives, memorials, and museums assisted us in locating the sources for this book. We thank the archivists and the staff at the Central Archives of the History of the Jewish People Jerusalem, the Diözesanarchiv and Diözesanmuseum Limburg an der Lahn, the Hadamar Memorial Museum, the Hessian Central State Archives Wiesbaden, the Institute for the History of Frankfurt (ISG), the Jewish Museum Frankfurt, the Library and Archive of the University of North Dakota, the Magistrat der Kreisstadt Limburg an der Lahn, the Stadtarchiv Limburg, and the USC Shoah Foundation Visual History Archive. Finally, we are sincerely grateful to the institutions and copyright holders who granted us permission to reproduce historical images and sources in Part I.

Nina Caputo and Ronald Schechter introduced us to the world of "Graphic Histories" and the series of the same name at Oxford University Press. Their works were our inspiration, and we thank them for their support and guidance. Like them, we had the honor and the pleasure to collaborate with Liz Clarke. We highly value her artwork and professionalism and would like to thank her for creating this graphic history with us. At Oxford University Press, Charles Cavaliere took on this project with enthusiasm. We tremendously benefited from discussions with him as well as with Carolin Cichy. We are grateful to both for their tireless support. They carefully read, edited, and commented on the manuscript, navigating it through its different stages with superb editorial skills. Jon Ashby and Lizzy Emerson went over our texts with sharp critical insight, and their honesty and attention to detail improved our manuscript stylistically. We thank Monika Holzscheiter, Jeremiah Riemer, and Deborah Pomeranz for translating historical sources. Their rigorous and meticulous work provides readers with access to source material hitherto unavailable in the English language. Our special thanks go to Deborah Pomeranz, who joined our team as a student assistant and soon developed into an invaluable team member who accompanied our project for several years. We could not have done it without her tireless work and dedication to professionalism. We are indebted to Klaus Hesse for offering his deep knowledge of the visual history of Nazism and its material culture, in particular symbols and uniforms. Jay H. Geller contributed his expertise to Part IV. Working with him has been a rewarding collegial and intellectual experience. We thank him for his dedication and support.

We thank Cornelia Aust, Rachel Furst, Christina Morina, Ulrich Prehn, Daniel Uziel, Diane L. Wolf, and Frank Wolff for providing us with precious feedback on different parts of our book. Other colleagues who were kind enough to share their expertise and advice include Dennis Bock, Ole Frahm, Maria Fritsche, Sylvia Fuks, Christine Gundermann, Hans-Joachim Hahn, Laura Jockusch, Angelika Königseder, Yael Kupferberg, Jürgen Lillteicher, Lina Nikou, Cornelia Shati-Geißler, Christian Schmittwilken, Björn Siegel, and Anna Ullrich. Our special thanks go to Irit Dekel for discussing an earlier version of the graphic narrative with her class at the Borns Jewish Studies Center, Indiana University. We also owe a special thank you to the reviewers commissioned by Oxford University Press: Volker Benkert (Arizona State University), Tobias Brinkmann (Pennsylvania State University), John M. Efron (University of California, Berkeley), Peter Fritzsche (University of Illinois), Sheer Ganor (University of Minnesota), Emily Gioielli (Worcester Polytechnic Institute), Norman J.W. Goda (University of Florida), Marjanne Goozé (University of Georgia), Laura J. Hilton (Muskingum University), Katherine R. Jolluck (Stanford University), Kristin Semmens (University of Victoria), Lisa Silverman (University of Wisconsin–Milwaukee), Helmut Walser Smith (Vanderbilt University), and Robert Shea Terrell (Syracuse University), as well as some readers who wished to remain anonymous. They offered invaluable advice on improving our manuscript. For their support in developing the comics part of our project we thank Barbara Yelin, Tobi Dahmen, and Jens Rasmus Nielsen. We are also grateful to Charlotte Schallié and all colleagues from the project "Narrative Art & Visual Storytelling in Holocaust and Human Rights Education" for an inspiring workshop and lots of encouragement. Laura Arnold Leibman and the women from the AJS Summer Writing Class 2021 provided rewarding feedback on segments of the graphic narrative. Over the last decade, we have been given the valuable opportunity to present our research findings to different audiences and research communities. We want to thank all our hosts for inviting us to discuss our work.

Our colleagues at our home institutions supported us in myriad ways. We want to acknowledge the advice offered at an early stage by Ruth

HaCohen and David Shulman at The Hebrew University of Jerusalem. We are grateful for the discussions with Margit Szöllösi-Janze at LMU Munich, which helped sharpen our argument. At Technical University Berlin and at Goethe University Frankfurt, Stefanie Schüler-Springorum, Uffa Jensen, and Christian Wiese provided a stimulating intellectual and ideal working environment. There, Zelig Jacob Dov, Percy Herrmann, Lasse Meyerink, Mason Reck, and Tobias Wehrle supported us in researching and writing the book. We thank them for their assistance at different stages of the project.

Essential backing during different periods of researching and writing this book was provided by many institutions, including the German Academic Exchange Service (DAAD), the Martin Buber Society of Fellows in the Humanities and Social Sciences at The Hebrew University of Jerusalem, the Selma Stern Center for Jewish Studies Berlin-Brandenburg, the Association for Jewish Studies, the Goethe University in Frankfurt am Main, the Institute for the History of the German Jews in Hamburg, and the Center for Antisemitism Research at Technical University Berlin. We acknowledge the generous funding of the Volkswagen Foundation, which transformed the idea of doing a research project on Oberbrechen into a full-fledged graphic history.

Our co-authorship has been an exciting, inspirational intellectual and collegial experience for over a decade. We thank each other for this joint endeavor. Over the years that lie between the project's beginning and end, our lives changed in different ways, and our friendship deepened. We thank those closest to our hearts, our families, for all the love and joy they bring into our lives. We could not have done it without them.

ABOUT THE AUTHORS AND THE ILLUSTRATOR

Stefanie Fischer holds a PhD from Technische Universität Berlin. She is a faculty member at the Center for Antisemitism Research at TU Berlin. Her fields of scholarly research are German-Jewish history and Holocaust Studies. Fischer is the author of *Jewish Cattle Traders in the German Countryside, 1919–1939: Economic Trust and Antisemitic Violence* (2024) and has published numerous articles on German-Jewish history and culture.

Kim Wünschmann is Director of the Institute for the History of the German Jews in Hamburg. She obtained her PhD from Birkbeck, University of London. Her research centers on German-Jewish history, Holocaust Studies, and legal history. She is the author of *Before Auschwitz: Jewish Prisoners in the Prewar Concentration Camps* (2015) and co-editor of *Living the German Revolution 1918–19: Expectations, Experiences, Responses* (2023).

Liz Clarke is a professional illustrator based in Cape Town, South Africa. She has contributed to a variety of graphic history publications, including several titles in the Graphic History Series published by Oxford University Press.

PART I
THE GRAPHIC HISTORY

CHAPTER 1
OBERBRECHEN

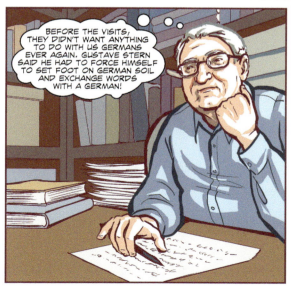

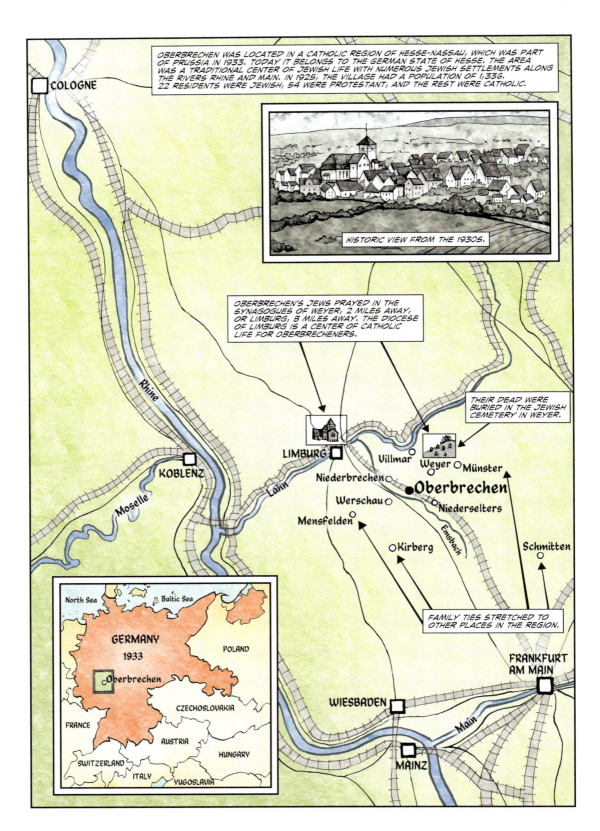

ACCORDING TO THE NEWSPAPER ARTICLE, KURT LICHTENSTEIN TOOK A WALK THROUGH THE VILLAGE WITH MAYOR KRAMM.

He also drove to the Jewish cemetery in Weyer where a number of his ancestors are buried...

...and he drove to Münster, where his father had been born...

...then on to Schmitten where his mother Flora and his sister Irene were born—and where, in 1925, he himself came into the world.

In the evening, Mayor Kramm arranged a meeting of their age cohort—all those who started school in 1932. Kurt Lichtenstein gave an account of the life he'd led since leaving Germany in 1937.

CHAPTER 2
NAZI PERSECUTION

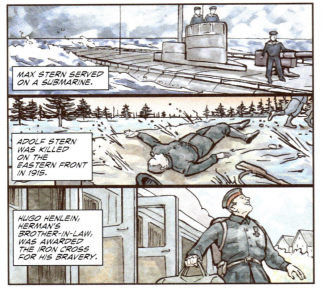

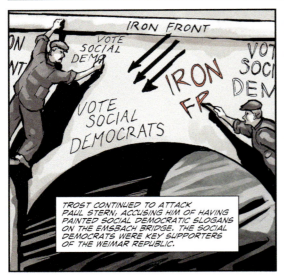

Venlo, Holland, 7/24/33

Dear Onkel:

You note I am in Holland, and I purposely came here to tell you a few things reg. conditions almost U N B E L I V E A B L E.

Before saying one more thing---I must warn you NEVER to refer to it in a letter to Giessen or Frankfort. When ever you write just say "I'm in reciept of your letter from Holland and glad to learn that every thing is O.K."

... On the street they holler "Send the stinking Jews to Palestine! Begone to Jerusalem, dirty Jews!" I know cases where six jews in one day committed suicide. My own Bother's bro in law committed suicide when these men came to arrest them.

... I tell you it is TERRIBLE. You say Rabbi Wise* talks about collecting two million dollars. While they need money these jews want to be safe of their life and NOBODY is safe. NO ONE is allowed to express his opinion. The new laws, ANYONE who gets or speaks AGAINST the new govornment or recieves sympathizing letters will GET SHOT TO DEATH.

... NEVER SAY ANTHING that you are sorry you heard about the cruel treatments. If you do write this and the letter happened to be censured they will be SHOT to death SHOT SHOT to death.

There is no civilization. All I can tell you is the jews suffer terribly.

... I could tell of hundreds of cases too cruel to write. I purposely came to holland spent my Railway fare an extra Visa, a special permit from Polizei Presidium just to write from a neutral country where mail will not be censured.

... It is simply terrible and the jew is boycotted worse today than 90 days ago. ON the bill borads large signs

> The Jew has ruined Germany
> The Jews: Germany's Ruin
> The Jew must be annihilated
> Don't buy from Jews

* RABBI STEPHEN S. WISE OF THE JEWISH WORLD CONGRESS RALLIED AGAINST NAZISM AND CAMPAIGNED FOR SUPPORT FOR GERMAN-JEWISH REFUGEES.

Most stores have signs in their windows: "A Christian German Business"

... And again Please tell them in Fargo SOMETHING must be done to help the jew (Not with money) that is all a mistake. They get assistance here most of them, BUT the Rishes,† the Torture etc. etc.

... for God's Sake tell Alex or any one NEVER to write to any one in Germany to say he feels sorry. It means DEATH

as ever

The Chammer

† "RISHES" IS YIDDISH FOR "MALICE," "MEANNESS." IT SERVES AS AN UMBRELLA TERM FOR ANTISEMITISM AND ANTISEMITIC ACTS.

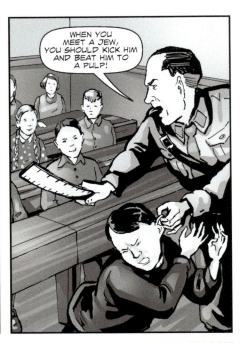

CHAPTER 3
WAR, HOLOCAUST, AND RESCUE

IN MARCH 1938, THE WEHRMACHT INVADED AUSTRIA AND THE COUNTRY WAS INCORPORATED INTO GERMAN TERRITORY. AT MUNICH ON SEPTEMBER 29-30, 1938, HITLER CONFIRMED GERMANY'S ANNEXATION OF THE SUDETENLAND (A PART OF CZECHOSLOVAKIA LARGELY POPULATED BY ETHNIC GERMANS). FEARFUL OF ANOTHER WAR, THE KEY EUROPEAN LEADERS—NEVILLE CHAMBERLAIN (BRITAIN), ÉDOUARD DALADIER (FRANCE), AND BENITO MUSSOLINI (ITALY)—SOUGHT TO APPEASE HITLER BY AGREEING TO THIS EXPANSION.

THOUGH THIS POSTPONED WAR, THE OUTBREAK OF RENEWED HOSTILITIES WAS ONLY A YEAR AWAY.

WHILE NAZI GERMANY GEARED UP FOR WAR, EUGEN HARVESTED POTATOES WITH HIS FAMILY IN THE FIELDS JUST OUTSIDE OBERBRECHEN.

FROM EUGEN CASPARY'S MEMOIR:

For days and then weeks we could observe the troop movements, a 'spectacle' that, for months on end, got us children spending all our free time playing soldier. We couldn't understand the adults' trembling countenances and apprehensive conversations about the dangers of a new war.
To us children, being a soldier seemed a glorious thing, and war appeared to fulfill dreams of danger and adventure.

When, nevertheless, around the end of the potato harvest the peace was saved by the Munich Conference (at least for the time being), it was not just the potato pickers who were gratified and rejoiced.

I SERVED IN THE GREAT WAR AS A SOLDIER, AND I STILL HAVE NIGHTMARES ABOUT IT. A NEW WAR WILL BE EVEN WORSE.

OUR FÜHRER WILL WIN THE WAR WITHIN WEEKS.

My dear Father was in the Buchenwald concentration camp for 4½ weeks.

Just recently, the [Nazi] Party forced dear Father to sign an empty page. We were supposed to sell our gardens. The mayor wanted to set the price after dear Father had already signed.
Eight days later a law was passed decreeing that Jews are no longer allowed to own property.
Now dear Father must sell the house too. You can't call it selling, as the Party decides the price. Everything goes way below its value.

I'm writing to you on behalf of your brother Moses. You shouldn't send dear Moses any money before he asks you.

EVEN BEFORE KRISTALLNACHT, THE STERNS HAD SOLD THEIR HOUSE UNDER PRESSURE TO THE SCHMIDT FAMILY. MOSES CONTINUED TO LIVE THERE AS A TENANT.

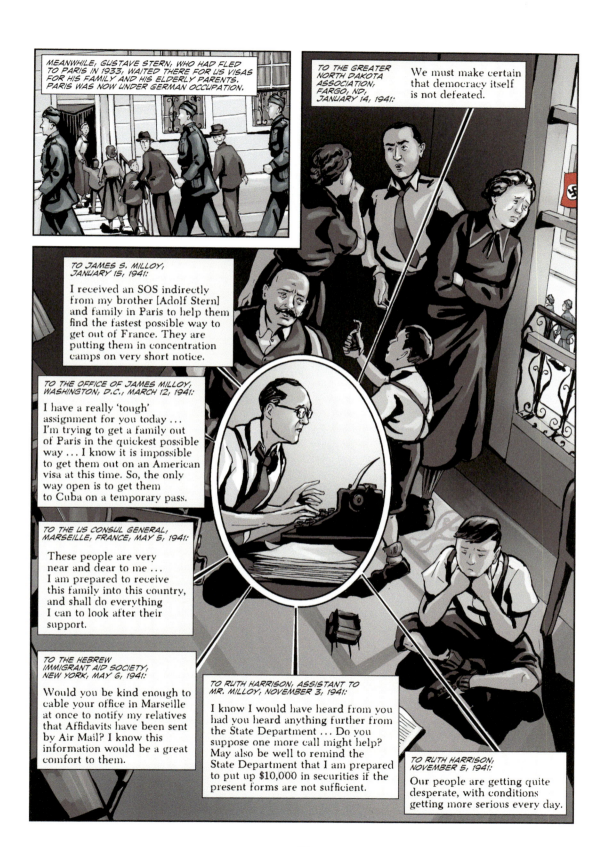

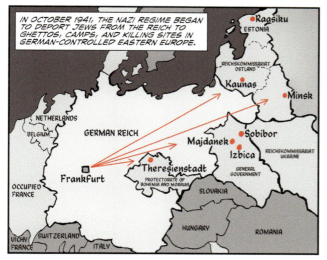

AFTER THE ALLIED LANDINGS IN NORMANDY ON D-DAY—JUNE 6, 1944—GERMAN TROOPS RETREATED FROM FRANCE AND THE LOW COUNTRIES. THE BATTLE OF THE BULGE IN THE WINTER OF 1944/45, GERMANY'S LAST MAJOR OFFENSIVE, WAS MEANT TO STOP ALLIED ADVANCES ON THE WESTERN FRONT.

BACK IN OBERBRECHEN, EUGEN'S WAR EUPHORIA CAME TO AN END WHEN HE VISITED THE WESTERN FRONT WITH THE LOCAL HITLER YOUTH GROUP IN THE WINTER OF 1944.

IN NOVEMBER 1944, EUGEN DESCRIBED HIS FEELINGS AT THE END OF THE WAR IN A PASSIONATE DIARY ENTRY:

I often find myself beset by uncontrollable fantasy, but I will try my best to suppress it. The war, which surrounds us and which we despise, is careering onwards, annihilating, trampling the earth, sparing no blood, ravaging peoples. The whole world is caught up in the terrible frenzy of "war, fighting, blood, death, a desperate struggle for existence."

CHAPTER 4
JUSTICE?

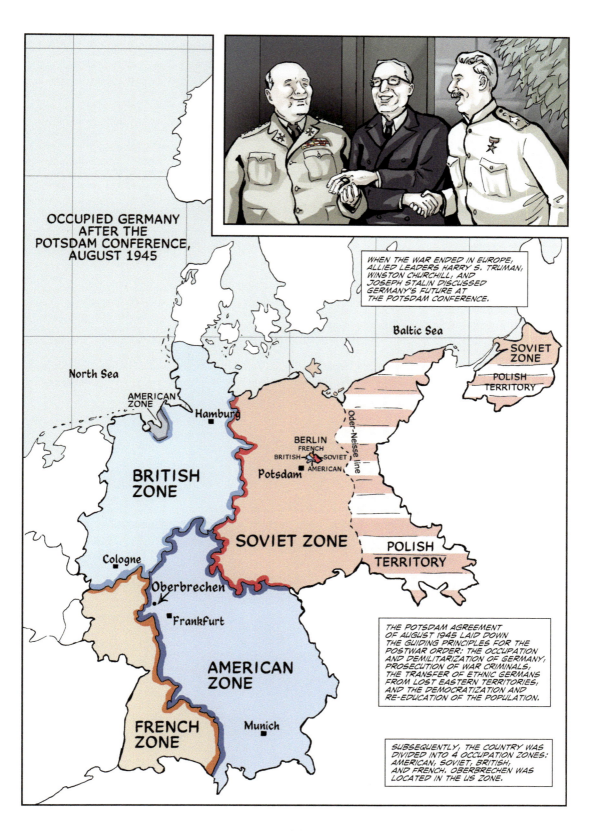

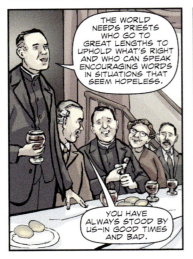

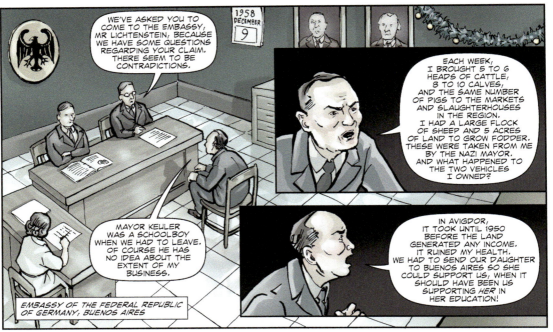

CHAPTER 5
THE ORANGE BOOK

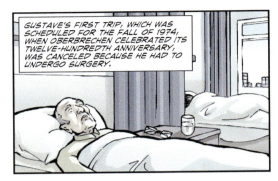

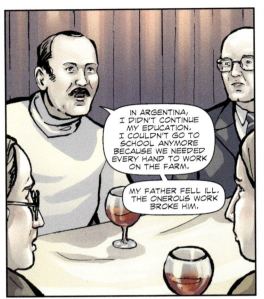

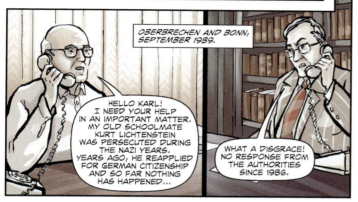

CHAPTER 6
EPILOGUE

PART II
THE PRIMARY SOURCES

DOCUMENT 1: LETTER FROM AN UNKNOWN RELATIVE, VENLO, THE NETHERLANDS, TO HERMAN STERN IN VALLEY CITY, NORTH DAKOTA, JULY 24, 1933

This source appears in Chapter 2 of the Graphic History, where it is partly reproduced on page 25. Here it can be read in its full length. As an urgent cry for help, the letter was written under an assumed name and in broken English, and the following transcription retains all mistakes and typographic choices that appear in the original. It describes the Nazis' anti-Jewish violence in Germany in 1933, which resulted in legal discrimination, social exclusion, economic boycotts, and professional bans that drove Jews into isolation and despair. Knowledge about the Nazis' violent acts traveled abroad through early testimonies like this, which pleaded for support from the United States to save Jewish lives.

This image shows the upper half of the first page of the original letter sent to Herman Stern.

Venlo, Holland
7/24/33

Dear Onkel:

You not[e] I am in Holland, and I purposely came here to tell you a few things reg. conditions almost U N B E L I E V EABLE. Before saying one more thing—I must warn you NEVER to refer to it in a letter to Giessen or Frankfort. When ever you write just say "I'm in reciept of your letter from Holland and glad to learn that every thing is O.K.

Well—the Jehoodems[1] and d o n e for in Germany and this is what happens everyday. In Nuernberg last Thursday four Jews were shot at and killed(no arrests nor did any police interfere) A low down southern nigger is a gen[t]lemem compared with a german jew.[2] On the street they holler "Raus nach Palestine mit den stink[i]schen Juden, Fort nach Jaerusalem mit den dreckische Judde"[3] I know cases where six jews in one day committed suicide. My own Bother's b[r]o in law committed suicide when these men came to arrest them. Listen to this. In Frankfurt they arreste[d] 45 Jewish business men and locked them up. To two o[f] them they told "Now get away. Run like Hell" and then the guards shot them to death and the papers naturally said jews tried to escape. Leoplold Stern was twice taken to clean bill-boards all day. The next time they got him again to scrub etc he fainted, took sick and was taken to the hospital. Burt Hirsch was knocked down. His bother was overtaken. He fled to Giessen and remained two week. Leopold fled to Coblenz. I tell you it is TERRIBLE. You say Rabbi Wise talks about collecting two million dollars. While they need money these jews want to be safe of their life and NOBODY is safe. NO ON[E] is allowed to express his opinion. The new laws, ANYONE, who gets or speaks AGAINST the new govornment or recieves sympathizing letters will GET SHOT TO DEATH. A Jew in Worms was locked up in a pigs pen all nite. I[n] Darmstadt and Hessen it is terrible. Now FOR GOD'S SAKE when you write NEVER say that you feel sorry for them. BUT you tell them in Giessen that you recieved

---

1   The origin of the word "Jehoodems" remains unclear. It is supposed to mean "Yehudim"—Jews in Hebrew. The Dutch word for Jews would be "Joden," or "Jodendom" for Jewry or Judaism (the German word for Jodendom is "Judentum"). We may suggest the author meant to say "the Jehoodems are done for . . . " (not "and").

2   The author compares the situation of Jews in Germany with that of Black people in the Southern United States. The use of deeply racist language in this context reflects the author's awareness of the dramatic situation of Jews in Germany but also conveys a lack of sensitivity toward people of color.

3   This sentence translates as "Out to Palestine with the stinking Jews, away to Jerusalem with the dirty Jews."

a letter from Herman in Holland and they all understand. Marta, Hans & Leopold and I all were together Sunday where Leopold is in a hospital he is a sick man poor condition. Sally M. also Leopold want their sons to come to U.S.A.

NEVER~~Y~~ SAY ANYTHING that you are sorry you heard about the cruel treatments. If you do write this and the letter happened to be ce censured they will be SHOT to death SHOT SHOT to death.

This letter is meant for you to tell Sam F. Bill Stern, Alex and Morris. All are charitable and Jews at heart. I wish Bill or Alfrd K. Stern could do something polically (not with a Rabbi) but with Senators or Congress or the PRESIDENT. There is no civilization. All I can tell you the jews suffer terribly. No one goes out at nite. They are not looking for money from the U. S. They want their liberty. I Just can't write more. I could tell of hundreds of cases too cruel to write. I purposely came to holland spent my Railway fare an extra Visa, a[s]pecial permit from Polizei Presidium just to write from a nutral contry where mail will not be censured.

One more SAY NOTHING in any letter that you write.

It is simply terrible and the jew is boycotted worse today than 90 days ago. On the bill borads large signs

Der Judd hat Deutschland Ruiniert
  Der Jude: Deutschlands Ruination
    Der Judd muss vernichted werden
      Kauft nicht beim Judd[4]
Most store have signs in their windows "Ein Deutsch Christxxx liches Geschaft"[5]

My own bother, the doctor, had to quit. My Bother the lawyer wanted to get his black robe from the courthose and was refused admission, Kein Jude erlaubt in Amts Gericht.[6] My sisters xxxx son, four years a lawyer, his sign was xxx torn down office closed. In fact I can't or wont write more. And again Please tell them in Fargo SOMETHING must be done to help the jew (Not with money) that is all a mistake. They get assistance here most of them, BUT the Rishes,[7] the Torture etc. etc.

---

4   These four German phrases can be translated as "The Jew has ruined Germany," "The Jew: Germany's ruination," "The Jew must be annihilated," and "Don't buy at the Jew's."

5   This phrase means "A German Christian business."

6   This phrase means "No Jew allowed in District Court."

7   The word "Rishes" refers to the Yiddish term *rishus* that comes from the Hebrew רישעת and means cruelty.

I spent my good Geld[8] to come to Holland and tell you a few things you haven't heard Half and for God's Sake tell Alex or any one <u>NEVER</u> to write to any one in Germany to say he feels sorry. It means DEATH

as ever

The Chammer.[9]

Source: Department of Special Collections, Chester Fritz Library, University of North Dakota. Herman Stern Papers, Series 1, Box 9, Folder 3.

DOCUMENT 2: LETTER FROM DORA AND MOSES STERN, OBERBRECHEN, TO HERMAN STERN IN VALLEY CITY, NORTH DAKOTA, DECEMBER 31, 1933

Jewish reactions to Nazi persecution were varied and depended on social status, economic ability, health, age, gender, and many other factors. This source attests to the difficult decisions on staying or leaving home in the face of growing discrimination and anti-Jewish violence. It illuminates the broader family background of Herman Stern's rescue activities and Klara Stern's flight from Nazi Germany discussed in Chapter 2 of the Graphic History. It is also a rare testimony of the older Stern siblings' situation in Oberbrechen in the early 1930s.

Oberbrechen, December 31, 1933

My Dear Ones,

We received your lovely letter and understand that all is well with you. I can report from our side that all is still well here, too. Also, thank you for the nice things you sent me. The overcoat is standing me in good stead, and the nice underpants are also keeping me very warm. When a third man is missing to play skat [in the village], I am always ready to fill in. I am glad that I can walk better again with my leg. Dorchen will write you with all other news. I am not a friend of writing.

Warm greetings to all of you,

Moses

Yes, things concerning Palestine are not so easy. Everywhere you hear that people who aren't able to take any money along have to work hard, that is, if they can find any work at all. Skilled craftsmen are among the professions

---

8 Geld is the German word for money.

9 The word *Chammer* comes from Yiddish and means donkey. It can also refer to a stubborn person or a simple person who does not know a lot; see Heidi Stern, *Wörterbuch zum jiddischen Lehnwortschatz in den deutschen Dialekten*, Reprint 2012 (Berlin: De Gruyter, 2013), 71.

sought after.[10] I already said that I wouldn't go there if it came to that, I'd rather go to America. There they won't have much use for old aunts. Here we are better off. My eyes are not good anymore. My eyesight is bad, I cannot read or write anything without glasses. Over Christmas I was in [Bad] Schwalbach for two days. [The family there] is doing well. Hugo [Henlein] still has an elderly aunt of 85 years with them, she is causing d[ear] Jettchen much work. Jettchen is such a good person.[11] Yes, Erich [brother of Klara Stern] is a big boy.[12] I myself haven't seen him for two years. He should get the suits you sent. When Klara comes, she should take them with her. I think that's all there is to report.

With many greetings to all you dear ones, I remain

Yours,
Dora

Source: Department of Special Collections, Chester Fritz Library, University of North Dakota. Herman Stern Papers, OLGMC 217, Series I, Box 9, Folder 51. Transcribed from handwritten original with the help of Paul Dillmann. Translation by Jeremiah Riemer.

DOCUMENT 3: LETTER FROM ILSE STERN, [NEW YORK], TO HERMAN STERN IN VALLEY CITY, NORTH DAKOTA, MARCH 15, 1939

The testimony given by Ilse Isabella Stern in this letter she sent to her uncle Herman Stern is illustrated at the beginning of Chapter 3 of the Graphic History. The 17-year-old refugee had arrived in the United States

---

10 This refers to the British control of Jewish immigration to Mandatory Palestine. The authorities issued immigration certificates based on applicants' economic ability or the skills needed in the country.

11 Jette "Jettchen" Henlein née Stern (1884–1977) is one of the eight children of Mina and Samuel Loeb Stern. She is the sister of Moses (1872–1942), Dora (1883–1934), and Herman Stern (1887–1980). Jettchen was married to Hugo Henlein (1864–1939). They lived in Bad Schwalbach in the Taunus Mountains, some 40 km southwest of Oberbrechen, until their flight from Nazi Germany with their daughter Lotte (1925–2004) in the fall of 1936. With Herman's help the family immigrated to the United States. (See Terry Shoptaugh, *"You Have Been Kind Enough to Assist Me": Herman Stern and the Jewish Refugee Crisis* (Fargo: North Dakota State University, Institute for Regional Studies, 2008, 140–142.)

12 Klara (later Clara) (1915–1995) and Erich (later Eric) Stern (1918–1984) were the children of Gustav Stern (1880–1944), another of the eight Stern siblings from Oberbrechen and brother of Moses, Dora, Jettchen, and Herman. Gustav and his family lived in Gerolzhofen, Bavaria. Klara Stern, who had received her visa for the United States in December 1933, was one of the first Jewish refugees who could escape Nazi Germany thanks to the support of Herman Stern. She arrived in the United States in early February 1934. The visit Dora mentions in her letter might well have been Klara's farewell visit to family members in Germany.

only shortly before penning her account of the violent events that unfolded in Oberbrechen in the aftermath of the November Pogrom, the Nazis' nationwide attack on Jews on November 9, 1938. She reports on the arrest of her father Siegfried and his deportation to the SS concentration camp of Buchenwald, and how the family was pressured to surrender their property. When she wrote this letter, Ilse's parents, her aunt, and Moses Stern were the last Jews still living in Oberbrechen.

March 15, 1939

Dear Uncle Hermann!

I hope you and your d[ear] family are in the best of health.—I have already been here for a few days and I like it a lot. D[ear] uncle, thank you so much for the papers. It is so wretched over there now. The conditions have gotten worse since November 9. My d[ear] father was in the Buchenwald camp for 4½ weeks. Unfortunately, he went through a great deal there. Your dear brother Moses did not go. He was there when d[ear] father was arrested. In the district, Jews up to 60 years old were taken. Nothing in Oberbrechen was destroyed, but the surrounding area is really horrible. It's indescribable. There is new turmoil out there every day. Just recently the police wanted to force d[ear] father to sign a blank page. It was supposed to be the sale of our gardens. The mayor wanted to set the price after d[ear] father had already signed. Eight days later a law was passed that Jews were no longer allowed to own property.[13] Now father must sell the house and gardens. One can't call it selling, as the party decides the price. Everything goes for below its value. Afterwards my d[ear] parents [and] aunt cannot stay in Oberbrechen. They want to move to Frankfurt am Main. That is not so easy either. They have a high number and, barring any changes, will have their turn in 1½ – 2 years.[14] It's very bad that they have to stay over there for so long.—I'm supposed to

---

13   The Decree on the Utilization of Jewish Property of December 3, 1938, forced Jews in Nazi Germany to sell or liquidate their businesses. Bank accounts were to be blocked and stocks and securities deposited with foreign exchange banks. Jews were forbidden to purchase or sell precious metals and jewels, which had to be delivered to the state.

14   This refers to the quota system introduced by the United States in the 1920s to control immigration. The quota restricted the number of immigrants that could come to the United States from each country. The restrictions placed on immigration were often based on race (*de facto*) or nationality (*de jure*). In 1938, the number of 27,370 was set for immigrants from the entire German Reich—an allowance that was far too small for the tens of thousands of Jews and non-Jews attempting to flee Nazi persecution. If the quota number for one country was exhausted for a year, one would get a quota number for the next year or the year after. People often had to wait more than three years until they could enter the United States. For many, the call of their quota number came too late—that is, only after the Nazis started the systematic deportations of Jews from the Reich in October 1941.

write you on behalf of your brother Moses. You shouldn't send d[ear] Moses money before he writes to you. He also wants to move to Frankfurt am Main. Moses still has his sense of humor. I've often said to my d[ear] father that I wish he also had such humor. D[ear] Moses visits all the Jews in the area. Every Sunday he's someplace else. When he's at home, he can be found at our place.—On behalf of my d[ear] parents and d[ear] aunt I'm supposed to thank you for their papers. If only they could leave Germany for another country soon! Over there it's getting worse by the day.—I have a housekeeping position and must start on April 15. Meanwhile I'll be with my d[ear] aunt to learn about running an American household properly. D[ear] Kurt is at work and sends his most cordial greetings, as do my other relatives.

I wish you, especially, all the best, and thank you once again for everything, from your,

Ilse Stern

Best wishes to the Henlein family too. I'll have a letter sent to them soon.

Source: Department of Special Collections, Chester Fritz Library, University of North Dakota. Herman Stern Papers, Series 1, World War II, Sub-Series A, Box 9, Folder 50: Correspondence—German Political Refugees: Stern, Kurt and Ilse (1938–1941). Translation by Deborah Pomeranz.

DOCUMENT 4: LETTER FROM HERMAN STERN, VALLEY CITY, NORTH DAKOTA, TO JAMES S. MILLOY IN WASHINGTON, D.C., JANUARY 15, 1941

Herman Stern's restless activities to rescue Jews from Nazi oppression are depicted in Chapter 3 of the Graphic History. An important ally for Stern was the businessman and journalist James S. Milloy. They had met in North Dakota where the Canadian-born Milloy served as secretary of the Greater North Dakota Association, a state chamber of commerce. In 1931, Milloy started working for the Minneapolis Tribune and was sent to Washington, D.C., as a correspondent. His influential network reached into government institutions like the State Department, which was responsible for the allocation of visas. In Stern's words, Milloy was "a man who can get results." When their collaboration intensified during the refugee crisis triggered by the 1938 November Pogrom, this "marked a turning point in Stern's mission to help Jews."[15]

---

15 Herman Stern to James Milloy, November 13, 1938, quoted in: Shoptaugh, *"You Have Been Kind Enough to Assist Me"*, 222. See ibid. 45–46, 221–223.

Mr. James S. Milloy

Hamilton Hotel
Washington, D.C.

Dear Jim:

Thanks very much for your telegram.

I received an SOS indirectly from my brother and family in Paris to help them the fastest possible way to get out of France. They are putting them in concentration camps on very short notice.

I am following directions of telegram to see what can be done.

Dr. Lavine was very grateful for your fine reception and the valuable information you gave him.

Is it worth while to follow up that project?

I hope the New Year is starting nicely for you and your family.

With kindest regards, I am

Sincerely yours,
Herman Stern
HS:C
Jan. 15, 1941

Source: Department of Special Collections, Chester Fritz Library, University of North Dakota. Herman Stern Papers, Series 1: World War II, Sub-Series A, Box 9, Folder 46: Correspondence—German Political Refugees: Stern, Gustav and Adolf (1940–1942).

DOCUMENT 5: LETTER FROM HERMAN STERN, VALLEY CITY, NORTH DAKOTA, TO RUTH HARRISON, OFFICE OF JAMES S. MILLOY, IN WASHINGTON, D.C., MARCH 19, 1941

The rescue of Herman Stern's brother Adolf and his nephew Gustave and their families is depicted in Chapter 3 of the Graphic History. This letter is addressed to Ruth Harrison, who was James S. Milloy's assistant at the time. She was instrumental in finding ways to bring the family from their exile in France to the United States, which proved to be an especially difficult mission.[16] Quotes from other letters between Herman Stern and Ruth Harrison can be found in the same chapter.

Mrs. Ruth Harrison

Office of James Milloy
Hotel Hamilton
Washington, D.C.

My dear Mrs. Harrison:

I have a really "tough" assignment for you today, but I know that the more difficult they are, the better you like it.

I'm trying to get a family out of Paris in the quickest possible way. They are: Adolf Stern and his wife, Dora Stern; Gustav Stern and his wife, Gertrude, and their two sons, Ralph and Hans.

I know it is impossible to get them out on an American Visa this time. So, the only way open is to get them to Cuba on a temporary pass.

I am prepared through the nearest relatives to put up the required deposit which the Cuban Government will demand, as well as to pay for their passage.

Now, one of the difficult things is to get in direct touch with these people in Paris. The only way open is by the Diplomatic Channels. Their address is Square D—Aquitaine No. 8—Paris—C-19.

When I saw Mr. Milloy in Chicago, I understood that that was the quickest way to get people out of Europe at this time. As I stated before, their nearest relatives are prepared to pay the bill, and put up any amount that is necessary to get the temporary refuge in Cuba.

If this matter can be handled by cable, I would be very much pleased.

I expect to be in New York, and Washington sometime next month, and at that time, I will tell you how much I appreciate the many courtesies you have shown me during these past few years.

May I also congratulate you on your nice promotion and advancements since Mr. Milloy's new connections. You are very deserving of every promotion that is coming your way.

---

16 Shoptaugh, *"You Have Been Kind Enough to Assist Me,"* 280.

With kindest personal regards, I am,

Very sincerely yours
HERMAN STERN
hs;j
March 12, 1941
AIR MAIL

Source: Department of Special Collections, Chester Fritz Library, University of North Dakota. Herman Stern Papers, Series 1: World War II, Sub-Series A, Box 9, Folder 46: Correspondence—German Political Refugees: Stern, Gustav and Adolf (1940–1942).

DOCUMENT 6: LETTER FROM HERMAN STERN, VALLEY CITY, NORTH DAKOTA, TO U.S. SECRETARY OF STATE CORDELL HULL IN WASHINGTON, D.C., AUGUST 27, 1941

In search of support for his tireless rescue efforts (Chapter 3 of the Graphic History), Herman Stern turned to the highest political places. This source documents his correspondence with Cordell Hull, who served as U.S. Secretary of State in the administrations of President Franklin D. Roosevelt from 1933 to 1944.

Honorable Cordell Hull
Washington, D.C.

My dear Mr. Hull,

This is to certify that in the event that the attached affidavits for immigration visas are not found fully sufficient, I shall be prepared to deposit $10,000 in recognized securities okayed [?] by all National Banking institutions to the credit of Adolph and Dora Stern; Gustav and Gertrude Stern.

Yours truly,
HERMAN STERN
Hs;j
August 27, 1941

Source: Department of Special Collections, Chester Fritz Library, University of North Dakota. Herman Stern Papers, Series 1: World War II, Sub-Series A, Box 9, Folder 46: Correspondence—German Political Refugees: Stern, Gustav and Adolf (1940–1942).

DOCUMENT 7: EUGEN CASPARY, DIARY ENTRY, NOVEMBER 16, 1944

Toward the end of Chapter 3 in the Graphic History, we learn about how Oberbrechen's youth experienced the final stages of the Second World War (see page 48). This account is based on Eugen Caspary's diary. Eugen was 15 years old when he wrote the following diary entry.

It has been more than two months since I last took this book in hand and set down my thoughts. Today I want to try to briefly describe the past and to chronicle some important facts about the present that encircles and besieges me. I'll try to rein in, as well or as badly as I can, the fantasy that often issues forth so vehemently from me.—

The war, which surrounds us and is despised by all, charges ahead; crushing and trampling the earth, not sparing blood, ravaging nations. The whole world is caught up in the terrible frenzy of "war, fighting, blood, death, desperate struggle for existence." "Fighting, life, death," those are harsh words; they accompany the war,—at every turn. Men in their prime, youth in their bloom—yes, the most brutal part of this only-out-for-extinction struggle between nations—old men, women, children, and young babes must be martyred because they are too weak to fight, because they are bound to lose this struggle for existence, overcome by the violence of enemies—at home and abroad. Who asks after the losses, amassing daily—at the front and at home! Who stays the bomber formations almost constantly flying over our heads! Who will put an end to their criminal game! The grief is only expressed in words, but—"the fight goes on!" Such is the call after every new defeat, and no one wants to yield, they would sooner allow the streams of German blood to flow on.

We as individuals can undertake nothing against this tyranny. Our words and deeds would get lost among the masses under the blows of the ruthless and unrestrained power of the ruling demagogues. The onslaught, the rebellion of the people as a whole must necessarily bring about their fall, but the pressure exerted from above is too strong to allow an uprising, a righteous insurrection, to emerge. Let us allow God and Time to decide. We must wait, wait for the liberation of our people from the yoke of a brutal reign. . . .

Source: Estate of Eugen Caspary. Translation by Deborah Pomeranz.

DOCUMENT 8: CARL REIFERT, ENTRY IN THE OBERBRECHEN SCHOOL CHRONICLE DETAILING EVENTS IN 1945, UNDATED

Head teacher Carl Reifert's entry into the Oberbrechen school chronicle informed the depiction of the village's transition from war to peace at the beginning of Chapter 4 of the Graphic History. His account of Oberbrechen under Nazism, delivered in front of U.S. military personnel, is shown over several panels. It provides insights into the postwar narrative of complicity and victimhood taking shape in the local community.

As 1945 dawns and not a soul believes in victory anymore—which we would gladly have experienced for the sake of Germany—the last reserves (even teachers of this school: Herr Reifert, teacher Kengel) were deployed for the *Volkssturm*[17]. . . .

When I was a *Volkssturm* man, I was caught off guard by the incursion of the Americans by the Rhine, and in an unparalleled nighttime ramble (during the day we were in the woods) I slogged through with five comrades eastward to Oberbrechen, where the Americans [had] already [been] for 3 days (in March 1945). . . . Houses (with baths) had to be evacuated, an American command post was set up, and every citizen from here had to register at the mayor's office in order to verify whether he belonged to the Nazi Party or not. Former party members were required to perform community service work by the Americans. . . . .

There were no lessons in school. First of all, the Americans ordered that all teachers be carefully scrutinized for ties to the Party, and as lessons began on Oct. 1, 1945, it was announced at a district teacher's conference whether each individual on the teaching staff was accepted or rejected. . . . Relations were very good, the Americans . . . behaved very politely and correctly toward us, even if now and then they judged the Germans abusively and emphasized the collective guilt of the German people. . . .

One day I (head teacher Reichert) was ordered to speak in front of a broader circle of Americans on the subject: Why were so many in Oberbrechen Nazis or militarists (synonymous with criminals). . . .

"*Gentleman!*[18]
Your comrade, a colleague of mine, has invited me to say a few words to you. I regret that I do not speak English very well, but I hope you will understand me. I shall read my thoughts out loud:

I've been a teacher in this village since March 1, 1916. In 1929, I became headmaster, and since 1929 I've acted as the organist in the Catholic church here.

---

17 The *Volkssturm* was a militia created by Nazi Germany toward the end of the Second World War. It was made up of men between the ages of 16 and 60 who did not serve in the military.

18 The text shown in italics appears in English in the original source, which is otherwise written in German. Reifert translated this first part of his speech, but his English is broken and contains spelling mistakes. In the interest of readability we decided to provide a corrected version.

There were no Nazis in Oberbrechen until 1930. There were traveling speakers who came into the village. They preached National Socialism. Their propaganda was addressed to the unemployed.—Oberbrechen has 1,400 inhabitants, of which 25 are farmers, most of the others artisans. From 1929 through 1933 the artisans were without work, there was hunger and poverty in the families, children were undernourished. Nazi propaganda was primarily addressed to the unemployed. The word[s] 'work' and 'bread' got through to the masses, and many people in town and country believed Hitler. The Church issued a serious warning: Hitler means war. Here in Oberbrechen most people followed the summons of the Church, and the number of Nazis remained small. The Nazis in the village were mostly strangers, newcomers. The poorest hoped for an improvement of their condition and became Nazis.

In 1933 Hitler came to power. With his followers he set up a dictatorship, which also had an impact in Oberbrechen: The mayor, a Catholic and man of the Center (member of a religious party), was forcibly removed. Without any court ruling! His appeal was unsuccessful. A dedicated Nazi became mayor and acted dictatorially. He had the power to 'rule' the municipality without the municipal representatives.[19] Yesterday's democracy was done in with a single blow. People felt how they lost their rights and opposition grew.

There were Jews in the village. They were no longer allowed to trade. Our village denizens didn't do anything to the Jews. In my class there was a Jewish girl, 14 years old. She was intelligent, good, and popular.[20] The schoolchildren had to join the so-called 'Hitler Youth.' Whether unemployed fathers got paid jobs was made dependent on 'voluntarily' joining the 'Hitler Youth.' In the Hitler Youth, agitation against Jewish children was organized (even against teachers who were not in the party—head teachers). A bleak time began for these Jewish children. Our teachers (3 of 4) supported these children—and that was "Staatsgefährlich" [seditious]— and the girl fell under the personal protection of the class teacher (head teacher Reifert) from home to school and back. The harassment became unbearable for the child. I stood up in a big way for the child, as a result of which I myself got into unbearable interrogations, and so I decided to release the child, who was legally required to attend school, early, before the expiration date for compulsory attendance, without informing the authorities, in order to end her torment. The child received her school leaving certificate with the best grades, and she was happy when the school door

---

19   After this sentence, the original reverts to German.
20   Reifert speaks of Irene Lichtenstein here.

closed behind her for the last time. The family emigrated to Argentina, which was fortunate, for otherwise the children and parents would have fallen victim to annihilation.—Village denizens thought the attitude of the headmaster was all right, but the Nazis rampaged against the 'Jew lackey' who also had to put up with the name 'Pope lackey.'—Politically I was declared 'unreliable,' and that started in 1933. Charges were brought against me by the party. Result: 10 hours of interrogation by the government. In addition: 10 hours of interrogation by the Gestapo (Secret State Police). The Nazis wanted to remove me from office. I defended myself, and here I had the good fortune of having people before me whom I could grab by their conscience. . . .

The Nazis, gentlemen, were not Germany. They were also not fighting for Germany, but for their power, to save their heads. The fallen sons of Germany and the many from our municipality [who died in the war] did not fall for Germany's greatness, but for the deluded idea of the Nazis who grabbed power through lies and deception. The party was not Germany, and Germany was not the party, and Americans need to know that.

According to Göbbels' propaganda, 99% stood behind Hitler. We knew that the votes at the elections were partly extorted, that invalid ballots were regarded as valid and included in the count as yes votes. Whoever talked openly about this ended up in a concentration camp. Whoever got out of the camp dared not talk about his suffering, for otherwise he went back there for good. There was no public opinion. Especially not in the war.—We were unable to remove the dictatorship of the Nazis by our own efforts. The dictatorship prevented that. What propped up Hitler was not 100 million Germans, but the SS, the Gestapo, who—for money and the best provisions—risked everything for their Hitler and beat to death every opinion.

Today the war is lost. It is a tragedy for our people. The greatest tragedy, however, is that foreign powers had to liberate us from an unwanted government that we were unable to get rid of by our own efforts.

A lost war is terrible, the guilty parties should and will be punished. But our people is blameless for the war. Certainly, there is an indirect guilt, in that we let ourselves be deceived and elected those responsible in good faith. Guilt is borne alone by these—I'll say this again clearly—Nazi-leaders elected by us in good faith. . . .

Every nation has a right to live and to be respected, and, gentlemen, hopefully the time will come when we as Germans again have an honorable name, and I wish and hope that you, the nation of freedom and democracy, will help us in this effort. The honest Germany has the will to this end!"

My remarks, which I made with a certain inner disquiet, left behind an impression in the ensuing discussion—conducted in English by Miss Spoo—that may be described as good. They certainly contributed to changing the preconceived opinion of the Yanks that all Germans are criminals. When I assess the behavior of the Americans subsequently, then this "address" was, after all, a bit of reconciliation.

Whether my prognosis was right can only be ascertained in the years or decades to come. In any event, for the time being there can be no thought of a change of attitude toward Germany among its enemy nations due to the terrible crimes committed especially against the Jews; this hate against Germany as a party liable for collective guilt has grown immeasurably.

Source: Oberbrechen Municipality Archives. Translation by Jeremiah Riemer.

DOCUMENT 9: FATHER ALOIS KUNZ, STATEMENT IN THE DENAZIFICATION CASE OF FORMER OBERBRECHEN MAYOR HUGO TROST, APRIL 29, 1948

This source inspired the scene in the first part of Chapter 4 of the Graphic History in which we see Oberbrechen's Catholic priest deciding to support former mayor Hugo Trost in his denazification hearing (see page 59). Alois Kunz's statement intervenes in favor of Trost, and with it the clergyman defends his former opponent. His act reflects a general tendency of the Catholic Church to issue so-called Persilscheine—*that is, attestations to whitewash former Nazis and other Germans implicated in Hitler's regime.*

Cath[olic] Parish office, Oberbrechen
Oberbrechen, 29 April 1948

Attestation
Concerning: Hugo Trost, Oberbrechen

Mr. Hugo Trost has been well-known to me since 1932. Though he had been *Stützpunktleiter* [local base leader of the Nazi Party] since 1933,[21] he was never one of those evil, disreputable Nazis. Indeed, that is the almost unanimous judgment of the people of Oberbrechen. I cannot recall

---

21 The investigation initiated by the Limburg denazification board found that Trost held the office of Nazi Party local base leader since December 14, 1932. Statement of claim, April 2, 1948, HHStAW, 520/38, Nr. 58640, 7.

that he caused anybody particular trouble or inconvenience. That also applies to me, both personally and in my position as Catholic priest of Oberbrechen. It would have been easy for him to turn me over to the Gestapo, especially as complaints about me were repeatedly brought to him as *Stützpunktleiter*. Nevertheless, he never forwarded a single one of these complaints. Furthermore, he regularly made ornamental wreaths and trees from the municipal forest available to the Catholic community for Corpus Christi and Christmas, contrary to the party's instructions. As mayor he could have easily obstructed this. Additionally, in Oberbrechen there was never a hint of anti-Jewish actions. Even during those infamous days, none of the local Jews were harmed in the slightest, nor were their homes or businesses damaged at all.[22] Although Mr. Trost left the Church, as far as I am aware he took this step due to irregularities about the requisition of the church tax.[23] He sent his son to Catholic religious instruction all the same.

I attest to the truth of these statements

The Cath. Parish Office
A. Kunz, pastor

Source: Hessian Central State Archives Wiesbaden, denazification file Hugo Trost. HHStAW, Best. 520 Nr. 58640. Translation by Deborah Pomeranz.

DOCUMENT 10: LETTER FROM FRANZ PABST, FLÖRSHEIM AM MAIN, TO THE DENAZIFICATION BOARD IN LIMBURG AN DER LAHN, MAY 22, 1948

The oppression that the Catholic clergy in Oberbrechen suffered under Nazi rule is depicted in Chapter 2 of the Graphic History. The following letter by Chaplain Franz Pabst is referenced in Chapter 4 in the scenes showing the denazification hearing of the village's former mayor Hugo Trost. Pabst had been asked by the denazification board to testify about his experiences in Oberbrechen between 1936 and 1939, and in particular about the role and behavior of Trost.

---

22 The reference here is to the 1938 November pogrom.

23 In Germany, a tax is paid by the members of religious communities registered as a cooperation of public law. It is collected by tax offices and is meant to fund the work of the religious communities.

Flörsheim am Main, May 22, 1948

To the Denazification Board
in Limburg an der Lahn
Schiede 14

Re: Denazification Board proceeding against Ortsgruppenleiter [Nazi Party local group leader] Hugo Trost from Oberbrechen

It is a fact that I, together with Herr Chaplain Schlitt, was reported to the authorities in 1937 in the manner to which you testified. Just as it is a fact that, as of May 29, 1937, I was no longer allowed to visit the school.[24] Whether the former *Stützpunktleiter* [Nazi Party local base leader] Hugo Trost took part in this suspension I do not know. I can only suspect that a certain teacher Semrau reported me to the authorities on a specific matter at that time.[25] Whether the former *Ortsgruppenleiter* and mayor took part in this I do not know.

F. Pabst,
Chaplain

Source: Hessian Central State Archives Wiesbaden, denazification file Hugo Trost. HHStAW, Best. 520 Nr. 58640. Translation by Jeremiah Riemer.

DOCUMENT 11: LETTER FROM KURT STERN, NEW YORK, TO THE DENAZIFICATION BOARD IN LIMBURG AN DER LAHN, JULY 12, 1948

Chapter 4 of the Graphic History discusses the denazification hearing of former Oberbrechen mayor Hugo Trost. Kurt Stern, who had fled anti-Jewish persecution in the village in 1936, intervenes into the proceeding with a letter addressed to the denazification board. In the relevant panels, he can be seen composing this letter in July 1948 in his home in New York (see page 60).

---

24 Pabst here refers to the withdrawal of his permission to teach Catholic religion in the Oberbrechen school. The withdrawal was issued by the President of the Wiesbaden governmental district of Hesse-Nassau on May 29, 1937. The same authority—much to the displeasure of the Nazis—had granted Pabst permission to teach in July 1936. Trost indeed had a hand in bringing about the withdrawal. (Letters of President of the Wiesbaden governmental district to Franz Pabst, Oberbrechen, July 9, 1936 and May 29, 1937, HHStAW, 411, 3060.)

25 Bruno Semrau was transferred from Berlin to Oberbrechen in 1935 and was a teacher there until his departure from the village in 1938. Semrau regularly clashed with Pabst over the indoctrination of Oberbrechen's youth with Nazi ideology and their joining of Nazi youth organizations.

New York, July 12, 1948

To the Denazification Board, Limburg/Lahn
(Case of Hugo Trost, formerly Nazi mayor)
(in Oberbrechen)

I recently received several letters from Oberbrechen and the surrounding area requesting that I be a witness in the case of Trost whom you in Limburg/Lahn are trying to acquit. Hugo Trost is a criminal and he belongs in prison. In May 10, 1934 Hugo Trost knocked me down in our garden in the Eichenborn [sic] district without any reason at all.[26] No. 2 Hugo Trost arranged to have the county governor [*Landrat*] suspend my father's trade license [on the grounds of his] being an enemy of the state. My father took on the lawyer Dr. Hilf Limburg with several appointments in Wiesbaden which cost us much money [but] we got the trade license back. Hugo Trost tried everything in his power to prevent it. No. 3 Hugo Trost said to my father when he was still in Oberbrechen living in our house: you must sell the house to the town for 6000 Marks, [and] if you sell it to private individuals or your neighbors I will have you imprisoned immediately. My father had a heart condition which Dr. Hilfrich in Dauborn can confirm for you. Mayor Hermann/Dauborn knew my father very well; both were together in the Great War. I ask that the honorable district court judges evaluate my statements and you [will] see that Trost is guilty in all cases. I am an American and will also contact the military administration in Frankfurt and inquire why Trost as 1 Nazis was released.[27]

I am prepared to provide additional information.

Sincerely,
Kurt Stern

Source: Hessian Central State Archives Wiesbaden, denazification file Hugo Trost. HHStAW, Best. 520 Nr. 58640. Translation by Deborah Pomeranz.

---

26 The Oberbrechen area of gardens and meadows is called Eichelborn, not Eichenborn. Stern's letter contains several odd-sounding "Americanisms" and typographical errors in the original German. A number of phrases also run into each other without proper punctuation. The English translation captures some features of this idiosyncratic style, which are conspicuous in either language. Others have been corrected in the interest of readability.

27 The meaning of "Trost als 1 Nazi" is unclear. It could mean that Kurt Stern regarded Trost as "a number 1 Nazi." One could also read it as Stern calling Trost "the first Nazi" in Oberbrechen. It is also possible that Stern was thinking of the category I, the major offenders, according to denazification legislation.

DOCUMENT 12: LETTER FROM ALBERT SCHMIDT, OBERBRECHEN, TO HERMAN STERN IN VALLEY CITY, NORTH DAKOTA, JULY 20, 1948

The second part of Chapter 4 of the Graphic History deals with the complex process of reparation to Nazi victims. It opens with a scene in which the Schmidt family receives a letter from the authorities regarding the restoration of property acquired from former Jewish owners. The panels in which we see them discussing what to do and consulting with Alois Kunz, the village priest (see page 62), are based on the letter reproduced below. This letter from the Schmidts to Herman Stern was accompanied by a note of support from Kunz typed underneath the Schmidts' message to Stern on the same sheet of paper.

Oberbrechen, July 20, 1948

Dear Herr Stern!

I approach you with a request:

You must certainly be aware that we purchased your parental home from your brother, Moses Stern, in 1936. A trustee has been imposed on us who has been demanding rent from us since March 1948. We thus come under the law on Jewish property, retroactively from 1933, with a requirement to have reported this by May 5, 1948.

We would be grateful for clarity about this. Should you make use of the law, by lodging an additional claim on us, we ask you to let us know [personally] or by notary, also when you lodge the claim. At the time, we made the sale peaceably and hope that we can now also come to an agreement with you peaceably. You must certainly be aware of the purchase, since you sent your brother powers of attorney to the sale in 1936. In addition, you must have taken notice of how your brother lived with us until 1941 almost as one of the family, and that we got along quite well. I certainly believe that your brother from Montabauer [sic] and the Altmann family, the daughter of Isaak Stern, will confirm this. The buyer of Herr Isaak Stern's property has also contacted the Altmann family and been notified that they regard the sale as legally valid and are not placing any claims.

We ask you again to let us know your answer more specifically, as it is very important for us so as it pertains to the authorities and questions now facing us. Looking forward to your answer, greetings to you from

Your Albert Schmidt

[typed underneath]
Cath.[olic] Parish Office Oberbrechen.
Oberbrechen, July 20, 1948

Dear Herr Stern!

The information provided by Herr Albert Schmidt is fully and completely true. The purchase of the property at the time was done in a thoroughly legal way. No kind of pressure was in any way exerted by the buyer. The purchase price corresponded to its value at the time. The buyer, a simple worker, hardly had it easy raising the sum. Herr Schmidt, who is an invalid as the result of an accident, has no assets other than his relatively small pension. He therefore deserves having you meet his request.

With best greetings, I am your devoted
A. Kunz Pastor

Source: Department of Special Collections, Chester Fritz Library, University of North Dakota. Herman Stern collection—Correspondence—German (1925–1978), Herman Stern Papers, OLGMC 217, Series 1, SubA, Box 9, Folder 3. Translation by Jeremiah Riemer.

DOCUMENT 13: MINUTES OF THE PUBLIC SESSION OF THE APPEALS COURT IN WIESBADEN, REVIEWING THE DECISION OF THE DENAZIFICATION BOARD IN LIMBURG AN DER LAHN, DECEMBER 13, 1949

This source informed the scene at the end of the first part of Chapter 4 in the Graphic History in which we see the Appeals Court in Wiesbaden clearing former Oberbrechen mayor Hugo Trost of charges brought against him in his denazification hearing. The Court's reference to the amnesty for returning POWs issued in April 1948 is quoted in the scene (see page 61).

Wiesbaden, December 13, 1949

On the basis of the Law for Liberation from National Socialism and Militarism of March 5, 1946, the Appellate Panel issues . . . the following verdict against the estate manager Hugo Trost . . . on the basis of the oral hearing:

On appeal of the concerned party, the verdict issued on June 7, 1948, by the Denazification Board Limburg/Lahn is suspended and the legal proceedings are abandoned on the basis of amnesty for repatriates.

The costs of the entire proceedings are borne by the state.

. . .

Sgd. Dr. Marckwald
Colonel
Kalbhenn

Opinion:

Further, in the view of the Appellate Panel, an act of inflammatory behavior against the Church itself (Art. 7/II/5 BG) cannot be ascertained in the established case record. Speaking against any such conduct is the attestation of the Catholic pastor in Oberbrechen (page 60 of the file), according to which his behavior was irreproachable not only toward him, but also toward the Church. . . .

Retroactively, as an additional incriminating circumstance, a letter has been received from the Jewish gentleman Herr Kurt Stern from Niederbrechen [sic], now living as an American in New York, in which he reports that the concerned party had knocked him down on May 10, 1934, in his garden in the Eichenborn [sic] district without any reason.[28] The concerned party had also shown himself to be spiteful against his father and also demanded of him that he needed to sell his house to the municipality; if he did not do this, he would immediately arrest him. The concerned party admits having boxed the young Stern on the ear one time in 1933 or 1934. The occasion for this had nothing to do with political things, especially [not] with Stern's being a Jew. He had supplied statutory declarations in which his version of this matter is confirmed. The Appellate Panel regarded the matter as insufficiently resolved for the purpose of accepting an incriminating charge against the concerned party based solely on the letter made available by the Jew Stern. That no antisemitic attitude on the part of the party concerned is available in general emerges from the statutory declaration of the practicing physician Dr. Hilfrich in Dauborn, according to which, during a sick bed visit for Herr Stern in Oberbrechen on the day after the persecution of the Jews, the patient had told him that, as a result of the notification made by then Mayor Trost urging shops to be closed in the afternoon and pedestrians to stay off the street, no riots against the Jews had taken place.[29]

Source: Hessian Central State Archives Wiesbaden, denazification file Hugo Trost. HHStAW, Best. 520 Nr. 58640. Translation by Jeremiah Riemer.

---

28 "Niederbrechen" should read "Oberbrechen" and "Eichenborn" should read "Eichelborn."

29 Reference here is to the violent events of the 1938 November pogrom.

DOCUMENT 14: IRENE LENKIEWICZ, NÉE LICHTENSTEIN, ACCOUNT OF HER LIFE UNDER NAZI PERSECUTION AND IN EXILE, COMPOSED IN CÓRDOBA, ARGENTINA, NOVEMBER 25, 1958

The testimony that Irene Lenkiewicz, née Lichtenstein, gave in the context of her claim for compensation provided important information for Chapters 1, 2, and 4 of the Graphic History. We learn about the persecution of the Lichtenstein family in Oberbrechen depicted in Chapter 2, in particular about the harassment Irene had to suffer in the village school (see page 29). The source also provides details about the family's escape from Nazi Germany and their struggle to begin a new life in Argentina, which can be seen in Chapter 1 (see pages 13–14). As a compensation claim for postwar reparation, the source is part of the second half of Chapter 4.

LIFE STORY

The undersigned, Irene Lenkiewicz née Lichtenstein, was born on June 9, 1922, in Schmitten/Taunus as the daughter of Mr. Siegfried Lichtenstein and his wife Frau Flora née Hess. Several years later [in 1927] my parents changed their residence when they moved to Oberbrechen, where I attended school from 1928 to 1936. In that same school I was subjected to major harassment after 1934, so that Rector Reifert, out of sympathy, repeatedly excused me from instruction.

My parents were in a position to provide me with a good education, yet that was quite impossible because of the prevailing political circumstances at that time.

In the meantime my parents lost the foundation for their livelihood in Germany and in May <u>1937</u> we emigrated to Argentina on the ship *Antonio Delfino*.

We arrived here without any money and without knowledge of the language and, in order to establish a new livelihood, we had to start as farm workers, clearing previously uncultivated land.

Since earnings were not sufficient, in 1940 I went to Buenos Aires, where I worked as a domestic servant to support my parents.

. . .

These statements are in accordance with the truth, and I make them to the best of my knowledge and in good conscience.

Irene Lenkiewicz née Lichtenstein

Instruction according to [illegible] §7 BEG [*Bundesentschädigungsgesetz*, the 1956 Federal Compensation Act], §31 BWGöD [*Gesetz zur Regelung der Wiedergutmachung nationalsozialistischen Unrechts für Angehörige des öffentlichen Dienstes*, the 1951 Act Governing Compensation for National Socialist Injustice for Public Sector Employees] has been applied.

I hereby notarize the above personal signature of the seamstress Irene Lenkiewicz née Lichtenstein, residing in Córdoba/Argentina, as executed in my presence.

Córdoda, the 26th of November 1958
Alfred Otto
Consul
[Seal of the Consulate of the Federal Republic of Germany, Córdoba]

Source: Hessian Central State Archives Wiesbaden, Compensation file Irene Lenkiewicz. HHStAW, Best. 518 Nr. 81953. Translation by Jeremiah Riemer.

DOCUMENT 15: LETTER FROM CARL REIFERT, OBERBRECHEN, TO THE COMPENSATION OFFICE IN WIESBADEN, APRIL 30, 1960

This letter from Carl Reifert, a former head teacher of Oberbrechen's school, to the Compensation Office in Wiesbaden concerns the case of Irene Lenkiewicz, née Lichtenstein. The source is presented as lying in an unopened envelope among various papers in a panel on page 66. It took Reifert several months to respond to the authorities. His account of the persecution that Irene suffered in the village school was vital for deciding the case, and it also informed the scenes of harassment depicted in Chapter 2.

Oberbrechen, 4/30/60

To Mr. District Administrator
Restitution Office
in Wiesbaden
[?] No. 32

Regarding: Your letters from 11/23/59 and 4/28/60

The claimant, Mrs. Irene Lenkiewicz, née Lichtenstein, lived in Oberbrechen and was enrolled in school in Oberbrechen in 1928 under my administration. In her last two years of school—1936–1938—she was a student in my class. Even two years before 1933, we had lots of National Socialists in Oberbrechen, and Hesse's future "Gauleiter" [Jakob] Sprenger, together with his Nazi friend [Eduard] Lutz, who owned an apothecary in Niederselters and was [the Nazi Party's] propaganda speaker for the district after 1933, held many regional party meetings in Oberbrechen, and after one such (outdoor) meeting, I myself had to appear in court in Limburg as a witness against Sprenger, for defamation of the then Reich Chancellor

[Heinrich] Brüning. It is understandable that the "Old Fighters'"[30] hatred was directed at me, the "lackey of the priests and Jews," especially once I had to defend my Jewish student (the claimant Mrs. Irene Lenkiewicz) from the rabble-roused throng of fellow students.

The four Jewish families who lived here, including the parents of Mrs. Irene Lenkiewicz, who made a living through trade, faced intensive boycotting. And, in 1932—after her elementary school years were over—the Lichtenstein parents, under the pressure of the agitation against the Jews, did not send their daughter Irene to high school. In 1933 the parents wanted to send the child to the Marienschule, a Catholic secondary school for girls in Limburg, but that was not possible for Jewish children.

So the child remained in the school in Oberbrechen.

It was demanded that I seat the Jewish girl alone on a separate bench! Since compulsory school attendance also applied to Jewish children, my conscience as an educator required me to also be a teacher to these children, and the Jewish girl stayed with the other children. When, after class one day, the rabble-roused fellow students doused the Jewish girl with ink, I had to punish them; I had to explain myself to the district leadership, but was met with a reasonable appraisal of my conduct.

I accompanied the student to and from school; I had to protect her from disparagement. And, as I did not want to expose the intimidated child to agitated youths, I dismissed her, with a certificate, <u>before</u> the official graduation and without the knowledge of my school inspector: in 1936.

The school inspector Fromm, who died in 1959 and was my school inspector in the Limburg district from 1919 to 1945 (at no time between 1933 and 1945 was he a Party member!), and whom I later privately informed of this, condoned my behavior.

All the parents' efforts to secure an apprenticeship for their child, which I supported, were unsuccessful. The father had the financial ability to provide his child with higher schooling, and the child's disposition would have allowed her to get her *Abitur*.[31]

I was head teacher here from 1929 until 1958 (I've worked here as a teacher since 1916), and I give, in lieu of an oath, the above account from my personal memories.

Carl Johann Reifert, retired head teacher Oberbrechen

Source: Hessian Central State Archives Wiesbaden, Compensation file Irene Lenkiewicz. HHStAW, Best. 518 Nr. 81953. Translation by Deborah Pomeranz.

---

30 *Alte Kämpfer* ("Old Fighters") was a term (of praise, though used here ironically) for the earliest and most dedicated members of the Nazi Party.

31 The *Abitur* is a German secondary-school diploma that allows students to enroll in university; it is acquired at secondary schools that are more selective and emphasize academic learning.

DOCUMENT 16: LETTER FROM THE COMPENSATION OFFICE, WIESBADEN, TO GERTRUD MARX IN OBERBRECHEN, JUNE 16, 1961

This letter was sent from the compensation office in Wiesbaden to Gertrud Marx, asking her to testify on Selma Altman's economic and professional standing before escaping Nazism in 1939. The compensation office determined how much compensation to pay to someone based on testimonies from people who knew claimants like Selma before the war. We learn about the friendship between Selma Altman (née Stern) and Gertrud Marx in Chapters 2 and 4.

Compensation Office

June 16, [19]61

Re: Compensation case of Selma Altmann née Stern, born August 7, 1900, formerly residing in Oberbrechen. Currently residing: Los Angeles/California.

Dear Frau Marx!

From the files on hand belonging to the claimant's husband, Max Altmann, I gather that you were in your youth a domestic servant for the parents of the claimant and occasionally helped out in the house of the claimant's husband until 1939, since Frau Altmann was ailing. From this it can be gathered that you were well instructed about the family's circumstances.

In the compensation proceedings pending here, Frau Altmann stated that she was a dressmaker by occupation and, as indicated by certificate, acquired her apprenticeship diploma in 1925.

As she goes on to state, she then worked as a domestic seamstress and also at home. In spite of her marriage, in 1931, to Herr Max Altmann, she claims to have continued practicing her trade. As a result of the political conditions after 1933, however, there was a sharp decline in her business.

I therefore request a reply to the following questions:

1.) Are you aware that Frau Altmann practiced her profession as dressmaker, in what way and how long?

2.) Did Frau Altmann continue to practice her profession even after her marriage to Max Altmann?

3.) Was Frau Altmann even in any condition to practice her profession as a result of her ailment?

4.) Can you provide information about the extent of her gainful employment?

On behalf of
signed [illegible]

Source: Hessian Central State Archives Wiesbaden, Vol. 1, Compensation file Selma Altman née Stern. HHStAW, Best. 518 Nr. 53361. Translation by Jeremiah Riemer.

DOCUMENT 17: LETTER FROM GERTRUD MARX, OBERBRECHEN, TO THE COMPENSATION OFFICE IN WIESBADEN, JULY 1, 1961

Selma Altman's former maid, Gertrud Marx, testified to the Compensation Office in Wiesbaden about Selma's professional life as a seamstress. From her letter, we also learn that Selma's business came to an end after 1933. This document informed scenes in Chapters 2 and 4.

To the District Administrator in Wiesbaden

Compensation Office

I worked in Frau Altmann's parents' house for many years and helped Frau Altmann until her emigration. She learned the profession of seamstress in Limburg, where she earned her apprenticeship diploma. Frau Altmann then sewed at home and also sewed at other places. After her marriage to Herr Altmann she continued to practice her trade because they had a business; she then had to sew for their business. But after 1933 it became less, then suddenly it was over, because in a small village, where everyone knows everyone else, everyone was scared to go there.

Frau Gertrud Marx

Source: Hessian Central State Archives Wiesbaden, Vol. 1, Compensation file Selma Altman née Stern. HHStAW, Best. 518 Nr. 53361. Translation by Deborah Pomeranz.

DOCUMENT 18: LETTER FROM MAYOR JOSEF KEULER, OBERBRECHEN, TO THE DISTRICT ADMINISTRATOR IN WIESBADEN, JUNE 26, 1961

This letter from Oberbrechen's mayor Josef Keuler to the District Administrator attests to Selma Altman's economic and professional standing before escaping Nazism in 1939. In contrast to Gertrud Marx

(Document 17), Mayor Keuler denied Selma's economic activity as a seamstress. Female economic activity was rarely "on the books" but significantly contributed to a family's income and a community's economic life. We learn about Selma's business activity and struggle for compensation in Chapters 2 and 4.

The Municipal Council for the Municipality of Oberbrechen
Limburg District
Oberbrechen, June 26, 1961
To the District Administrator (*Regierungspräsident*)
<u>Wiesbaden</u>

<u>Re:</u> Compensation case Selma Altmann, née Stern

<u>Regarding:</u> Your letter of June 16, 1961

Frau Selma Altmann resided in Oberbrechen, Langestr. 16, until her emigration to England on December 15, 1939 [sic].[32] When she declares that she worked here as a seamstress, she can only have worked in this occupation clandestinely, since she was never taxed as a tailor by profession.

Together with her husband, Max Altmann, Frau Altmann operated a grocery and general store and would hardly have been in a position to work as a seamstress on the side, since the clientele was spread out across the entire day and her husband also traded in textiles outside the house.

Keuler

Source: Hessian Central State Archives Wiesbaden, Compensation file Selma Altman née Stern. HHStAW, Best. 518 Nr. 53361. Translation by Jeremiah Riemer.

DOCUMENT 19: MEDICAL OPINION FROM NEUROLOGY SPECIALISTS FOR SELMA ALTMAN, THE HACKER CLINIC, BEVERLY HILLS, CALIFORNIA, MARCH 1966

This document is a neurological report on Selma's health from the 1960s. Medical reports like this were created during the compensation process. This example documents Selma's suffering during the 1930s and how she and her husband escaped Nazism. It also portrays how Nazi persecution affected Selma's economic, social, and emotional life and how the

---

[32] Selma and Max Altmann left Germany on February 15, 1939. See Document 19: Medical Opinion from Neurology Specialists for Selma Altman, The Hacker Clinic, Beverly Hills, California, March 1966.

experience of violence and persecution continued to harm her after escaping Germany. It is a key source in Chapter 4 and also informed the history of violence narrated in Chapters 2 and 3.

The Hacker Clinic
Psychiatry
160 Lasky Drive
Beverly Hills, California 90212
Medical Opinion from Neurology Specialists

For Submission to the Reparations Authorities and Courts of the Federal Republic of Germany
March 1966

Re: Frau Selma Altman, née Stern

At the behest of Frau Altman and her attorney Herr Dr. jur. Fritz Goode, the patient was seen in our clinic on February 15 and 18, 1966. On this occasion an extensive case and life history was recorded and a psychiatric examination undertaken. In addition, an objective anamnesis was collected from the patient's husband on February 23, 1966.

. . .

ANAMNESIS AND LIFE HISTORY

Mrs. Selma Altman, neé Stern, was born in Oberbrechen on August 7, 1900. . . . and she lived there until 1938. . . . [Her father] ran his own upholstery shop, where he also engaged some employees. Their financial situation was good; they lived in their own house and always had a maid. This maid helped her a lot later, when she was persecuted. They are still in contact with one another, by letter.

. . .

There were four other Jewish families living in the village, including her father's brother's family. Her uncle had a cigar shop in town. Her religious upbringing was liberal; on Saturdays she would go to the synagogue in Limburg, which was 20 minutes away by train.

. . .

After the [Nazi] seizure of power, there were riots and Jews were harassed in her small village. In April 1933 there was a boycott of her business. SA men stood in front of the shop and did not let anyone in. Afterwards more and more customers started to stay away, as many officials could no longer risk buying from them. Beginning in 1934, they were harassed on their way home many times. SA men jostled her, she fell and then was trod on by them. She told her husband about this, and he initially wanted to confront the SA men. But there would not have been any point in that, and he would only have been punished for it. The situation became more and more dangerous and lawless. Their old friends and acquaintances abandoned them; only their maid, who . . . had worked in their house for 17 years, stood by them. Because she was married and over 45, she was able to continue working for them for a time.[33]

Her brother was arrested in 1933 and thrown in jail for several weeks. Because of these terrible experiences, he emigrated to Holland in 1934.[34] She subsequently visited him in Holland multiple times; she had planned to emigrate as well, but their mother had a heart condition and she did not want to leave her.

Starting in 1935 their house was searched repeatedly, allegedly for hidden weapons. 20 SA men invaded their home, ransacked and nosed through everything. The SA men brandished their weapons at them and threatened that if they made a sound, they would be shot. Because of the boycott, their business declined more and more. They had to lay off their chauffeur and sell their car.

In 1937 their business was liquidated. Outstanding bills had not been paid in a long time, and they also did not have much stock left. They rented out the lower floor of their house and lived only on the upper floor. Her sister had gotten married at the time, and lived in Wiesbaden. Her husband took a position as a salesman in a Jewish shop in Limburg, where people still went because of the good quality [of the wares]. Antisemitism had not taken hold as strongly in Limburg as it had in her small, rural village.

She herself cared for her mother in 1937/38. She no longer went out at night, and then also during the day, out of fear of assaults. She avoided everyone and was constantly suffering under the fear that something could happen. The ostracism she faced from everyone in the village in these years hurt her deeply.

---

33 The 1935 Nuremberg Laws prohibited Jews from hiring domestic servants under the age of 45.

34 Other sources indicate that Max Stern had fled to the Netherlands already in 1933. The municipality's official register of departure gives the date of September 20, 1933. Certification of Oberbrechen mayor Josef Keuler, March 1, 1962. In the context of Selma and her sister Hedwig's attempt to claim compensation for the murder of their brother, Selma stated that Max Stern fled from Germany "head over heels" after his release from imprisonment in Limburg an der Lahn in early 1933. See HHStAW, 518, Nr. 5347, 25, 28.

Her mother died in April 1938. On the one hand, she was despondent over her death, but on the other hand, she was comforted that her mother was at peace. There were incidents at her mother's funeral, in a different village. Locals, in particular Hitler Youth boys, threw stones at the coffin and their car, and the chauffeur was unable to drive on. They buried her mother quickly in the Jewish cemetery. Aside from the scared family, the only person there was a rabbi. She was very agitated and full of indignation about it all not even the dead were allowed their rest. Her gallbladder troubles began at this time.

On November 9, 1938, all the Jewish businesses and homes were demolished during the so-called Kristallnacht. Her husband had come home earlier from Limburg. In the early morning on November 10, 1938, he was hauled out of his bed and taken away by the SA. She was, of course, tremendously upset by this. The maid advised her not to stay there, but rather to go to Limburg. She followed her advice and went to see her widowed sister and her cousin in Limburg. The riots had been just as terrible there. They fled to the attic, but were found there by patrols. She was dragged by the hair, and SA and SS men hollered at them: "you've brought it upon yourselves, and now you must suffer for it."

They were all taken away to jail. On the way there, they were spat on and kicked by passersby on the streets of Limburg, and objects were thrown in their faces. Once they arrived at the Limburg jail, they were put in a cell where they had to sleep on the floor. Otherwise, the police did not do anything to them. They were told that their husbands were in a work camp, and that they would also be sent there. Over the next few days in the Limburg jail she endured terrible fear, and was constantly thinking of her husband, and what must surely have happened to him. After three days she was released, along with her sister and cousin. They stayed together in Limburg, fearing for their husbands, who had been apprehended and taken away.

The following weeks were an agonizing ordeal. She was hardly able to sleep, started at every creak of the steps, and would have hidden herself away if the doorbell had rung. The anxiety kept getting worse. She was overpowered by it. Even before this, she was rarely able to sleep well; now it was all but impossible. She hardly went outside; her cousin did most of the shopping. She once received a note from her husband, from the Buchenwald concentration camp. That was it. She heard from other Jewish families in Limburg that they had received urns sent from Buchenwald. She became convinced that her husband would never return either.

Eventually he returned around Christmastime 1938, as did her cousin's husband. Her husband looked raggedy, filthy, and completely distraught. He seemed dazed and told her only that he was constantly beaten.

Subsequently he had to report to the mayor's office in Limburg, and later in their hometown, every day.

They were told that if they had not emigrated in six weeks, they would both be sent to the camp. They called and sent cables, and eventually their relatives in France provided a visa for England. The papers for America had already been ready before this, but were rendered invalid by the arrest of her husband. Her name was also listed on her husband's visa, so they had to leave the country together, at any price. However, to be able to leave she still needed her passport, which the mayor of Oberbrechen refused to give her. Their departure date, February 15, 1939, got closer and closer, and still she did not have her passport. She was dreadfully worried about this and became more and more nervous and anxious. It was clear to her that without her passport she would be deported to a camp.

Finally, she plucked up her courage and went to the county office [*Landratsamt*] in Limburg. A clerk there asked her what her husband had told her about Buchenwald. She answered that she did not know anything and had not asked him. He eventually said that he would call Wiesbaden, at her expense, and managed to have her passport handed over to her. She was afraid until the last that something could go amiss.

They left for Holland via Cologne on the specified day, February 15, 1939. They were only allowed to bring 10 Marks with them.

. . .

HUSBAND'S STATEMENT

. . .

In April 1938, his mother-in-law passed away, after suffering a long period of illness. They were not able to get a hearse. Eventually, a farmer from their village agreed to drive them to the neighboring town, where the Jewish cemetery was, in his muck wagon. As they drove through the village streets there was a disturbance. The SA and Hitler Youth threw things at them and at the coffin, and their driver and the farmer did not want to drive any further. Finally, they managed to reach the Jewish cemetery, and Rabbi Laubheimer [sic] from Bad Ems quickly performed the burial.[35] These events brought his wife great sorrow. She brooded over them for months, how something like that could have happened, withdrew more and more and was very frightened and in low spirits. This is when his wife's first gallbladder troubles appeared.

---

35   Dr. Friedrich "Fritz" Eliahu Laupheimer served as Rabbi of the Ems and Weilburg rabbinical district from 1931 to 1939. He fled to Mandatory Palestine.

In Oberbrechen at this time, they were harassed and sometimes spat on every day. They were, of course, called all sorts of names. Overnight, former friends became enemies. He wondered how it was possible for this to happen to German culture. Until November 9, 1938, he lived in Oberbrechen and went to work in Limburg every day.

On November 9, 1938, Mr. Loewenberg's business in Limburg was destroyed, and this man advised him to go home.[36] This was a Thursday. Friday morning, November 10, 1938, he was suddenly hauled from his bed and taken away. He did not know then what exactly had happened to his wife; he learned only later that she had been in jail for several days and had been very worried about him.

He himself ended up at the Buchenwald concentration camp. He was transported there together with other Jews, and when they arrived at the camp they were beaten brutally. Many were unable to escape and dropped dead. The treatment continued to be inhumane during the weeks he spent in the concentration camp. He was housed in Barrack 3a and had to witness, again and again, how Jews were hauled out at night and shot to death in the corridors. He still remembers one man from Frankfurt who was so badly choked that he died that night. The worst was that they got no water. They were so thirsty that one night, when it was raining, one prisoner collected the rain in a small bowl and they all drank from it. They were beaten day and night. He only told his wife a fraction of what he experienced there, in order not to upset her further.

Around Christmastime 1938, he was released from Buchenwald and returned to Limburg. The next day he was obligated to report to the police station. There it was categorically explained to him that if he said anything about what happened at Buchenwald, he would be immediately sent back and shot. Additionally, he was told he must leave Germany within six weeks, or he and his wife would be sent to a concentration camp. In the following weeks, he had to report to the police station in Oberbrechen every day, because that was his hometown. Thus he had to travel back and forth between Limburg and Oberbrechen every day. His wife's reaction was indescribable. She was afraid to so much as breathe. Every day there was the chance that something terrible would happen. She was hardly able to sleep. Even before this, her sleep had been greatly disturbed.

---

36   The G. Löwenberg Department Store, founded by Moritz Löwenberg in 1897, was located on Neumarkt in Limburg an der Lahn. After the forced sale, it became the Vohl & Meyer Department Store. Moritz Löwenberg was deported from Frankfurt am Main in October 1941 together with his daughter Ilse. He died in the Lodz ghetto. His wife, Emmy Löwenberg, was killed in the Sobibor death camp. *Stolpersteine Guide*, last accessed February 17, 2023, https://stolpersteine-guide.de/map/biografie/927/familie-lowenberg.

They had received a visa for England via their relatives, but then faced further nerve-wracking complications. His wife's passport, which they desperately needed in order to emigrate, was being withheld by the mayor of Oberbrechen. Finally his wife plucked up her courage and went to the county office in Limburg, where a clerk had her passport delivered via Wiesbaden.

...

In 1965, his wife traveled to Oberbrechen, in order to look after her parents' graves there. She had long felt guilty that she had not done anything for them. She stayed with their old housemaid. Afterwards she went to the spa town [Bad] Kissingen for a course of treatment. He himself did not have anything against that, but was not able to accompany her. He would have probably told some people in Oberbrechen the truth. So he preferred to stay home.

...

PSYCHIATRIC FINDINGS
...

During the interview, the patient displayed the following defense mechanisms: avoidance, repression, suppression, rationalization, and reaction-formation. The conflict between strong emotions and these defense mechanisms emerges with special clarity in the patient's statements about visiting her hometown last year. She added that she had long felt guilty that she had not taken care of her parents' grave. She was born there, and loves the country. Her husband and sister were very skeptical about her visit to Germany, and did not want to come along, but she wanted to see her parents' grave, no matter what. She traveled to Oberbrechen via Frankfurt with a cousin from Paris, and stayed in her former maid's house. During the postwar years she had regularly sent her packages, and in this manner helped her and her children through the most difficult period. In Oberbrechen she avoided speaking to any of her former acquaintances. She looked away; she did not want to re-open old wounds.

A neighbor, who had been six years old at the time and was then a senior official [Oberregierungsrat] in Bonn, drove her from Frankfurt to Oberbrechen.[37] Neighbors brought her flowers and fruit, and she also spoke with one neighbor. She did not feel hatred; one must resign oneself

---

37 This is a reference to Karl Jung, the official who was also instrumental in restoring German citizenship to Kurt Lichtenstein. He was the grandson of Peter Jung, known as "Peter, the baker," or *Bäcke Petisch* in the local dialect. The Jung Bakery in Lange Straße 18 was located directly next to Selma and Max Altmann's house in Lange Straße 16. The Jung and Altman families stayed in contact after Selma and Max were forced to leave Oberbrechen. (Summary of interview with Ria Schneider, née Jung, interviewed by Doris Hecker, April 2022.)

to things and cannot in any case bring back the dead. She loves the forest, and the countryside. After her visit to her hometown, she went to Bad Kissingen, where the natural springs did her good.

It would have been pointless to speak with Oberbrecheners or other Germans about the past. Today, they say no one did anything, and everything is denied. Then again, there were also decent Germans. Her husband had warned her against going to her hometown. Maybe she would encounter somebody who had driven them out.

She has always brooded over the fate of her twin brother [Max Stern], with whom she was particularly close. Why did he not make it out of the calamity? He was such a good fellow who helped everyone.

. . .

Frederick J. Hacker, M.D.
Diplomate American Board of Neurology and Psychiatry in Psychiatry
Professor of Psychiatry at University of Southern California

Dr. med. Klaus D. Hoppe
Doctor of Neurology and Psychiatry
Member of the International Psychoanalytic Association

Source: Hessian Central State Archives Wiesbaden, Vol. 1, Compensation file Selma Altman née Stern. HHStAW, Best. 518, Nr. 53361. Translation by Jeremiah Riemer.

DOCUMENT 20: LETTER FROM SELMA ALTMAN, LOS ANGELES, CALIFORNIA, TO MAYOR JOSEF KRAMM IN OBERBRECHEN, NOVEMBER 26, 1973

In November 1973, Selma Altman responded to a letter from Mayor Josef Kramm asking her about Jews living in Oberbrechen before 1942. In this letter, Selma Altman provides Kramm with biographical information on Jews living in Oberbrechen, which allowed Eugen Caspary to compose his chapter about the Jews of Oberbrechen. This correspondence also set in motion a long-lasting written exchange between Altman and Kramm. The letter is a key source in Chapter 5 of the Graphic History.

Los Angeles, California
Novbr. 16, 1973

Dear Mr. Mayor,

We have received your letter and send our best regards and all good wishes for the Christmas holiday to you and to the community from our present home in Los Angeles.

I respond to your letter with the following, which you can perhaps use for your book.

In Oberbrechen there lived a family Blumenthal, Bahnhofstr.

<u>Family Samuel Stern Langgasse</u> (Moses Stern). Their relatives are scattered all over the world.

Family Siegfried Stern; these are the parents of Kurt and Ilse Stern. Kurt Stern lives in New York and is best placed to provide information. . . .

<u>Siegfried Lichtenstein</u> Bahnhofstr. There are 2 children, Irene & Kurt . . .

The Blumenthal family moved to Erbenheim near Wiesbaden with three sons Bernhard, Karl, & Richard. Karl lives in Chicago . . .

The children of the family of <u>Si[e]gmund Stern</u> live in New York; they are <u>Maurice Stern</u> . . . , <u>Cilly Strauss née Stern</u> . . .

<u>Isaak & Rosa Stern were my parents, 4 children</u>, <u>Adolf Stern</u> born December 1895, died in battle on November 7, 1915 in Dunaburg in Russia. <u>Hedwig Stern, married to Adolf Löwenstein in Kirberg.</u> <u>Max Stern</u> emigrated to Holland and was deported from there to Auschwitz and gassed.

<u>Selma Altman née Stern</u> [and] <u>Max Altman</u> ran a store in Oberbrechen and, like all Jewish families, we had to give it up because of Hitler. We emigrated in 1939 to England and then to America. As to what was done to Jewish families, chasing them abroad with 10 marks, in order to save their lives—I don't want to go into this in any greater detail.

Kind regards
Yours Max & Selma Altman née Stern

Source: Estate of Eugen Caspary.

DOCUMENT 21: LETTER FROM EUGEN CASPARY, NIEDERSELTERS, TO HERMAN STERN IN VALLEY CITY, NORTH DAKOTA, JULY 7, 1974

This letter marked the beginning of the long-lasting written and personal exchange between Eugen Caspary and the Stern family, which is depicted in Chapter 5. Gustave Stern had referred Eugen Caspary to Herman Stern, who remained deeply connected to the village after emigrating to the United States in 1903. In this letter, Eugen openly addressed the persecution of the Jews during Nazism and expressed his interest in learning about and documenting the history of Jews in Oberbrechen.

July 7, 1974

Dear Mr. Stern,

You will certainly be astonished to receive this letter from someone who is a complete stranger to you. So, allow me to begin by introducing myself. My name is Eugen Caspary; I was born in 1929 in Oberbrechen. I am the deputy head teacher at the Philippinum secondary school in Weilburg/Lahn. I have lived in Niederselters since 1956.

The mayor of Oberbrechen, Mr. Josef Kramm, who took over from his predecessor, Mr. Josef Keuler, in this position approximately one year ago, requested that I write a chapter about the former Jewish residents of Oberbrechen for a local history chronicle, which will be published on the occasion of the 1,200th year anniversary of the town. In the course of my inquiries, I was referred to your address, namely by your nephew in [Seattle,] Washington, Gustave Stern, whose address I obtained from the Duisburg municipal archive. I learned of your unusual and impressive professional and social career from Mr. Gustave Stern in an extremely friendly letter. He also encouraged me to approach you. He wrote that you would certainly be willing to provide information in support of my undertaking.

For my account of the history of the Jews of Oberbrechen since ca. 1700, which is largely completed (approx. 70 pages), I am primarily interested in the personal reasons for your immigration to the USA in the year 1903, and the general relations between Jews and Christians in Oberbrechen at this time.—In the aforementioned letter, your nephew called you the "most eminent member of the family" and described you with deep reverence as a "humanitarian" who enabled more than 100 people to escape the criminal Nazi regime.

Would it be possible to hear more about these events in a time that was terrible for Jews who lived in Germany or in countries occupied or threatened by Germany?

Dear Mr. Stern, please don't think of my questions as an unseemly expression of my personal curiosity. Their only goal is to make this chapter of the Oberbrechen chronicle a worthy memorial to the former Jews of this community and, in so doing, contribute to the triumph over any prejudices that may still exist. My intention is to sketch out, as objectively as possible, the most important stations in the timeline of the centuries-long history of the Jews of my birthplace.

Dear Mr. Stern, I would be very grateful if you would share with me matters worthy of recording from your store of memories. We will, of course, send you a copy of the chronicle after its publication (likely in October of this year).

Sincerely yours,
Eugen Caspary

Source: Department of Special Collections, Chester Fritz Library, University of North Dakota. Herman Stern Papers, OLGMC 217, Series I, Sub-Series A, Box 9, Folder 4. Translation by Deborah Pomeranz.

DOCUMENT 22: LETTER FROM GUSTAVE AND GERTRUDE STERN, SEATTLE, WASHINGTON, TO EUGEN CASPARY IN NIEDERSELTERS, JULY 11, 1974

In this letter to Eugen Caspary, Gustave expresses his mixed feelings about Germany that oscillated between cutting ties with present-day Germany and a deep love for and rootedness in German culture and music. This aspect of the source informed Chapter 5. Gustave's description of how he played with other children in the village during his visits to his grandparents' house before 1933 shaped a scene at the beginning of Chapter 2 (see page 19).

Gustave Stern[38]
5521 Pullman Avenue Northwest   Seattle, Washington 98105
July 11, 1974

Dear Herr Studienrat![39]

I find it moving of you to be so engaged with the fate of a Jewish family. That makes me forget many terrible things and believe in Schiller's words: "All people become brothers."[40]

At first I should like to mention that I never spent the night in Niederselters. My grandfather Samuel took us children along to Niederselters, where he butchered goats. Ordinarily we went to an inn and had sausages, bread, and beer. (Maybe it was the Hotel Caspary?)

I will now attempt to answer your questions to the best of my knowledge.

1.) I believe that the financial situation of my great-grandparents forced all the children to go abroad in order to earn their daily bread.

2.) Moses was 14 years old when he began his life on a variety of steamers. In 1911 he returned to Oberbrechen for the first family reunion. As far as I know, he then stayed in Oberbrechen and became a butcher.

My father Adolf was a butcher and later cattle and horse trader in Duisburg. I do not know the reason why he settled in Duisburg. He was always an enthusiastic singer, and for a time he was vice-president of the choral society there. He was also a respected member of the Jewish

---

38 The letter is typewritten on Gustave Stern's stationery, but signed (with a handwritten note appended) by Gertrude Stern.

39 Formal title for secondary school teacher with civil service status.

40 An allusion to Schiller's "Ode to Joy" (*Ode an die Freude*), the poem used in the final choral section of Beethoven's 9th Symphony: "All people become brothers / Where thy gentle wing abides" (*Alle Menschen werden Brüder/Wo dein sanfter Flügel weilt*).

religious community. A kindly Providence saved my parents from the gas chamber. They had traveled to North Dakota to visit their brother Hermann. On their return trip to Germany, they visited us in Paris. There [my] father Adolf was run over by a car and was in the hospital for a long time. In between there was the so-called Krystallnacht [sic] (during which a very valuable collection of pictures and antiques was thrown out the window and disappeared) and additional acts of persecution, so that we no longer let our parents go back to Duisburg. In Duisburg my father had married Debora née Kann. The couple had 2 sons: I was the elder one and [then there was] my brother Julius, who died a year and a half ago. At the instigation of Uncle Hermann Stern, Julius emigrated to the United States in 1925. In Chicago he married Herta, née Tand, from Leipzig. Those two also had 2 sons, Larry and Franklin, who both live and work in Chicago.

In 1928 I myself married Gertrud, née Vasen, from the Ruhrort district of Duisburg. We also have 2 sons. The elder one has a menswear business, and the younger one is an attorney, both in Seattle.

Now as to myself: I was never an actor, although the other statements are correct[:] conductor, choirmaster, and singing teacher. I was a piano student of the famous musician Dr. Otto Neitzel, who taught at the Conservatory in Düsseldorf. Scheinpflug, Teichmueller[,] Graener, and Nikisch were the masters with whom I studied in Leipzig and Cologne. I was a répétiteur, conductor, and singing teacher at different theaters in Germany. In addition, I conducted choirs in Duisburg. In 1933 we emigrated to Paris, where I had different artistic jobs. After quite a few adventures and escaping from occupied to unoccupied territory, Uncle Hermann made it possible for us to get to the United States. We lived in New York, Chicago, and then in Fargo, North Dakota, where I worked for two years as a salesman in one of Uncle Hermann's businesses. In 1945 we moved to Seattle, where I finally was able to practice my profession again.

I was an instructor at the local Catholic university, conducted and managed operas and operettas and was music director for the city of Seattle until 1971, produced and conducted the Broadway musicals from those years with famous personalities. I also gave private singing lessons, and some of my former students sing on the stage. Now, at 73, I have withdrawn from public life.

Now back to my uncles and aunts from Oberbrechen.

- J u l i u s was a cattle trader and moved to Montabaur. I asked his son Gustav to give you a more detailed account of his family. He lives in New York.

- S a l l y was a cigar maker in Oberbrechen and later moved to Essen. He[41] married there, died between 1920 and 1930.[42]
- G u s t a v became a merchant. I asked his son, who lives in Chicago and has a menswear shop there, to give you a more detailed account.
- J e t t c h e n lives in New York. I asked her daughter for more detailed information.
- From Uncle Hermann you will be hearing in person.

I would love to come to Oberbrechen with my dear wife in order to attend the celebration. I probably still have some friends there, since I spent my vacation every year in Oberbrechen and fell into "the creek" down in the village with "other children."[43]

I hope very much that all your questions will be answered with the assistance of my diverse relatives.

With best regards,
Your
[signed] Your Gertrude Stern[44]
[Handwritten note appended to typewritten letter:]

Dear Herr Studienrat!

I am ending this letter because my dear husband is in the hospital & was operated on yesterday. Hopefully he will soon be recovering and can come back home in 8 days.

With best regards
Your
Gertrude Stern

Source: Estate of Eugen Caspary. Translation by Jeremiah Riemer.

---

41 Sally is, in this case, a man's name. It is similar to the English name Solly (often an abbreviation of Solomon).

42 Sally died on February 14, 1919. See Geni website, last accessed January 4, 2023: https://www.geni.com/people/Sally-Stern/342934657750012263.

43 Gustave Stern has put "the creek" ("die Bach") and "other children" ("andere Kinda") in quotation marks to indicate that he's spelling and pronouncing these terms in a local Hessian dialect. In proper High German, this would be "andere Kinder" falling into "den Bach."

44 The first typewritten "Your" is masculine ("Ihr")—possibly to indicate that Gustave Stern wanted to sign the letter, but the handwritten signature has a feminine "Your" ("Ihre") in front of his wife Gertrude's name.

DOCUMENT 23: LETTER FROM GUSTAVE STERN, SEATTLE, WASHINGTON, TO MAYOR JOSEF KRAMM IN OBERBRECHEN, AUGUST 1, 1974

In this letter to Mayor Josef Kramm, Gustave Stern thanks him for condemning Germany's Nazi past and expresses his admiration for German culture and music. Gustave also proposes to visit Oberbrechen on the town's 1,200th anniversary, asking for financial assistance from the municipality to help cover his travel expenses. The authors critically discuss the source in Chapter 5 of the Graphic History. This document is also discussed in Part III, The Historical Context, and Part IV, The Making of Oberbrechen.

Gustave Stern
5521 Pullman Avenue Northwest   Seattle, Washington 98105
August 1, 1974

Mayor Josef Kramm
OBERBRECHEN

Dear Mr. Kramm,

Your letter of July 25 moved me very deeply because of your efforts to rebuild the bridges which were torn down by incompetent hands. We <u>have</u> forgotten—but still <u>cannot</u> understand, that <u>t h e</u> Germany of Goethe, Schiller, Lessing, Heine, Beethoven, Brahms, and other great scholars could be so deceived by a (master???) painter and decorator.

I can remember the name Kramm <u>very</u> well, as well as the "Schitze Mathes" (Oberbrechen dialect) and the baker Peter in the Langengasse,[45] where I would pick up <u>good</u> fresh bread every morning. My grandparents lived two houses down. I have many memories of Oberbrechen, and am certain I still have old friends there.

I would be glad to participate in your celebration, even as a performing artist, if it would be possible to receive financial assistance for the trip. This is just an idea, which nevertheless could be wonderful.

Once again, Josef Kramm, I am <u>sincerely</u> delighted at your letter, and that of Mr. Caspary (<u>please</u> <u>send him my regards</u>), and hope that we will

---

45   He refers to Lange Straße here, which in the local dialect is also termed "Langgass." The bakery was the one belonging to Peter Jung in Lange Straße 18.

be able to shake hands in person, one old Oberbrechener to another in friendship as ever.

Yours,
Gustave Stern

Source: Estate of Eugen Caspary. Translation by Deborah Pomeranz.

DOCUMENT 24: LETTER FROM GUSTAVE STERN, SEATTLE, WASHINGTON, TO EUGEN CASPARY IN NIEDERSELTERS, SEPTEMBER 28, 1974

In this letter to Eugen Caspary, Gustave Stern thanks Eugen for sharing the chapter manuscript with him. Deeply impressed by Eugen's research and writing, Gustave offers him his friendship and asks Eugen to address him by his first name. (In Germany, adults traditionally address each other by family name, and only children, family members, and friends are on a first-name basis.) This source is a key document in Chapter 5 because it echoes what a good reception Eugen's chapter about the Jews from Oberbrechen got from some Jewish families.

Seattle, September 28, 1974

Dear Mr. Caspary,

The manuscript arrived this morning and I studied it in the afternoon. First of all, allow me to congratulate you "for a job well done."[46] The style is exceedingly clear and, reading between the lines, one learns your character quite well. In a word—I would like very much to meet you in person and shake your hand. I would like to tell you in person how much I value such difficult and comprehensive work. You and I have stayed in touch since you first wrote me, something I unfortunately cannot say of the mayor, who didn't even bother to confirm his receipt of the letter I sent him. Oh well, it takes all sorts (a Duisburg saying).[47]

From my reading I learned many things that I had not known, and I will study the original even more closely when it arrives. Names like Maibach, Blumenthal, Moritz, Paul, and so many other names have come

---

46 The phrase in quotes was entered in English by the letter's author.
47 The saying Stern invokes here is "es giebt sonne und sonne"—which is Ruhr dialect for "es gibt so eine und so eine" ("there is such a one and such a one").

back to me and have awoken in me a longing that sends my thoughts back to Oberbrechen and the cemetery in Weyer.

In my last letter, I asked if it would be possible can get [sic!] copies of various things (my German—my spelling!!!!!!!)[48]

If you happen to meet people who still remember me, please send them my greetings.

I am very proud to have made your acquaintance, even if only through written correspondence, and in this spirit offer you my friendship. I suggest that I call you Eugen, and that you say Gustav to me.

So, dear Eugen, sincerest thanks once again for sending the manuscript. Would you like to have it back?

Once again, I must thank you for this painstaking work. You have rendered a great service to your hometown, the surviving Jews, and humanity in general.

Gustave

Is it possible to photocopy the parish register?

Source: Estate of Eugen Caspary. Translation by Deborah Pomeranz.

DOCUMENT 25: EUGEN CASPARY, "JEWISH CITIZENS IN OBERBRECHEN, 1711–1942: A SURVEY," 1975

This source presents excerpts from Eugen's chapter about "Jewish Citizens in Oberbrechen." In this chapter, Eugen presented the history of the Jews in Oberbrechen, from its beginning in 1711 to its end in 1942. This source also exemplifies Eugen's use of apologetic language when discussing the Nazi years. The authors critically reflect on this source in Chapters 1, 5, and 6 of the Graphic History.

I. INTRODUCTION

Following the traces of the Jews who once lived and worked in Oberbrechen was a laborious, time-consuming enterprise, undertaken at every moment under the sword of Damocles of futility and failure. Often enough, it seemed as if it would be impossible to realize my plan of putting together a well-rounded overall picture compiled from the scattered and more or less random mosaic pebbles of written and oral testimony. Nevertheless, the thought of resignation was never really considered, in spite of all the

---

48 Stern is drawing attention to his embarrassment at bumbling the ending of this sentence in German. It looks as if he couldn't make up his mind if he wanted to complete his request by asking "if it *would be possible to* get copies of various things" or "if I *can* get copies of various things"—so he jumbled the two together.

difficulties involved in taking the material already available from local history and reshaping it (within a framework transcending regional history) into an account that is readable and can simultaneously be regarded as factual.

The need to use this opportunity, which is not likely to repeat itself in the immediate future, provided by the prospect of publishing a comprehensive local history, but above all the special obligation to record the darkest era in the life of the Jews, the stations of their deepest humiliation and subjugation to state-organized inhumanity, drove the continuation of this work and the recording of its results.

For nearly two and a half centuries, demonstrably, Christians and Jews in this municipality experienced everything together: holidays and everyday life, cheerful and sorrowful days, peace and war. To Jewish families residing in Oberbrechen for at least eight generations, this village in the center of the Golden Ground[49] meant their livelihood, security, and place of refuge, in a word: home [Heimat], the daily reality of life they could take for granted—much the same as for the long succession of Christian families that resided here.

. . .

VI. THE JEWS OF OBERBRECHEN IN THE NATIONAL SOCIALIST STATE (1933–1945)

Aliens in their ancestral homeland—New homeland abroad—Suffering and death

With the kind permission of the county governor [Landrat] of the former Limburg county . . . I was able to look at the Jewish files preserved in the archive of the county administration office (approx. 650 pages), files that provide highly interesting information about what was ordered and implemented in the framework of National Socialist Jewish policy in the Limburg county under the direction and control of the Gestapo in Frankfurt am Main: a shocking documentation of an ingeniously designed tactic for defaming and persecuting in small, increasingly clever and outrageous steps aimed with growing severity at the goals of boycotting, exclusion, deportation, or emigration, and finally annihilation. . . .

It may be noted with great relief that, in contrast to many of the county's other municipalities where Jews lived, there is no really incriminating

---

49 Goldener Grund ("Golden Ground") is the name of the area known for its rich soil and minerals in the Limburg Basin that includes Oberbrechen.

material about Oberbrechen that contains more than the registration of numbers and that would reveal antisemitic initiatives and activities of an especially spectacular kind. Thus, the name Oberbrechen is also missing from the official compilation of the names of Jewish citizens who were harmed during the night of November 9, 1938. This reinforces the credibility of those Oberbrechen citizens who emphasize, when questioned about the relationship between Jewish and "Aryan" inhabitants of the municipality, that the efforts of the National Socialists to stage "spontaneous" anti-Jewish actions here did not resonate with the locals. Even in the camp of [Nazi] party supporters, including the local party leadership, people were restrained, to the extent this was even possible. In any event, such being the case, there were also no serious attempts undertaken to force the Oberbrechen population, not even party members, to participate actively in anti-Jewish measures. What was undertaken against Jews by officialdom always transpired within the realm of compulsory exercises that could not be evaded. As I was assured by different persons all agreeing with each other, the mayor at the time (Hugo Trost) knew how to boycott radical anti-Jewish actions. He was decisively committed to keeping things quiet in Oberbrechen on the night of November 9, 1938. Oberbrechen was not, in any event, a place in which that "spontaneous popular rage," in reality an action organized by the party, could have grown, that rage that ran riot during the notorious *Kristallnacht* ["Night of Broken Glass"] as Jewish businesses and home furnishings were wrecked, Jewish fellow citizens were brutally maltreated or even murdered. . . . However, hardly noticed by anyone, on the following day, November 10, 1938, two Jewish citizens of Oberbrechen—Siegfried Stern and Max Altmann—were arrested by officials of the Frankfurt Gestapo and brought to Frankfurt, from which they were delivered to concentration camps . . .

The majority of Oberbrechen's citizens reacted to these capricious actions carried out across the entire territory of the Reich—to these alarming signs of a relapse into pre-Enlightenment, indeed pre-civilized practices—with disconcerted silence, with mute incomprehension. Yet in isolated instances and in small circles accusations were also articulated. . . . Concerning Franz Pabst, at the time the chaplain working in Oberbrechen (and today the parish priest in Fischbach im Taunus), we know that he said the following to the nine- through thirteen-year-old Oberbrechen youngsters sitting as passengers in his Opel P 4[50] on the

---

50 Opel is a German automobile manufacturer.

afternoon of November 10, 1938, in front of the charred remnants of Limburg's synagogue: "What you see here is a work of criminal arson. And the worst thing is that there is nothing one can do about it." Dangerous words expressed here! . . .

If people in Oberbrechen were not prepared to let themselves be misused as active participants in an inhumane action, it goes without saying that people also did not have the courage to criticize publicly or even to express solidarity with their Jewish fellow citizens who were being expelled and denounced. Whatever was provided in the way of assistance and comfort occurred, with one exception—this was the case of Gertrud Marx, who carried on in plain view and without any reservations the work she had done for years as domestic servant for the Stern and Altmann family—whatever, in other words, was shown toward Jewish fellow citizens in the way of assistance and comfort happened in secret, in seclusion, for fear of the consequences that had to ensue for "Aryans" practicing this kind of humanity. Whoever would have dared to satisfy the Christian duty of neighborly love would have stood alone, without the institutional protection—this, too, must unfortunately be emphasized—of his church . . .

In Oberbrechen—as in the "Golden Ground" altogether—there was no tradition of open opposition against authorities. Dangers linked to risks that endanger livelihoods are not sought out; especially not when the prospect of success is minimal or even nil, as is the case in the era of the National Socialist state. The tendency, rather, is to conform to the prevailing political, social, or clerical order of the day—admittedly without commitment, without abandoning the distance toward everything official. . . . The regulations are observed, so that one isn't affected by their severity day-to-day. . . .

To seek to characterize this fundamental attitude typical of Oberbrechen as merely cowardly, egoistic, and conscience-free would be one-sided and unjust. For such an interpretation disregards the motive of social responsibility that is important for this behavior and the Christian sympathy—even if concealed—that absolutely needs to be invoked in any attempt to explain the peculiar lifestyle of the Oberbrechen citizenry. Alongside the effort to save one's own skin, dodge dangers, and take refuge in the merely private, in the course of historical development over centuries under the auspices of Absolutist or totalitarian tutelage, a growing skepticism toward everything unconditional and ideologically one-track had taken shape. This kind of mistrust may create in the everyday life of normal times an atmosphere of unworldliness and hostility to progress, small-town narrowness and peasant dullness, but in dangerous times it prevents radical orientation either toward unreserved subordination to the will of the rulers or toward unreserved resistance. Situated midway between these poles of uncritical commitment and committed criticism, there was no place in Oberbrechen for misanthropy to be cultivated and for the eruption of violence to be organized. Neither verbal pathos nor inflammatory denigration nor prepared riots against fellow citizens without the ability to defend or protect themselves ever had a real chance in Oberbrechen! What flared up in the way of antisemitic activity was essentially hatred derived from youthful fanaticism that did not grow out of its own volition but must rather be understood as the result of massive party propaganda, as an emotional commitment to the only saving virtue of Germanic lordliness, of which it was suggested to people that this is manifested in the German people in unadulterated form. . . . That blind trust in the correctness of National Socialist ideology within Oberbrechen's youth was also expressed in actions of an antisemitic kind uncontrolled by reason is attested and must therefore be stressed. . . .

Moses Stern gave the impression of being restrained, rather shy. That he wanted to earn money in his trade is obvious, but that he might have availed himself of dishonest methods therein is unthinkable; and that is something everyone who had a business relationship with him knew. It pains me to this day that I occasionally found myself among the children who crudely harassed him on his travels through the village. As much as I am ashamed of this, I am happy (on the other hand) that I can say there were enough people in Oberbrechen who unequivocally and energetically forbade us children from doing this kind of thing.

. . . What these former fellow citizens of the Oberbrechen municipality experienced after their forced resettlement to Frankfurt is something I could ascertain only in bare outline. I tried getting leads and concrete information from different offices and persons about the time they spent in the Frankfurt ghetto.[51] From the family members living in America I received only meagre clues. The result of these investigations

---

51 Research applies the term *ghetto* to designated areas established by the Germans to concentrate Jews in occupied Eastern Europe. Due to the heterogeneous and complex nature of the ghetto phenomenon during the Holocaust, definitions remain broad. The *Yad Vashem Encyclopedia*, for example, defines a ghetto as "any part of a pre-existing settlement occupied by Nazi Germany where Jews were forcibly confined for at least a few weeks." In German cities, Jews were required to live in so-called *Judenhäuser* ("Jewish houses") from 1939 onward. These are not considered to form a ghetto. Frankfurt am Main thus did not have a Jewish ghetto during the Nazi era. Guy Miron and Shlomit Shulhani (eds.), *The Yad Vashem Encyclopedia of the Ghettos During the Holocaust* (Jerusalem: Yad Vashem, 2009). XL; Kim Wünschmann "Exploring the Universe of Camps and Ghettos: Classifications and Interpretations of the Nazi Topography of Terror," *Studies in Contemporary Jewry* 27 (2015), 251–263, here 258.

is therefore scanty. All we know for sure is that Siegfried, Sophie, Jette, and Moses Stern resided in Gagernstraße or Schickhausstraße [sic] in Frankfurt from 1940 or 1941 until 1942.[52] On June 20, 1942 they were deported to the east: Moses Stern to the Theresienstadt concentration camp; he died here on October 9, 1942; Jette Stern was initially brought to Theresienstadt and then "transferred" on September 29, 1942 to Maly Trostenic. From that point on all traces of her are lost. Of Siegfried and Sophie Stern we only know that they were deported east on June 20, 1942. But it is certain that they died in the gas chamber. Upon application of Kurt Stern, their son living in New York, Siegfried and Sophie Stern were declared dead on June 16, 1952 by the Frankfurt District Court.

. . .

Source: Eugen Caspary, "Jüdische Mitbürger in Oberbrechen 1711–1942: Eine Bestandsaufnahme," in: *Geschichte von Oberbrechen*, ed. on behalf of the Brechen municipality by Hellmuth Gensicke and Egon Eichhorn (Brechen-Oberbrechen: Gemeinde Brechen, 1975), 157–231.[53] Estate of Eugen Caspary. Translation by Jeremiah Riemer.

DOCUMENT 26: *NASSAUISCHE LANDESZEITUNG*, REPORT ON KURT LICHTENSTEIN'S FIRST POSTWAR VISIT TO OBERBRECHEN, APRIL 24, 1978

The local newspapers covered visits of the Jews who were originally from Oberbrechen to the village. These newspaper clippings usually portray the visits as success stories, sidelining questions about bystanders, perpetrators, or robbery of Jewish property during the Nazi years. The article below, published in the Nassauische Landeszeitung, *covers Kurt Lichtenstein's 1978 visit. It was preserved in Eugen Caspary's archive of local documents and casts the village community in a highly positive light. Stefanie and Kim critically discuss this source in Chapters 1 and 5 of the* Graphic History.

---

52 Siegfried, Sophie, and Jette Stern's last residence was in Schichaustraße 4, close to the Eastern Station (*Ostbahnhof*) in Frankfurt am Main. According to the present state of research, this was not a *Judenhaus*. (Email from Rico Heyl, Institut für Stadtgeschichte Frankfurt am Main, to Kim Wünschmann, November 4, 2021.)

53 This translation of excerpts from Eugen Caspary's seventy-five-page chapter in a history of Oberbrechen published in 1975 was undertaken independently of a previous translation of both overlapping and entirely different excerpts (amounting to just sixteen typewritten pages, plus introductory material) done by Justin J. Mueller in 1999 and archived at the Leo Baeck Institute New York. An online (searchable) scan of Mueller's translation may be found at https://archive.org/details/jewishcitizensin1384unse.

Brechen-Oberbrechen.—Kurt Lichtenstein (right), with his wife Susi and married couple Anita and Paolo Landau (on the left), visited his old home village for the first time since emigrating forty-one years ago. Photo: Josef Kramm.

Overwhelmed by the Good Reception
Kurt Lichtenstein Visits His Former Home Village after Forty-one Years

Brechen-Oberbrechen—Kurt Lichtenstein, who came back to Oberbrechen for the first time since his emigration forty-one years ago, was deeply impressed by his former home village. He, along with his parents and sister, had to emigrate in 1937, during the Hitler regime, and found a new homeland in Argentina. Together with his wife, Suse, and some friends, the couple Anita and Paolo Landau, whose ancestors also come from Germany, he visited the family home on Frankfurter Straße and was shown around the community by Mayor Josef Kramm, with whom he had attended school for several years.

It was the recently published village chronicle, which the mayor had sent out to all former Oberbrechen residents, that was "to blame" for this reunion. A lively correspondence arose from this, leading to the current visit.

Kurt Lichtenstein said that he still remembered the landscape and some individual things, but everything else had become foreign to him. He and his companions were especially impressed by how well-organized everything was.

The visitors from Latin America appeared overwhelmed by the warmth with which they were received and the hospitality afforded to them, especially by the mayor and his family.

After initially difficult years in a jungle camp, Argentina has become a new homeland for him and his family, explained Lichtenstein. He moved to the capital Buenos Aires in 1958, where he set up a business. Argentina has everything that a country could have, he thought, from a European climate in the south with plenty of snow in winter, to a tropical climate in the north, not to mention 45 million cattle, 48 million sheep, five million horses, and more than three million hogs. The transformation from an agricultural to an industrial state, pushed in recent years, has led to severe setbacks, he opined of the situation in the South American country. Reality is often ignored in the planning, as demonstrated by, for example, nine Argentinian automobile factories for only 25 million inhabitants. Lichtenstein staunchly repudiated the, in his opinion, often biased and inaccurate reporting on the political circumstances in his country.[54] Under the new government, the situation has begun to calm down, and the number of kidnappings and crimes has declined. After years of uncertainty and confusion, there is once again a clear program, which could help provide the country with a sorely needed economic upturn.

Source: Estate of Eugen Caspary. Translation by Deborah Pomeranz.

DOCUMENT 27: CHRISTMAS GREETINGS FROM SELMA ALTMAN, LOS ANGELES, CALIFORNIA, TO JOSEF KRAMM IN OBERBRECHEN, DECEMBER 1980

This source exemplifies Christmas greetings sent by Jewish refugees from Oberbrechen to Mayor Josef Kramm. Max and Selma Altman regularly sent greetings on Easter and Christmas holidays. The sources do not testify to non-Jews sending greetings on Jewish holidays to the Jews from Oberbrechen scattered around the world. The source is discussed in Chapter 5.

---

54 On March 24, 1976, a military coup d'état toppled the government of President Isabel Péron and led to the establishment of a dictatorship that ruled until 1983. Political dissidents were persecuted, and tens of thousands of people "disappeared" in kidnappings and killings.

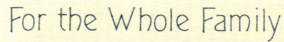

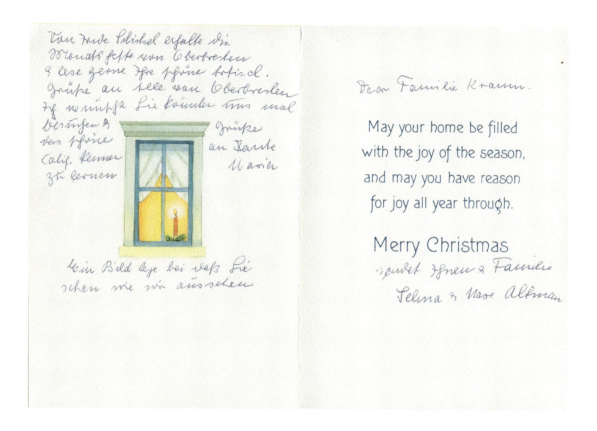

Dear Kramm family,

[pre-printed text] "May your home be filled with the joy of the season, and may you have reason for joy all year through. Merry Christmas"

To your family, from,
Selma & Max Altman

I get the Oberbrechen monthly from Trude Schickel & am always happy to read your lovely articles. My regards to everyone in Oberbrechen. I wish you could visit us sometime, and experience beautiful California.

Regards to Aunt Maria.[55]

---

55 Reference here is probably to Maria Roth née Kramm, who together with her husband Alois Roth had bought the house in Lange Straße 16 when the Altmanns had to sell it under duress.

Enclosed, a photo, so you can see what we look like, taken August 1979.
1 relative[,] I with our dog
                & my husband
in remembrance

Source: Family archive Wünschmann/Kramm-Abendroth. Translation by Deborah Pomeranz.

DOCUMENT 28: PROVISIONAL MINUTES OF A MEETING ON "CATHOLIC RESISTANCE AGAINST THE HITLER YOUTH AND THE REPERCUSSIONS OF THE NATIONAL SOCIALIST SEIZURE OF POWER IN OBERBRECHEN," JULY 30, 1984

These minutes of a conversation between Herr Kramm, Herr Roth, Herr Caspary, Herr Müller, and Herr Hacker, which took place in Kramm's house on July 30, 1984, reveal their experiences as young boys in the Catholic Youth movement, Jungschar. As passionate followers of chaplains Graulich and Pabst, they were reluctant to join the Hitler Youth before it became mandatory in 1936. They reflect on the disruption of

Catholic social and religious life under Nazism. Caspary also attests to borrowing a Hitler Youth uniform (against his father's will) to watch a movie presented by the local Hitler Youth group. This scene is depicted in Chapter 2 (see page 30), and the authors critically discuss how Oberbrecheners simplistically recall this process as Catholic resistance in Chapter 4.

MR. CASPARY: . . . I was born in 1929, and at home with our family we really kept our distance from the "browns." For example, we never had that blank spot from when "the picture"[56] had to be taken down afterwards. I can recall that one was influenced, naturally, by the Catholic Youth and participation in the *Jungschar*[57]—that was not open to debate; it was self-evident that one would join. But just as great, all the time, was interest in joining the others—the *Jungvolk*.[58] One just wanted one of those uniforms. Back then, that's how movies where shown, and the rule was: children were only allowed into the movie when they were in the Hitler Youth, that is, when they had a uniform. But my father said: "Whether or not you see the movie, that's not so important; and a uniform, just because of the movie and in other respects and in general, we don't need that." So, I secretly put on a uniform before the movie, and after the movie was over, I took it off again.

MR. HACKER: But you had to conceal this from your father.

MR. CASPARY: Yes, but there were also major reservations about the Hitler Youth in various other families. There were also, to be sure, certain families where this was not the case.

MR. KRAMM: There were really only very few who had a uniform. . . .

MR. HACKER: What, then, from your perspective, was the cause for the attraction that the Hitler Youth, weapons, and uniforms would have exerted at that time on young people in Oberbrechen?

---

56 Meaning portrait of Hitler as *Führer* displayed in German homes.

57 The *Jungschar*—literally "Youth Flock"—was the youth group for Catholics from around age 8 to 14.

58 The *Jungvolk* was the branch of the Hitler Youth for nearly the same age range (10 to 14) as the Catholic *Jungschar*.

MR. ROTH: Here there was never any fascination with the HJ [Hitler Youth] on the part of young people. After all, we had chaplains who were so good that we didn't need any HJ. We had, e.g., Chaplain [Oswald] Graulich; that was the first one. He inspired us with so much enthusiasm—as chaplain and as a human being; and he said, on Sunday we're going to Obertiefenbach and spend the night there in a barn; and he slept along with us there, and we hiked with him enthusiastically. But we had already joined the HJ by necessity then. That was in 1938.

MR. CASPARY: I still even have the document, that was compulsory, back then.
. . .

MR. KRAMM: We were standing at the train station, and it was said there can't be any dual membership. Whoever wants to stay in the *Jungschar* should step forward. But then everybody stepped forward, which basically meant that we would all be staying in the *Jungschar*; and from this time forward one can say that it was approximately one tenth. At its dissolution in September 1937, we still had ninety boys in the *Jungschar*. And maybe ten to eleven were in the *Jungvolk*, in the HJ. And in the *Jungvolk*, it was this way, whoever had a uniform—there were a couple who had a uniform—there was nothing left for them than to take a couple again, since otherwise nobody joined them.
. . .

MR. ROTH: Yes, at that time, Saturday was the day for doing service in the HJ, and at the same time there was the excursion with the chaplain; and we all went with Chaplain Graulich. It was wonderful, and as we came home, it was said: "So, you didn't join in the service, so you're all thrown out of the HJ." So we were all thrown out, and after a quarter of the year we were all forced back in. Because then the Limburgers said: "What, you don't have any HJ? No way!" And so we were taken back in.

MR. KRAMM: We in Oberbrechen had something way better than what the HJ had. It was so poorly organized, the way nobody was there. And those who went there, these were people who were not at all recognized by us. At this dissolution, in November 1937, this gives us a picture of what organization was like within the Catholic youth. At that time it didn't even take an hour until we were all gathered in the parish house, where it was revealed to us that all of the Catholic youth was dissolved. Within a short time the entire village—and that was approximately ninety young people we had—all had been informed.

MR. CASPARY: And at that time that was Chaplain [Franz] Papst [sic],[59] and I still remember that he said the following: "The front door is closed, and we're opening it up again in the back."

MR. ROTH: . . . The chaplains, they simply fascinated us. They went swimming with us: at that time, this was something quite new.

MR. CASPARY: Chaplain Papst [sic] drove a motorbike—a BMW 500. He whizzed around the way they whiz around today. He drove at 100–120 [km/h] along the B8 [interstate road], which was still under construction.
. . .

MR. KRAMM: After that there was not a single day where I was not together with Papst [sic]. At that time we actually wanted to make a complaint when he was transferred. We were with him in the room every day, one was simply at home. Our attitude was quite simply against them. The reasons why, maybe we can't even say.

MR. CASPARY: . . . Autumn of '44, we were at the Westwall. And when we returned, it was all over with our enthusiasm for the Fatherland. The ordinary soldiers in the bunkers who didn't have a single shot of ammunition and were only waiting for the Yanks to come. They talked about golden pheasants, by which they meant the party bosses, . . . That was our HJ deployment in the west. When we returned, doing service with the HJ was supposed to go on. But in Oberbrechen this didn't happen any longer. That was then disclosed during the Church service, during High Mass. But then we were all at Mass.

Source: Estate of Eugen Caspary. Translation by Jeremiah Riemer.

DOCUMENT 29: *NASSAUISCHE NEUE PRESSE*, REPORT ON KURT LICHTENSTEIN'S VISIT TO OBERBRECHEN, NOVEMBER 29, 1986

This newspaper article documents how non-Jewish Oberbrecheners reported on Kurt Lichtenstein's visit to Oberbrechen in 1986. The article covers Kurt's bearing witness to how his family rebuilt their lives in Argentina in the 1940s and later. Kurt's testimony and the non-Jewish view on these visits found their way into the Graphic History in Chapter 1 and Chapter 5.

---

59 The chaplain's name was Pabst, not Papst (the German spelling for Pope).

Ein Wiedersehen mit früheren Schulkameraden

Wiedersehen mit früheren Schulkameraden feierte Kurt Lichtenstein, der mit seiner Familie im Dritten Reich nach Argentinien emigrieren mußte, im Haus des früheren Bürgermeisters Josef Kramm in Oberbrechen. Über alte und neue Zeiten plauderten Walter Möbs, Walter Hennecker, Alois Roth, Kurt Lichtenstein, Hubert Schönbach (sitzend, von links), Josef Kramm und Richard Roth (stehend, von links). Foto: Königstein

Kurt Lichtenstein, who had to emigrate to Argentina with his family during the Third Reich, celebrated a reunion with former schoolmates in the house of former mayor Josef Kramm in Oberbrechen. Walter Möbs, Walter Hennecker, Alois Roth, Kurt Lichtenstein, Hubert Schönbach (seated, from left), Josef Kramm, and Richard Roth (standing, from left), chatted about old times and the present. Credit: Ursula Königstein.

A REUNION WITH PAST SCHOOLMATES
WOUNDS HEAL, SCARS REMAIN

Brechen-Oberbrechen.—"The wounds heal, but the scars remain." With these words, Kurt Lichtenstein described the feelings that came over him when he met with some of his former classmates, in former mayor Josef Kramm's house, for the first time since he emigrated to Argentina during the Third Reich.[60] Though he had been back to Germany before, he had hesitated to visit his old hometown. The same was true for other Jews from Oberbrechen. Josef Kramm deserves some of the credit for helping to break the ice.

---

60 This was actually not Kurt Lichtenstein's first postwar visit to Oberbrechen. The first visit took place in 1978.

The Lichtenstein family had moved to Oberbrechen in 1927, where they bought a house on Bahnhofstraße.[61] The father was from Münster. During his time in Germany, Kurt Lichtenstein also visited his grandmother's grave there.

The Jewish family lived on amicable terms with the townsfolk.

THE SUFFERING BEGAN

After the National Socialists seized power, the suffering began. A teacher who had been sent to Oberbrechen from Berlin incited the school children against their Jewish classmates and made their lives miserable. Soon Kurt Lichtenstein could no longer risk going to school. His father took him to relatives in Frankfurt, where he attended middle school.

The family emigrated to Argentina in 1937, when Kurt Lichtenstein was twelve.[62] His father had bristled at this idea until the bitter end. He could not fathom the developments in Germany. "After all, we Jews always fulfilled our duties as citizens, during the First World War and later, and always felt like good Germans," he would always say, uncomprehendingly.

A NEW START IN THE CAMP

It was not easy for the immigrants from Oberbrechen to establish themselves in the South American country. They joined a group of German Jewish émigrés in "Camp Avigdor," a colony in the Entre Rios province located about 800 kilometers from the capital. A foundation provided 75 hectares of land and ten horses and cows each to every settler. 30 percent of the revenue had to be paid out as interest. The work was hard, and often in vain. More than once, swarms of locusts devoured the entire crop. Nevertheless, "Camp Avigdor" became a model colony that was known throughout the country.

The settlers had to do without many things that they had been used to in their old homeland. There was no infrastructure in the remote area. There were no streets, schools, or hospitals. The nearest train station was 25 kilometers away. The Germans tried to create a piece of homeland abroad. They established sport teams, a library, a band, and an amateur theater troupe.

Kurt Lichtenstein met his future wife Susi in the camp. She was the daughter of Hans Lang, who once played left halfback for

---

61 The official name of the street was Frankfurter Straße. It was the street that led to the train station, the *Bahnhof*.

62 In May 1937, Kurt Lichtenstein, who was born in November 1925, was only eleven years old.

Wormatia Worms and qualified several times for the German national football team.

The Lichtenstein family moved to Buenos Aires in 1958, after they had sold their farm. There, Kurt Lichtenstein built a respectable life for himself. He operates his own shop for interior décor, which is associated with a small atelier in which a few employees make curtains. He also builds and sells a label-making machine. In addition to that, the sixty-one-year-old is a partner in a company that distributes German products in Argentina.

His oldest daughter recently moved to the Aschaffenburg area with her family. Her husband, also an Argentinian with German Jewish roots, works there as an engineer.

TALENTED ATHLETE

In his limited free time, Kurt Lichtenstein is an active board member of the Jewish congregation founded in 1936 by German immigrants in Argentina. He is also a member of the renowned football team "River Plate." Once an outstanding athlete, he was supposed to represent Argentina in the 100 meter sprint and four-by-100 meter relay in the South American Championships in Peru, around the end of the Second World War. However, because he refused to change his name to something more Spanish sounding, he was removed from the lineup.

Kurt Lichtenstein does not feel hatred for Germany or the Germans, despite the suffering that he and his family endured here—he has family members who perished in the concentration camps. If there had been no Third Reich, his parents would certainly have stayed, and he might also still be living here, he reckoned.

Source: Estate of Eugen Caspary. Translation by Deborah Pomeranz.

DOCUMENT 30: LETTER FROM EUGEN CASPARY, CAMBERG-ERBACH, TO KIM WÜNSCHMANN IN JERUSALEM, JULY 3, 2013

This letter marked the beginning of Kim and Stefanie's collaborative project. Even before their road trip from Las Vegas to Denver, Kim had reached out to Eugen about his contacts with Jews from Oberbrechen. In response, Eugen handed over parts of his correspondence to Kim, who shared it with Stefanie. After Eugen passed away in 2019, his son Christof and daughter-in-law Yvonne gave the authors access to Eugen's papers and private collections. This source found its way into the Graphic History in Chapter 1, which also includes Eugen's memories of Moritz Stern's postwar visit (see pages 8–9).

July 3, 2013

Dear Kim,

Your missive from far-off Jerusalem came as a surprise, of course, but at the same time as a very happy one. There is no need for you to be reserved with me, even if I am—in comparison with your youth—an ancient creature; my reason is completely intact, in contrast to the rest of my constitution! So I would be exceedingly glad if I could be of some help to you.

Before I get into your list of questions, I would like to say something about your grandfather, and his central role in Oberbrechen as well as in the region well beyond the district borders. He was always proposing important ideas, and actively galvanizing and keenly organizing the variety of projects he initiated. Of course he faced obstacles, and some of his contemporaries, with their "who-needs-it-mentality" that was so typical for our region, may have thought Jupp Kramm's dedication and many of his impetuses in the social and cultural field to be too much of a good thing; but these barriers could neither disrupt nor, in the long term, inhibit his innate drive to act in the interests of the community.

As far as his endeavor to establish contact with the former Jewish citizens of Oberbrechen is concerned, as early as right after the war he regarded this as a self-evident necessity. For example, I remember that it was thanks to him that a German Jew visiting Oberbrechen (Moritz Stern) was able to reconnect to his old *Heimat* once again. Moritz Stern was visiting Oberbrechen incognito. Without even knowing the "stranger," Jupp had struck up a conversation with him, in the course of which the identity of the visitor returning from exile became clear. Jupp managed to entreat the demurring guest to accompany him to an Oberbrechen inn, where he was introduced to a group of older Oberbrecheners gathered there. In a more reconciliatory frame of mind than when he arrived, Moritz Stern returned to his new *Heimat* in America.

You are certainly well aware that your grandfather was abundantly endowed with that rare ability to spontaneously strike up a conversation with anyone, no matter how unfamiliar; and that he relished the opportunity to expand and intensify those first fleeting instances of rapprochement. And this gift stood his tenure as mayor, initially of Oberbrechen when it was independent and then later of the larger municipality Brechen into which it was merged, in good stead.

. . .

One of his greatest and lasting achievements is the publication of the history of Oberbrechen during his tenure in local politics. The release of such a comprehensive work, both critically acclaimed by experts and well-received by the general public, would not have been possible without his support as mayor.

It is true that Jupp and I, prior to the chronicle's publication, got in touch with former Jewish Oberbrecheners or their descendants; a correspondence that, in some cases, intensified beyond just establishing contact and gathering facts. Indeed, real friendships arose with (for example) Jupp's schoolfriend Kurt Lichtenstein (whom you mentioned), Seattle-based music director Gustave Stern (whose father belonged to an old Oberbrechener Jewish family), and Adolf Besmann from Nahariya/Israel (whose mother was an Oberbrechener by birth), friendships that were deepened during repeated visits to Oberbrechen and car trips together. The aforementioned had actually abandoned any connection to Germany and were in fact firmly resolved, before they accepted our invitation, to never have anything to do with Germany or Germans ever again.

Once they had overcome, during their first encounter and conversation with us, their pent-up aversion and reservations toward the country and the people who had expelled and persecuted them and who had murdered their families and friends and millions of people of their faith and heritage, an atmosphere of everyday normality soon set in. Gustave Stern, for example, once said something to the effect that he had to outright force himself to set foot on German soil again. He had actually not thought it possible that he might exchange even one word with a German ever again. Unconsciously, so to speak, he had deemed all Germans potential criminals and regarded them with contempt, indeed even with hate. He was happy to have overcome these barriers through his encounters with us, our families and friends, and to have been able to summon up hope for a restoration of a humane relationship between Jews and Germany. He was grateful to us for this feeling, despite the impossibility of forgetting the horrors that took place in the name of Germany.

. . .

There is nothing I can say about the question of *Wiedergutmachung* (reparations). In Oberbrechen, Weyer, Münster, and other towns in our region there was no restitution of former Jewish property whatsoever, as far as I am aware. Whether claims to this effect were ever filed by families in the United States or Argentina or Israel I do not know. I am, however, aware that your grandpa provided Kurt Lichtenstein and his family in Buenos Aires with regular financial support, although his schoolmates did not honor Jupp's request that they also participate in these contributions. Jupp apparently also utilized his diverse ties to public and private entities for the benefit of the Jews who became his friends.

I have already indicated how our contact with the former Oberbrechener Jews came about. It started in the context of the research for the Oberbrechen history, and, once taken up, it evolved into friendly sincerity over the years, indeed for as long as the Jewish correspondents residing overseas remained alive. As I have mentioned, Gustave Stern, Adolf Besmann, and Kurt Lichtenstein visited us—in particular Jupp Kramm—on multiple occasions. There must still be photos and newspaper articles from these visits. Years ago, when my nephew Helmut Caspary, Hubert's oldest son, took a trip to the United States with his wife, he took my advice and visited Gustave Stern in Seattle, whose address I had given him. When he announced himself as Caspary from Oberbrechen and as my nephew, he and his wife were invited into the house and practically compelled to be his guests for a week.

Of particular help to me, as the writer who contributed the Jewish article to the Oberbrechen book, was Herman Stern. He had emigrated to the United States in 1903, as a 16-year-old, and made an impressive career for himself in North Dakota as a salesman, businessman, and politician. This allowed him, for example, to act as the guarantor sponsoring the indispensable pledge made by over 100 Jewish émigrés. When I wrote to Herman Stern to inquire about the life of Jews in Oberbrechen and the fate of the relatives who were able to escape, he readily provided me with information and let me know that he had instructed all of his relatives living in the United States to answer my inquiries in detail. In this way I obtained information, which is repeated in my contribution to the Oberbrechen book.

To be sure, these contacts were not directly of an official nature. But because your grandfather, as mayor, affiliated himself with these efforts directly with such special interest and care, thus granting them a suggestion of official support, they transcended the purely private. On Jupp's initiative, a meeting was arranged between Gustave Stern and old Oberbrecheners. The guest conversed easily with them and shared childhood memories about visiting his Oberbrechener grandparents and relatives as a child growing up in Duisburg.

On one of his visits, Gustave Stern directed the Oberbrechen music club's orchestra very spiritedly and professionally, and on another occasion he contributed—along with an American pianist joining him in a four-handed piano concert—to the Selters Culture Week.

At one time, Irene [sic][63] Stern, the daughter of Siegfried Stern, who was killed in a death camp, also visited her former *Heimat*. She had, together with her brother Kurt Stern, emigrated to the USA in 1935.[64] During her

---

63 Eugen Caspary confuses Siegfried Lichtenstein's daughter Irene (who also visited Oberbrechen with her husband after the Holocaust) with Ilse, later Isabella, the daughter of Siegfried Stern and Kurt Stern's sister.

64 The dates are confused. Kurt Stern emigrated from Germany in 1936, and Ilse Stern, later Isabella Nussbaum, in 1939.

visit, she met with her old classmates, including Gertrud Schickel, with whom she had a lifelong friendship and corresponded for decades.

Jupp was either directly or indirectly involved in all of these encounters and activities, which had the goal of supporting a new, humane, and peaceful Germany as far as his own lifetime and sphere of influence extended. This was also apparent, for example, when the descendants of the Lichtenstein family successfully appealed to Jupp for assistance with professional activities in Germany. Even after your grandfather died, there have been occasional queries or brief visits. For example, last year I was able to welcome the descendants of the Siegmund Stern family, who live in the USA, and assist them in their search for traces of their family history.

The town never gave an official apology. What took place while Jupp was mayor was certainly more valuable for relations with the former Jews of Oberbrechen than a formal gesture of official apology could have been. There are probably still documents about [Oberbrechen's] Jews in Jupp's papers. As for myself, I have kept all written material concerning Jewish matters that has accumulated, including the letters that have arrived from the USA, Israel, and Argentina, in binders, some of which are bursting at the seams. When you are back in the *Heimat*, all of my archival materials are at your disposal, and of course the publications, too.

. . .

Wishing you all the best and success in everything you wish for yourself,

Eugen Caspary

Source: Kim Wünschmann. Translation by Deborah Pomeranz.

PART III
THE HISTORICAL CONTEXT

Our study of Oberbrechen explores the dynamics of how a German village attempted to deal with its troubled past. It asks how Jewish and non-Jewish villagers experienced the momentous events of the twentieth century and how their experiences of Nazism and the Holocaust shaped the encounters they had with one another after 1945. Focusing our observation on a clearly defined place and set of actors, we approach Oberbrechen as a microhistory. This enables us to see the nuances of historical processes and to address in detail the complexity inherent in seemingly normative structures. It also brings into sharp relief people's attitudes, motivations, and behaviors.[1] To be sure, Oberbrechen should not be mistaken as *the* typical German village that could stand for the nation as a whole. As a medium-sized village in the west-central part of the country, it shared many commonalities with similar settlements—but it was, and still is, distinct. From our case study we can learn how the spread of Nazism affected villagers and ruptured existing Christian–Jewish relations in rural areas. It also tells us of grassroots attempts at reconciliation between Christians and Jews after the genocide, which were loaded with ambiguous dynamics that can also be observed in other localities.

This Part of the book contextualizes the events that occurred in Oberbrechen within a larger history of Jewish–non-Jewish relations before, during, and after the Holocaust. Its structure echoes the structure of the Graphic History (Part I), with identical headings for the five different sections of this text. In this way, the events graphically narrated at the micro level of the village can be situated onto the larger background of the underlying macrohistory, thereby connecting local, national, and indeed transnational history and historiography. We will relate Oberbrechen's confrontation with its Nazi past to the broader trends of Holocaust memory and the politics of history. We will explore how Germans, over time, tried to come to terms with their personal accountability, as well as with processes of denazification and reparation initiated by the Allied powers after the Second World War. At the same time, we will analyze how German-Jewish survivors, in turn, perceived these efforts on the part of non-Jewish Germans.

---

1   See Giovanni Levi, "On Microhistory," in *New Perspectives on Historical Writing*, ed. Peter Burk (Cambridge: Polity, 1991), 93–113.

Their varying responses to offers of reconciliation and rapprochement at the personal and local level were shaped by their very own struggles to live on after the catastrophe. We will examine their unsettling experiences with state-backed bureaucratic schemes of Holocaust compensation and restitution as well as the prosecution of Nazi crimes.

OBERBRECHEN

With almost 2,000 inhabitants, Oberbrechen is today a midsize village in the state of Hesse in the west-central part of Germany. In 2022, it celebrated the 1,250th anniversary of its foundation. In the last two centuries its population has roughly doubled, rising from 943 in 1834 to 1,336 in 1925 and (with the influx of expellees from eastern territories after the war) increasing to 1,703 in 1946. During this period, Oberbrecheners have lived under five different forms of government, with changing rulers and borders.[2]

It is hard to gauge what state-level political changes meant for the villagers and to what extent they identified as people of Nassau, as Hessians, or—prompted by the unification of 1871—as Germans (see Maps 1 and 2). After the 1866 Austro–Prussian War, Oberbrecheners were no longer subject to the Duke of Nassau. They had become and would remain Prussians for the next seven decades of empire, republic, and Nazi dictatorship.[3] The Prussian Province of Hesse-Nassau consisted of the two governmental districts (*Regierungsbezirke*) of Kassel in the north and Wiesbaden in the south. Oberbrechen was part of the Wiesbaden district. For most of the time, the village was located in the county of Limburg administered by the county governor (*Landrat*). With the 1944 reorganization, the two districts were separated and Oberbrechen became part of the Province of Nassau. After the Second World War, under U.S. occupation, the authorities redrew the borders yet again, with large parts of the former province now forming the westernmost region of Greater Hesse. This became what we know today as the state of Hesse, under the terms of the constitution adopted on December 1, 1946.[4]

---

2 For statistics, see *Historisches Ortslexikon*, Landesgeschichtliches Informationssystem Hessen, last accessed October 3, 2022, https://www.lagis-hessen.de/de/subjects/gsrec/current/1/sn/ol?q=Oberbrechen.

3 Hellmuth Gensicke, "Oberbechen im Wandel der Zeiten," in *Geschichte von Oberbrechen*, ed. on behalf of Brechen Municipality by id. and Egon Eichhorn (Brechen-Oberbrechen: Gemeinde Brechen, 1975), 248–266, here 259. On the territorial changes, see Eckhart G. Franz, "Zur politischen Landeskunde Hessens," in *Das Land Hessen: Geschichte–Gesellschaft–Politik*, ed. Bernd Heidenreich and Angelika Röming (Stuttgart: W. Kohlhammer, 2014), 15–32.

4 Franz, "Landeskunde," 32.

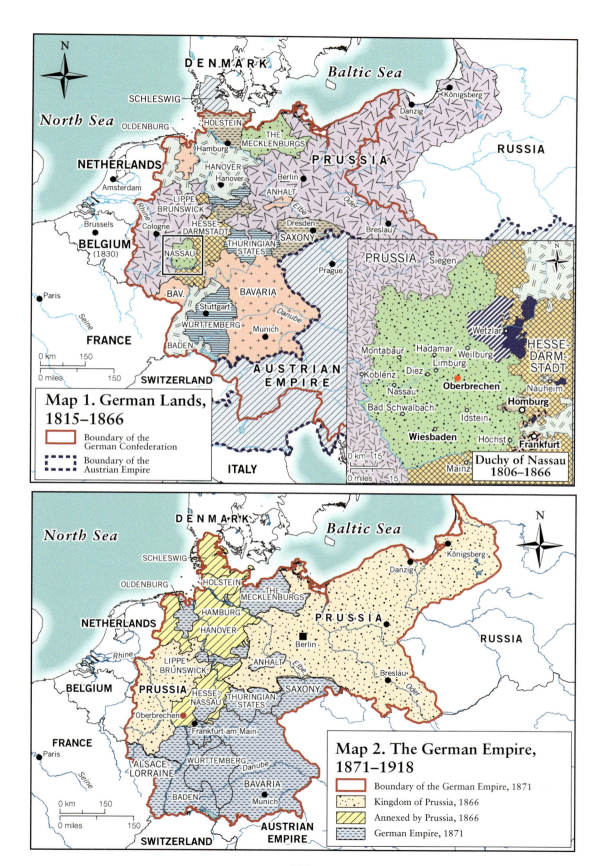

JEWISH LIFE IN OBERBRECHEN AND HESSE

Jewish life in the region surrounding Oberbrechen can be traced back to the High Middle Ages (c. 1000–1250). Records attest to Jews living in the area's urban center, Frankfurt am Main, in the twelfth century; and not far from Frankfurt, in the cities of Mainz and Worms, traces of Jewish life go back to the eleventh. However, from the very beginning of Jewish settlement in the lands of "Ashkenaz," we also find Jewish communities outside these urban centers along the rivers Rhine, Main, and Danube. But it was only at the beginning of the early modern period (c. 1500–1800) that such rural Jewish communities started to thrive.[5] The German lands were characterized by numerous small statelets and principalities whose rulers granted Jews rights to settle and establish communities in return for the payment of special taxes. By the sixteenth century, Jewish rural communities outnumbered those communities in urban centers. This settlement structure slowly started to change once again during the age of emancipation, which started at the beginning of the nineteenth century. In this context, "emancipation" refers to the extension of civic rights to Jews. This process of legal emancipation was accompanied by a process of social emancipation of the Jews that continued even after legal emancipation was concluded.

While the area surrounding Oberbrechen counted numerous Jewish settlements from very early on, traces of Jewish life in the village itself are first documented in the year 1711. Before discriminatory anti-Jewish laws were removed during the nineteenth century, the Jews of Oberbrechen, like those elsewhere in German lands, were limited in their movement and could not buy land or engage in craftsmanship. These prohibitions barred Jews from entering many occupations and from making a living in agriculture, as many Christians did. Instead, Jews were confined to trade and pawnbroking. We may note that Christian rural inhabitants were also subject to feudal restrictions at this time, and many struggled to make ends meet.

The majority of Jews made a living as peddlers, traders, or merchants at the eve of emancipation. In the German lands, emancipation was understood as a reciprocal process in which Jews were to be offered civic rights on the condition of their complete *Verschmelzung* (literally "amalgamation"— in the context of German Jewish emancipation, it can be best understood as assimilation) into German society. In other words, Jews were asked to give up their "Jewishness" in exchange for civic rights. At the core of this call for change was a demand for economic and cultural "betterment." In

---

5   Rainer Barzen, "Ländliche jüdische Siedlungen und Niederlassungen in Aschkenas: Vom Hochmittelalter bis ins 16. Jahrhundert. Typologie, Struktur und Vernetzung," *Aschkenas: Zeitschrift für Geschichte und Kultur der Juden* 2, no. 1–2 (2011) (Berlin: Walter de Gruyter, 2013), 5–36, here 18–19.

particular, the promoters of emancipation asked Jews to abandon making their living as peddlers and traders and to take up "productive activities," such as agriculture and craftsmanship, instead.⁶

Despite the removal of some of the restrictions from the early modern period, the livelihoods of Jews changed little in subsequent years. In 1841, there were 1,312 Jews living in the Duchy of Nassau; of these, 1,050 were traders, 3 were innkeepers, 101 made ends meet as craftsmen (including journeymen), 19 worked as farmers, 15 earned some money as day laborers, and 124 Jews were reported as being "poor" or without a job.⁷ In the countryside Jewish economic activity was chiefly confined to trade in agricultural products, such as hops and grain, and livestock (cattle, chicken, sheep, goats, and sometimes horses). Cattle trading in particular was widespread among Jews living in rural areas. Oral tradition even maintained that the majority of German Jews were descendants of cattle-trading families.⁸

In June 1841, special taxes that had previously been imposed on Jews were abolished in the Duchy of Nassau. The Jews of the Duchy, and with them the Jews of Oberbrechen, were granted full equality with regard to municipal and state taxes with the Christian population in 1849. But it was not until 1861 that the discriminatory Jew oath (*Judeneid*), which Jews were made to swear in court cases, was removed. On July 3, 1869, shortly after Prussia had annexed the Duchy of Nassau, Jews received full civic rights. A little while later, with the unification of Germany in 1871, Jewish emancipation was rolled out across the whole country.⁹ But this moment did not end formal discrimination completely. For instance, Jews were still excluded from high-ranking government positions until the end of the First World War.

Once settlement restrictions were lifted, the exodus of the Jewish rural population to urban areas that had already started before 1869 accelerated. More than any other group, younger Jews left rural communities to settle in medium-sized towns and cities, breaking away from traditional

---

6 David Sorkin, "Emancipation and Assimilation: Two Concepts and Their Application to German Jewish History," *Leo Baeck Institute Year Book* 35 (1990): 17–33, here 18.

7 Wolf-Arno Kropat, "Die Emanzipation der Juden in Kurhessen und in Nassau im 19. Jahrhundert," in *Neunhundert Jahre Geschichte der Juden in Hessen: Beiträge zum politischen, wirtschaftlichen und kulturellen Leben* (Wiesbaden: Kommission für die Geschichte der Juden in Hessen, 1983), 325–350, here 342.

8 Monika Richarz, "Viehhandel und Landjuden im 19. Jahrhundert: Eine symbiotische Wirtschaftsbeziehung in Südwestdeutschland," in Julius H. Schoeps (ed.), *Menora: Jahrbuch für deutsch-jüdische Geschichte* (Munich: Piper, 1990), 66–88.

9 J. Friedrich Battenberg, "Der lange Weg zur Emanzipation der Juden in den hessischen Ländern," in *Das Emanzipationsedikt von 1812 in Preußen: Der lange Weg der Juden zu "Einländern" und "preußischen Staatsbürgern"*, ed. by Irene A. Diekmann, 143–166 (Berlin: De Gruyter, 2013), 152; Kropat, "Die Emanzipation der Juden in Kurhessen und in Nassau im 19. Jahrhundert," 337, 341.

rural settlement patterns. In urban environments, they had access to better schooling and adopted a middle-class culture. Gustave Stern's father, Adolf Stern, was one of the young men who left the villages for business reasons.[10] In 1897 he moved to the city of Duisburg, where he expanded his cattle-trading business. While this move was driven by economic motivations, it went hand in hand with upward social mobility: he could now send his son, Gustave, to a selective high school (*Gymnasium*) that would allow him to access higher education—and this son later went on to study music at a conservatory. This rise into the cultured middle class differed considerably from the mobility of the non-Jewish population. The poor agrarian population, by contrast, usually migrated to the cities as workers.[11]

As elsewhere in the rural communities of Germany, the Jews who remained in Oberbrechen continued to follow pre-emancipatory occupational patterns. Jews who stayed in rural areas were often seen as unwilling to adapt to the process of modernization, preferring to stick to old patterns, while their apparently more advanced coreligionists took up academic professions in urban areas. Still, the fact that many rural Jews chose to remain in their pre-emancipation trade does not mean that they did not participate in the modernization process. On the contrary, they underwent a dramatic process of professionalization. Retaining an Orthodox Jewish lifestyle posed no contradiction to formation of a modern entrepreneurial culture, as the development of Siegfried Lichtenstein's business demonstrates.[12] Lichtenstein, who was known for retaining a traditional Jewish lifestyle, relocated his business from the neighboring village of Münster to Oberbrechen in 1927. There he could take advantage of the railway network, which linked remote farming villages with the major urban markets in cities like Frankfurt am Main, Wiesbaden, Gießen, and Koblenz. Lichtenstein's business had thus adapted to the demands of the times, from which his customers profited. Farmers participated indirectly in the transformation of rural areas but continued to use premodern animal power to work their fields. The Lichtenstein and Stern families, whose older generations were religiously Orthodox, operated in rapidly growing fields of businesses. In a rural society, they were both conveyors of old structures

---

10   As Steven M. Lowenstein emphasized, urbanization was frequently preceded by cultural and economic change; see Steven M. Lowenstein, "The Pace of Modernization of German Jewry in the Nineteenth Century," in id., *The Mechanics of Change: Essays in the Social History of German Jewry*. Brown Judaic Studies 246 (Atlanta: Scholars Press, 1992), 9–28, here 22.

11   Steven M. Lowenstein, "The Rural Community and the Urbanisation of German Jewry," in ibid., 133–151, here 140–141.

12   See also Stefanie Fischer, *Jewish Cattle Traders in the German Countryside: Economic Trust and Antisemitic Violence* (Bloomington: Indiana University Press, 2024), 58.

and agents of modernity. So, by the time the Weimar Republic drew to a close in the early 1930s, they were involved in a process of urbanization that made them participants in the shift to modernity experienced by the overall Jewish population. Preserving an Orthodox Jewish way of life did not stand in the way of this development.[13]

In rural areas, Jewish businesses were traditionally run as family businesses, involving men, women, and children alike. In the cattle-trading businesses, it was common for women to take on work in the stables and fields, along with managing the bookkeeping. Flora Lichtenstein, who had received training at a commercial school (*Handelsschule*) in Frankfurt am Main, took care of the bookkeeping and other office work in her family's business, including all correspondence with the authorities and business partners. Women assisted in running the family businesses to save on hiring additional personnel and so improve the economic foundation of the family.[14] In addition to carrying out managerial tasks, Flora Lichtenstein, like Christian peasant women, performed the hard physical labor in the fields that was required to produce cattle fodder.[15]

On the eve of the Holocaust, the number of Jewish communities in rural areas steadily decreased. In Hesse, thirty-eight rural Jewish communities had ceased to exist in the fifteen years from 1910 to 1925, while at the same time only nine new Jewish communities had sprung up.[16] To be sure, we lack exact numbers of the demographic development of Oberbrechen's Jewish population between 1711 and 1933, though one source suggests that the number of Jewish families declined from seven in 1912 to five families, or twenty-two individuals, in 1933.[17] This pattern differs from that of many other Jewish rural communities, which shrank more significantly or even ceased to exist after the abolition of settlement restrictions.

JEWISH RELIGIOUS LIFE

Religious life in Oberbrechen followed traditional patterns, as was common in rural areas. Oberbrechen's Jews belonged to the Jewish community of Weyer, which was part of the Ems-Weilburg rabbinate in the administrative district of Wiesbaden (Oberlahnkreis) in the Province of Hesse-Nassau.

---

13 Ibid., 202.

14 See also ibid., 47–55.

15 Affidavit by Flora Lichtenstein, Buenos Aires, November 22, 1966, Hessian Central State Archives Wiesbaden (hereafter HHStAW), 518, 82136, Compensation file Flora Lichtenstein née Hess, 5.

16 Paul Arnsberg, *Die Jüdischen Gemeinden in Hessen: Anfang, Untergang, Neubeginn* (Frankfurt: Societäts-Verlag, 1971), 20.

17 *Historisches Ortslexikon.*

The declining number of Jewish communities in rural areas made it almost impossible for the men of a single village to form a *minyan*—a quorum consisting of ten adults, which was traditionally required for public prayer and the performance of other religious rituals. As a result, Jews from several villages and towns had to come together to form a congregation. So, while the Jews of Oberbrechen celebrated Jewish holidays in their homes and sometimes went to synagogue in the distant county capital of Limburg on high holidays, the synagogue in the neighboring village of Weyer was the center of their religious life. We know little about the religious practices of the Weyer congregation, but we can assume that it followed an Orthodox liturgy, with men and women sitting apart from each other. While the reform movement in Jewish communities started to emerge in the nineteenth century, it remained an urban phenomenon in interwar Germany. In 1932, two Oberbrecheners, Siegfried Stern and Siegfried Lichtenstein, acted as the heads of the Jewish community (*Gemeindevorsteher*) in Weyer, and we know that Samuel Loeb Stern served as a cantor at the synagogue.[18] Max Altmann was the last head of this synagogue community before it ceased to exist in 1938/1940.[19] When Oberbrechen Jews died, they were buried in the Jewish cemetery in Weyer. Selma Altmann's mother, Rosa Stern (née Levita), was the last person to be put to rest there in spring 1938.

Jewish rituals and practices were part of everyday life in Oberbrechen's village community throughout the time Jews lived in Oberbrechen. Jewish women went about domestic chores in accordance with *halakhah*, which covers large parts of Jewish law and practice. They performed tasks such as preparing for the Sabbath and other holidays and guarding the *kashrut* (Jewish dietary laws) of the family home. We have no record that tells us where in Oberbrechen Jewish women baked *challah*—a bread baked for ceremonial occasions on Sabbath and Jewish holidays. But what we know generally of rural Jewry suggests that they likely would have done so in the village bakery, perhaps Peter Jung's bakery at 18 Lange Street, next to the home of Selma and Max Altmann.[20] Jewish daily life was particularly visible on holidays, for example, when families set up a decorated

---

18 Terry Shoptaugh, *"You Have Been Kind Enough to Assist Me": Herman Stern and the Jewish Refugee Crisis* (Fargo: North Dakota State University, 2008), 1.

19 Letter from Max Altman, Los Angeles, to Paul Arnsberg, Frankfurt am Main, September 5, 1966, in Archives of the Jewish Museum Frankfurt, Arnsberg Collection, 176 Weyer. Three people were still registered as members of the Weyer Jewish community on January 15, 1940. See Franz Gölzenleuchter, *Sie verbrennen Dein Heiligtum. Psalm 74,4: Synagogen und jüdische Friedhöfe im Kreis Limburg-Weilburg 50 Jahre später* (Limburg: Franz Gölzenleuchter, 1988), 88.

20 The reader will find two different forms of spelling for Selma's and Max's family name. We use "Altmann" with double "n" for the time before the couple's emigration from Germany and the anglicized version "Altman" which they used after their emigration.

sukkah outdoors during Sukkot or when they lit Chanukkah candles in their homes.[21] Samuel and Adolf Stern's kosher butchery was an ever-present part of the village's social and economic life. Our sources point to at least two kosher households in the interwar period (the Lichtenstein family and the Samuel/Moses Stern family), and there were probably more Jewish families in Oberbrechen who observed Jewish dietary laws.

As can be seen in Gustave Stern's case, the younger generation tended to distance themselves from Orthodox Judaism, but they often still did not allow themselves to eat pork or violate other Jewish laws. However, some continued practicing Orthodox Judaism later in their lives. Kurt Lichtenstein, for instance, described himself as growing up Orthodox in Oberbrechen and identified as religiously conservative in the 1990s.[22] However, in general, the observance of *kashrut* steadily declined in Germany in the 1920s and 1930s. The historian Trude Maurer suggests that, at this time, only about 15 to 20 percent of the overall Jewish population adhered to Jewish dietary laws.[23]

Issues of gender and family likewise shaped the religious life of Oberbrechen's Jews. To fulfill religious obligations, Jewish women were required to bathe themselves ritually in a *mikveh* (Jewish ritual bath) after their monthly menstruation, before marriage, and after childbirth. The sources do not refer to a *mikveh* in Weyer, but there are hints that Jewish women from Oberbrechen went to the *mikveh* in neighboring Münster in the nineteenth century. We do not know if they continued to purify themselves in a *mikveh* on a regular basis at the beginning of the twentieth century and, if they did, where they may have gone.[24]

SOCIAL AND COMMUNAL LIFE

Jews and Christians in the village shared public and social spaces, and interacted as neighbors, business partners, parents of young children, and playmates, or in other roles in daily life. These interactions were tried and tested, and oscillated between peaceful and difficult times. Often

---

21 A *sukkah* is a hut erected during the Jewish holiday of Sukkot. It marks the years of wandering after the Exodus from Egypt. Channukkah candles are lit during the Jewish holiday Channukkah, the festival of lights celebrating the miracle of the oil in the Temple.

22 Kurt Lichtenstein interviewed by Mirta Hecht de Yanco, May 6, 1996, Buenos Aires, Argentina, Interview Code 14451, Visual History Archive, USC Shoah Foundation.

23 Trude Maurer, "From Everyday Life to a State of Emergency: Jews in Weimar and Nazi Germany," in Marion A. Kaplan (ed.), *Jewish Daily Life in Germany, 1618–1945* (Oxford: Oxford University Press, 2005), 271–374, here 277–278.

24 Christa Pullmann and Eugen Caspary (eds.), *Das Gebinde des Lebens: Die jüdischen Kultusgemeinden Weyer und Münster in Hessen. Vom 17. Jahrhundert bis zu ihrer Vernichtung 1940* (Limburg an der Lahn: Gesellschaft für Christlich-Jüdische Zusammenarbeit, 2004), 66–68.

antisemitism and neighborliness existed in parallel with each other and shaped village life. The sources point to at least one antisemitic incident during the *Kaiserreich* (German Empire, 1871–1918) when businessman Hermann Blumenthal called pub owner Ernst R. (the source does not give his full name) the biggest antisemite in the entire region.[25]

Despite these tensions, an opening up to the non-Jewish world is also manifest in marriages between Jews and Christians. In Oberbrechen we know of Jenny Stern, daughter of Siegmund Stern and sister of Paul Stern, who married the non-Jew Lorenz Geiß. The couple migrated to New York in 1920. We can say little about the motives for their move—whether economic, political, or cultural factors drove them to the United States—but, to our knowledge, it was the only Jewish–Christian marriage that took place in Oberbrechen. In urban centers, the number of interfaith marriages was much higher. By 1927, "25 percent of Jewish men and 16 percent of Jewish women were marrying outside their religion" in Germany.[26]

MIGRATION

Jenny Stern and her husband were by no means the first to leave Oberbrechen to find a new home on the other side of the Atlantic. Some other villagers migrated to the United States much earlier than they did. One of them was Jenny's great uncle, Hermann Stern, who was among the 70,000 to 100,000 Jews from Germany who, in Avraham Barkai's estimate, entered the United States between 1890 and 1910.[27] Hermann's father, Samuel Stern, had made a living as a kosher butcher and cantor. His earnings were so low that he lived a life of poverty, and it was hard for the family to make ends meet. Herman Stern recalled that "before [he] was four-years-old his parents began sending him out to walk along the road leading into Oberbrechen, to pick up loose grain that had fallen off wagons. This 'gleaning' of grain . . . provided the family with something more to eat, together with the vegetables grown on the little piece of land they owned and some meat from the chickens and rabbits."[28] At the age of fourteen, Hermann started a two-year apprenticeship at a tailor's shop

---

25 Eugen Caspary, "Jüdische Mitbürger in Oberbrechen 1711–1941: Eine Bestandsaufnahme," in *Geschichte von Oberbrechen*, ed. Hellmuth Gensicke and Egon Eichhorn (Brechen-Oberbrechen: Gemeinde Brechen, 1975), 157–231, here 208.

26 Marion A. Kaplan, *Between Dignity and Despair: Jewish Life in Nazi Germany* (Oxford: Oxford University Press, 1998), 11.

27 Avraham Barkai, *Branching Out: German-Jewish Immigration to the United States, 1820–1914* (New York: Holmes & Meier, 1994), 126. Just as in the case of the Altmann/Altman family, the reader will find two different forms of spelling for the youngest of the Stern siblings. We use "Hermann" with a double "n" for the time before his emigration from Germany and the anglicized version "Herman" which he used after his emigration.

28 Shoptaugh, *"You Have Been Kind Enough to Assist Me,"* 3.

in the city of Mainz. While he worked there, his cousin, Morris G. Straus, owner of the Straus clothing store in Casselton, North Dakota, reached out to him asking for help at his store. Herman, who was not enjoying his apprenticeship in Mainz, quickly responded to his cousin's call and left for the United States in October 1903.

In this new country, an increasing number of German Jewish immigrants settled in remote, rural places, far away from metropolitan port cities on the East Coast, and made their living as small-scale entrepreneurs, just as many of them had previously done in Germany.[29] Another common pattern was to fall back on family ties to gain an economic foothold, and this is what Herman Stern (now with an anglicized first name) did as well.[30] He started working at his cousin's North Dakota clothing store, before achieving more economic stability when Straus handed the business over to him, shortly after 1907.[31] A lot of Jews were active in the same sector of business—as owners of dry goods stores and in selling clothing (though they also got involved in the manufacture of clothes). The stores were run by the whole family—male and female, old and young—as was typical for German Jewish middle-class businesses.[32]

THE FIRST WORLD WAR AND THE WEIMAR YEARS

Had Herman Stern stayed in Oberbrechen, he would probably have been drafted into the Kaiser's army during the First World War. His brothers Adolf and Julius Stern, along with his cousins, were among the up to 100,000 German Jews who participated in this mammoth conflict, joining different ranks of the German army.[33] When war broke out in 1914, many of them followed the Kaiser's call to fight for the fatherland: it was the first time, in a united Germany, that Jewish men could fight side-by-side with their non-Jewish comrades, and, for some of them, it was a way to demonstrate their loyalty and patriotism to their home country. Around 12,000 of them paid with their lives.[34] Jewish women also felt the hardships of the war, which left many of them mourning the death of loved ones at the front. One of the bereaved was Jette Stern, whose fiancé was killed in

---

29 Hasia R. Diner, "German Immigrant Period in the United States," Shalvi/Hyman, *Encyclopedia of Jewish Women*, December 31, 1999. Jewish Women's Archive, last accessed December 8, 2022. https://jwa.org/encyclopedia/article/german-immigrant-period-in-united-states.

30 Barkai, *Branching Out*, 135.

31 Shoptaugh, *"You Have Been Kind Enough to Assist Me,"* 6.

32 Diner, "German Immigrant Period in the United States."

33 Herman's brothers Adolf and Julius Stern no longer lived in Oberbrechen at the time of their draft. They are therefore not mentioned in the graphic part of this book (Part I).

34 Derek Penslar, "The German Jewish Soldier: From Participant to Victim," *German History* 29, no. 3 (2011), 423–444, here 432.

action at the front. She was shattered by this loss and never got married. Other Jewish women from Oberbrechen supported men on the battlefield from afar. One of them was Flora Lichtenstein, who worked in the office of the Free Association of Jewish Soldiers at the Front (*Freie Vereinigung jüdischer Frontsoldaten*)[35] (presumably in Frankfurt) from 1914 to 1918.

However, along with this heightened sense of national unity and belonging came the experience of fierce antisemitism with the so-called Jew count (*Judenzählung*) of 1916, which aimed at falsely accusing Jews of shying away from military service. On the other side of the Atlantic, Herman Stern, as a Jew who had come from Germany, experienced anti-German sentiments. After the United States entered the war in 1917, Herman no longer received letters from home, leaving him in the dark about the well-being of his family in Oberbrechen and beyond. At the end of the war, antisemitism in Germany worsened. Looking for a scapegoat, right-wing and nationalist-*völkisch* circles pinned the blame for the country's defeat primarily on the Jews and the Social Democrats and Socialists.[36] In short, Jewish Germans increasingly faced hostility no matter if they lived in Germany or abroad—either for being Jewish or for being German.

The postwar Weimar constitution guaranteed equal rights to all its citizens, including access to the highest state offices for Jews. During the years of the Weimar Republic (1919–1933), a flourishing and acculturated Jewish community was widely integrated into German society. In Oberbrechen, many Jews were actively participating in social and communal life inside and outside the village at this time. One of them was Paul Stern, who acted as board member for the local sports club (*Turn- und Sportgemeinde*) between 1926 and 1933. Some of the Jewish families traditionally hired non-Jewish maids to help them manage their households. One of these helpers was Gertrud Marx, who served as a maid in the households of Selma Altmann and Siegfried Stern. In many cases, such housemaids became part of the family for the duration of their employment. At the same time, the Weimar years were marked by economic and political turmoil, which provoked a growing, virulent antisemitism that gradually resulted in a complete reversal of this integration: the economic and social exclusion of Jews began in earnest.[37]

---

35 Affidavit by Flora Lichtenstein for the Wiesbaden compensation office, Buenos Aires, November 22, 1966, HHStAW, compensation file Flora Lichtenstein née Hess, 518, 82136, 5.

36 Werner T. Angress, "The German Army's 'Judenzählung' of 1916: Genesis–Consequences–Significance," *Leo Baeck Institute Year Book* 23 (1978), 117–138.

37 Anthony D. Kauders, "Weimar Jewry," in *Weimar Germany*, ed. Anthony McElligott (Oxford: Oxford University Press, 2009), 234–259.

NAZI PERSECUTION

THE GREAT DEPRESSION AND THE RISE OF NAZISM

Until 1928, Oberbrechen's population remained fairly stable, with a little over 1,330 residents. An occupational survey of that year recorded fifty-eight male and twenty female farmers, who worked with nine day laborers, two female agricultural assistants, one herdsman, and one agricultural laborer. The village had three general stores (*Kolonialwarenhandlungen*), twelve merchants, three traders, and three female salespersons. The number of working-class laborers in the community was small: just ten male and female factory workers. About sixty people had artisan jobs, among them Jewish women such as Selma Altmann and Flora Lichtenstein. Construction had become the largest economic sector in the region, with over 150 people from Oberbrechen working in this industry, either as employees or self-employed workers. This was also the sector hit hardest by the Great Depression, which followed the Wall Street Crash of October 29, 1929.[38] All over the world economic output sharply declined.

Farmers, too, were hit hard by the Great Depression. While most farmers had emerged unscathed from the 1923 hyperinflation, the late 1920s were devastating years for them.[39] A drastic fall in livestock prices created huge financial difficulties for many rural family farmsteads.[40] Jewish cattle traders felt the tensions of their dual role vis-à-vis farmers, who saw them simultaneously as "kindly" lenders and as "merciless" money collectors.[41] In the Nazi strongholds of Hesse, one interpretation of their economic position came to dominate: attacks, and insults were repeatedly hurled at Jews, either openly in the street or in taverns, to blame them and their business practices for the intensifying poverty of the rural population. This kind of harassment went hand in hand with a flurry of propaganda. In this way, the Nazis linked their agitation in the countryside to traditional anti-Jewish and *völkisch* (ethnic-national) stereotypes, propagating belief in a causal connection between the Great Depression and the economic position of Jewish businessmen.

---

38   Gensicke, "Handwerk und Gewerbe," in *Geschichte von Oberbrechen*, ed. id. and Eichhorn, 425–426; *Historisches Ortslexikon*.

39   Donald L. Niewyk, "The Impact of Inflation and Depression on the German Jews," *Leo Baeck Institute Year Book* 28 (1983), 19–36; Avraham Barkai, "Die Juden als sozio-ökonomische Minderheitsgruppe in der Weimarer Republik," in *Juden in der Weimarer Republik*, ed. Walter Grab and Julius H. Schoeps (Stuttgart: Burg, 1986), 330–346.

40   See Ulrich Kluge, *Agrarwirtschaft und ländliche Gesellschaft im 20. Jahrhundert* (Munich: Oldenbourg, 2005), 22.

41   See Gennady Estraikh, *Yiddisch in Weimar Berlin: At the Crossroads of Diaspora Politics and Culture* (London: Routledge, 2010); Dirk Walter, *Antisemitische Kriminalität und Gewalt: Judenfeindschaft in der Weimarer Republik* (Bonn: Dietz, 1999), 157–165.

By early 1932, over six million people were formally registered as being out of work in Germany, with the actual number estimated at around eight million. This makes for an unemployment rate of 37 percent, compared to 23.6 percent in the United States.[42] Oberbrecheners could not escape the rising social tensions triggered by this economic crisis. The local labor office was swamped when some 600 unemployed people from the surrounding area descended on the village twice a week to obtain the stamped certification that was needed to claim benefits.[43] One claimant who lived locally was Hugo Trost. In early 1931, when he was twenty-eight years old, he lost his job at a charity-run hospital in Frankfurt am Main. But Trost had already joined the Nazi Party in 1928. His case shows that it is difficult to construct a simple relation between rising unemployment rates and growing support for Hitler. Research has established that, in general, "unemployed workers were more likely to turn to Communism than to Nazism."[44] The bulk of the members of the Nazi Party (NSDAP) in these early years consisted of owners of small and medium-sized businesses, civil servants, white-collar employees, and freelance professionals. The NSDAP was thus the party of the small-town and petit bourgeois middle class, but not of farmers.[45]

NAZISM IN PROTESTANT AND CATHOLIC REGIONS OF HESSE

Unlike the case in other regions in Germany, National Socialism gained a strong foothold in Hessian territories quite early on. In all five national elections between May 1928 and March 1933, held in unusually quick succession after parliamentary terms had ended prematurely, votes for the Nazi Party were above average in Prussian Hesse-Nassau (Table 1). In Hesse-Darmstadt, they were above average from 1930 onward.

---

42 Harold James, "The Weimar Economy," in *Weimar Germany*, ed. McElligott, 102–126, here 104, 116–117; Michael Wildt, *Zerborstene Zeit: Deutsche Geschichte 1918 bis 1945* (Munich: Beck, 2022), 247; Historical US Unemployment Rate by Year, The Balance, last accessed March 5, 2023, https://www.thebalancemoney.com/unemployment-rate-by-year-3305506#toc-us-unemployment-rates-by-year.

43 History of the [Nazi] Party at the Oberbrechen local base, copy of an anonymous report, September 17, 1936, HHStAW, 520/38, 58640, Denazification file Hugo Trost, 9–14, here 11.

44 Niall Ferguson, "The German Inter-war Economy: Political Choice versus Economic Determinism," in *German History Since 1800*, ed. Mary Fulbrook (London: Arnold, 1997), 258–278, here 263.

45 Jürgen W. Falter, *Hitlers Wähler* (Munich: Beck, 1991), 55; Detlev J. K. Peukert, *Die Weimarer Republik: Krisenjahre der klassischen Moderne* (Darmstadt: Wissenschaftliche Buchgesellschaft, 1997), 227–228.

TABLE 1. NSDAP RESULTS AT REICHSTAG ELECTIONS, 1928–1933[46]

	5/20/1928	9/14/1930	7/31/1932	11/6/1932	3/5/1933
Hesse-Nassau	3.6%	20.8%	43.6%	41.2%	49.4%
Hesse-Darmstadt	1.9%	18.5%	43.1%	40.2%	47.4%
National average	2.6%	18.3%	37.3%	33.1%	43.9%

Historians have explored the thesis that Nazi electoral successes in Hesse "essentially originated in rural, Protestant, less industrialized and urbanized thinly populated regions."[47] The historical picture of a Hesse in which *völkisch*-nationalist and antisemitic voters in the countryside furthered the rise of Nazism through ballot-box successes becomes more nuanced when we take into account voting behavior in non-Protestant areas, such as the one in which Oberbrechen is located.[48] Like the organized labor movement, political Catholicism in the Weimar Republic stood, by and large, in opposition to Nazism, which had difficulties making inroads into both milieus until 1933. In 1925, 70.7 percent of Hessians were Protestant (compared with 64.1 percent in all of Germany), while 25.5 percent were Catholics (compared with 32.4 percent nationwide). At 2.1 percent, the share of Jewish Hessians was above the national average of 0.9 percent.[49]

The county of Limburg was a traditional stronghold of the Center Party (*Zentrumspartei*), which had represented political Catholicism in all of Germany with the exception of Bavaria since its foundation in 1870. As Table 2 shows, the Center Party gained a solid majority in this county in the four national elections held between 1930 and 1933. True to the Limburg pattern, Oberbrecheners responded to the growing crises of the early 1930s by increasing their support for the Center Party, which gained an absolute majority in the Reichstag election of July 1932 that it could retain in following elections. Among the neighboring villages, Oberbrechen was in a middle position between Niederbrechen, where, remarkably, the Nazi Party polled its nationwide low of a mere 3.1 percent in the 1933 Reichstag election, and Niederselters, where Hitler's

---

46 Numbers according to Eike Hennig, "'Der Hunger naht'–'Mittelstand wehr Dich'– 'Wir Bauern misten aus:' Über angepasstes und abweichendes Wahlverhalten in hessischen Agrarregionen," in *Hessen unterm Hakenkreuz*, ed. id., 379–432, here 384; Klaus Schönekäs, "Hinweise auf die soziopolitische Verfassung Hessen in der Weimarer Republik," in ibid., 45–60, here 58–59.

47 Hennig, "Wahlverhalten," 379, 382; Eberhard Schön, *Die Entstehung des Nationalsozialismus in Hessen* (Meisenheim am Glan: Anton Hain, 1972), 2.

48 Hennig, "Wahlverhalten," 379.

49 Schön, *Entstehung des Nationalsozialismus*, 2–3; Hennig, "Wahlverhalten," n. 22, 424–425.

TABLE 2. REICHSTAG ELECTION RESULTS FOR THE NAZI PARTY (NSDAP) AND THE CENTER PARTY (Z)[50]

	9/14/1930		7/31/1932		11/6/1932		3/5/1933	
	NSDAP	Z	NSDAP	Z	NSDAP	Z	NSDAP	Z
Oberbrechen	10.7	40.7	13.8	50.2	13.5	52.6	18.7	57.7
Niederbrechen	1.0	75.0	1.8	72.3	2.2	73.9	3.1	75.4
Niederselters	18.9	26.8	28.8	39.4	27.0	41.8	33.6	40.6
Limburg county	10.1	47.4	24.3	48.9	25.2	47.7	31.9	48.2
Hesse-Nassau	20.8	14.1	43.6	15.0	41.2	14	49.4	13.9

movement acquired a growing number of adherents, among them the later Nazi mayor Eduard Lutz.[51]

Hugo Trost's denazification file contains a detailed history of the Nazi movement's local branch written in September 1936. According to this history, the first two Oberbrecheners to join the party, Franz Josef Arthen and Karl Kremer, did so in 1928. By January 1933, 17 men from Ober- and Niederbrechen were card-carrying Nazis (0.5 percent of the Brechen population).[52] The historical account—most likely authored by Trost himself—recounts a difficult "time of struggle" (*Kampfzeit*), with the Center Party as the "strongest opponent" in the village community. Aggressive forms of agitation and clashes between political opponents did not stop short of physical violence. Given the intimacy of the spaces they shared, these events must have made a strong impression on both Jewish and non-Jewish Oberbrecheners.

Indeed, space was a crucial issue: until March 1933 the local Nazis often could not find public halls or pubs in which to hold their gatherings or to stage their propaganda spectacles—a pattern known from other places. Larger events, such as the first public rally with Gau leader Jakob Sprenger in Oberbrechen, were held outdoors.[53] In October 1932, the Nazis stormed

---

50 Frank Schmidt, *Wahlhandbuch Limburg-Weilburg 1919–1933* (Limburg/Lahn: Kreissparkasse Limburg, 1995), 66–69, 77–82, 86–87; Schönekäs, "Hinweise," 58–59.

51 Schön, *Entstehung des Nationalsozialismus*, 205; Eugen Caspary, *Bürgermeister Adam Graef: Bau-Gewerkschaftler und Sozialdemokrat *1882 Niederselters †1945 KZ Bergen-Belsen* (Camberg: Ulrich Lange, 1982), 61. See also Rudolf Morsey, "Die katholische Volksminderheit und der Aufstieg des Nationalsozialismus 1930–1933," in *Die Katholiken und das Dritte Reich*, ed. Klaus Gotto and Konrad Repgen (Mainz: Grünewald, 1990), 9–24, here 16–18.

52 History of the [Nazi] Party at the Oberbrechen local base, 9–11.

53 History of the [Nazi] Party at the Oberbrechen local base, 9–14. The report gives two different dates for Sprenger's appearance in Oberbrechen: 1929 and 1930. In both instances, the event is described as the Nazis' first public rally in the village. Following the event, Sprenger was reported to the police for insulting the national government. Ibid., 9. In the organization of the Nazi Party, a Gau leader was a party official who headed a regional party district termed *Gau*.

an event organized by the center-left Social Democratic Party of Germany (SPD), which had invited Berta Jourdan and Karl Wilhelm Erik Nölting, two prominent politicians and members of the Prussian parliament, to Oberbrechen as speakers. The party *History* records that they "were not able to finish their speeches and, together with the Jew Stern [possibly Paul, Moritz or Max Stern], had to escape through the window."[54]

The Nazis tirelessly constructed an image of themselves as a movement whose representatives did not just talk, like the others, but went in for action. Shock and repulsion in the face of Nazi violence could be assuaged when local or regional dignitaries supported or participated in the movement.[55] The influential churches had two options: they could either make Nazism seem acceptable or they could deny it an important public stage. The Protestant church saw itself as standing "outside of political party life" and did not interfere with party memberships among its congregants. This led to a highly "ambivalent attitude" toward Nazism.[56] In contrast, Catholic clergy mostly strove to keep the doors of their churches locked to demonstrations of Nazi power. In September 1930, the Diocese of Mainz, which was neighbor to that of Limburg, supported firm action by its local priests and declared the Nazi Party program to be "irreconcilable with Catholic doctrine." Congregants who joined the party were no longer to receive the sacraments.[57] The Episcopate was hesitant to follow this bold decision. In practice, no ecclesiastical penalties were issued to congregants who were party members.[58] Party-political Catholicism was *de facto* dead even before Hitler put his signature to the Concordat with the Holy See in Rome on July 20, 1933. The Concordat was meant to calm German Catholics, who were guaranteed free practice of their faith and the continuation of their right to give religious education. However, these chartered rights were not honored for long: over the years, the regime suppressed Catholic organizations, including faith schools, further and further.[59]

Research has moved beyond simplistic distinctions between Christian faith and Nazi ideology and between a basically supportive Protestant church

---

54 Ibid.

55 William Sheridan Allen, *The Nazi Seizure of Power: The Experience of a single German Town 1922–1945*, revised edition (New York: Franklin Watts, 1984 [1965]), 225, 308.

56 Resolution of Prussian State Synod, April 20, 1920, quoted in: Günther van Norden, "Die Stellung der evangelischen Kirchen zum Nationalsozialismus," in *Von Weimar zu Hitler: 1930–1933*, ed. Gotthard Japser (Cologne: Kiepenheuer & Witsch, 1968), 377–402, here 378. See also Schön, *Entstehung des Nationalsozialismus*, 191–192.

57 Schön, *Entstehung des Nationalsozialismus*, 189.

58 Morsey, "Katholische Volksminderheit," 13–14.

59 Ibid., 23–24; Dieter Albrecht, "Der Hl. Stuhl und das Dritte Reich," in *Katholiken*, ed. Gotte and Repgen, 25–47, here 28–29; Manfred Gailus, *Gläubige Zeiten: Religiosität im Dritten Reich* (Freiburg i. Br.: Herder, 2021), 41.

and a greater resilience in Catholic milieus. To be sure, the "Third Reich" was by no means a "godless time": Christian faith was held to be compatible with "belief" in Nazi visions of national destiny appealingly framed in eschatological rhetoric of the end of days, judgment, and redemption.[60] In Catholic-dominated areas of Germany such as Bavaria, Baden, Upper Silesia, Mainfranken, Westphalia, the Rhineland, and the Catholic parts of Hesse, it was Catholics who represented and implemented Nazi rule (see Map 3 for an overview of Catholic areas in 1925; Map 4 shows the distribution of the Jewish population in Germany in 1933 for comparison). In the staunchly Catholic town of Eichstätt in Central Franconia, for example, researchers observe a striking "Catholification of Nazism."[61] SA and Hitler Youth formations accompanied the Corpus Christi procession in Eichstätt in 1933—a "year of change" for Christians in all of Germany and a stark "religious revival" with people who had turned away from the faith now returning.[62]

The Catholic community of Oberbrechen also experienced religious renewal in 1933. Father Alois Kunz, consecrated as village priest in November 1932, managed to rouse the enthusiasm of his congregation for a longstanding, but so far stagnating, project: the refurbishment of the church.[63] Kunz swiftly succeeded in collecting donations and recruiting labor to rebuild the church, which the Bishop of Limburg would consecrate shortly before Christmas 1933.[64] His efforts to raise funds for this project put Father Kunz on a collision course with Oberbrechen's new mayor, Hugo Trost. Based on a contract between the municipality and the parish dating from 1902, the municipality was obliged to cover the costs for the church tower, which amounted to some 20,000 Reichsmark. Trost's apparent refusal to honor the municipal commitment can be interpreted as a first power struggle, setting the stage for what would become a difficult

---

60   Gailus, *Gläubige Zeiten*, 10. See also Olaf Blaschke and Thomas Großbölting (eds.), *Was glaubten die Deutschen zwischen 1933 und 1945? Religion und Politik im Nationalsozialismus* (Frankfurt am Main: Campus, 2020).

61   Markus Raasch, "Das schwarze Eichstätt ist braun geworden—katholische Lebenswelt und 'Volksgemeinschaft,'" in *Was glaubten die Deutschen*, ed. Blaschke und Großbölting, 83–111, here 83, 91. See also Evi Kleinöder, "Verfolgung und Widerstand der katholischen Jugendvereine: Eine Fallstudie über Eichstätt," in *Bayern in der NS-Zeit, vol. 2: Herrschaft und Gesellschaft im Konflikt*, ed. Martin Broszat and Elke Fröhlich (Munich: Oldenbourg, 1979), 175–236.

62   Gailus, *Gläubige Zeiten*, 15, 17–18; Raasch, "Das schwarze Eichstätt," 91.

63   Alois Kunz, "Die Pfarrkirche Oberbrechen im Wandel eines Jahrtausends: Zur Einweihung der neuen Kirche am Donnerstag," *Nassauer Bote*, December 20, 1933. See also Hellmuth Gensicke and Alfons Schmidt, "Die Kirche," in *Geschichte von Oberbrechen*, ed. Gensicke and Eichhorn, 124–135, here 124, 128.

64   Gensicke and Schmidt, "Die Kirche," 132. See also "Mit Meilensteinen des Schaffens gepflastert: Langjähriger Seelsorger von Oberbrechen trat in den Ruhestand—Ein Gruß an die Pfarrei," *Nassauer Bote*, March 9, 1961.

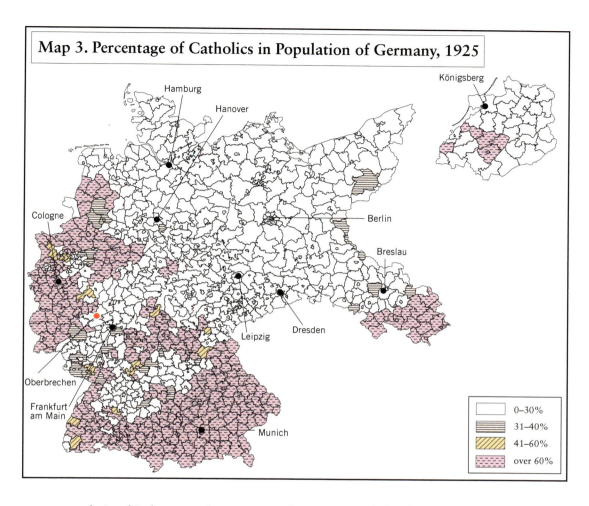

relationship between the two men who represented the clerical and political authorities in the village.⁶⁵

The religious renewal of 1933 was accompanied by radical political change in Oberbrechen. The circumstances under which the unemployed Hugo Trost became the village mayor cannot fully be reconstructed from available sources. What is clear, however, is that regular democratic procedures were circumvented when Trost, backed by the Nazi Party district leadership, ousted Otto Strüder from office. Strüder had won the municipal elections on March 12, 1933, as well as the reelections held on April 9. Trost not only prevented him from taking office as mayor; he also ignored an instruction from the county governor (*Landrat*) that another round of voting should take place before August 20.⁶⁶ A letter of protest sent to the

---

65 Copy of agreement between the Oberbrechen municipality and the parish, July 15, 1935, HHStAW, 411/3065, Gemeindeverwaltung Oberbrechen.

66 History of the [Nazi] Party at the Oberbrechen local base, 12.

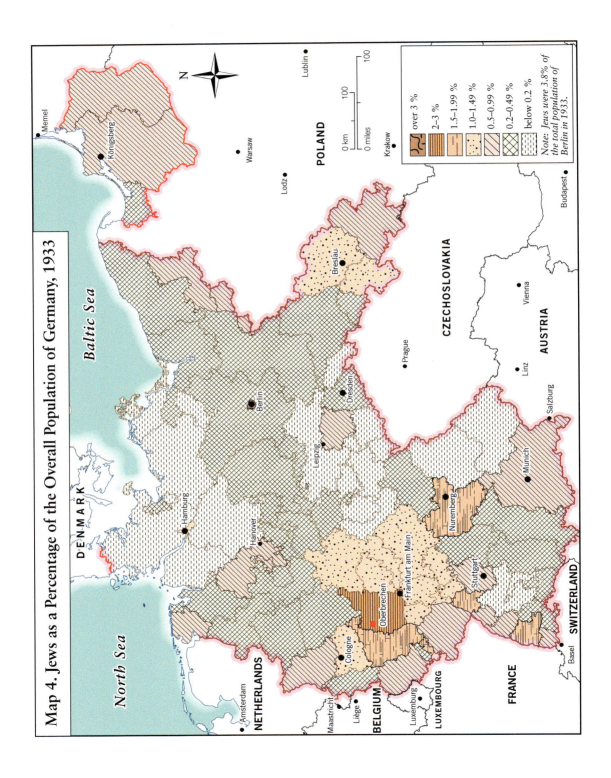

Map 4. Jews as a Percentage of the Overall Population of Germany, 1933

Landrat was "done away with when filed." The letter had been sent by the leader of the village workers' organization after Trost had suspended its six representatives from the municipal council in June. Soon afterward, he dissolved the council as a whole.[67]

What Trost, in 1936, proudly referred to as his thorough "cleansing of local politics" was nothing less than radical oppression enacted within an overall atmosphere of terror. His denunciation of the six dismissed workers' representatives as "Marxists" and his threat to "send them on vacation to a concentration camp" echoed violent measures undertaken by self-empowered Nazi potentates, paramilitary activists, and local state authorities all over Germany. In the spring and summer of 1933, the long-expected moment of reckoning came for all those regarded as the movement's enemies. Within months, tens of thousands were arrested and sent to improvised detention centers where they suffered abuse and torture. In the Hessian territories, early concentration camps were set up in Breitenau near Kassel (Hesse-Nassau) and in Osthofen near Worms (Hesse-Darmstadt). Their presence helped to spread an atmosphere of terror and turned Trost's announcement into life-threatening danger. Both camps held high proportions of Jewish prisoners from the region.[68]

ATTACKS ON JEWISH LIFE

Jews in Germany were among the first victims of Nazi terror. Soon after Hitler's assumption of power in January 1933, many Jews experienced a rapid breakdown of neighborly solidarity, and their increasing isolation throughout the first years of Nazi rule brought them ever closer to "social death."[69] Within weeks of assuming governmental power, the new regime issued legislation aimed at economic and professional discrimination against Jews. The category of "non-Aryan" was enshrined in the legislature as early as April 7, 1933, with the Law for the Restoration of the Professional Civil Service. This law was followed by a barrage of antisemitic regulations formulated to exclude Jews from the racially defined "people's community" in the making. The Nazis coupled a promise of gains and privileges for those they defined as "belonging" to this social utopia

---

67 Ibid., 12–14. Trost was acting mayor until officially appointed mayor in March 1934.

68 Ibid., 13; Statement of claim addressed to the Limburg denazification board, April 2, 1948, HHStAW, 520/38, 58640, denazification file Hugo Trost, p. 7. See also Jane Caplan, "Political Detention and the Origin of the Concentration Camps in Nazi Germany, 1933–1935/6," in *Nazism, War and Genocide: Essays in Honour of Jeremy Noakes*, ed. Neil Gregor (Exeter: University of Exeter Press, 2005), 22–41. On the camps of Breitenau and Osthofen, see Kim Wünschmann, *Before Auschwitz: Jewish Prisoners in the Prewar Concentration Camps* (Cambridge, MA: Harvard University Press, 2015), 46–49, 70, 74.

69 Kaplan, *Between Dignity and Despair*, 5.

with the ruthless exclusion of those held to be "community aliens."[70] Jews in Oberbrechen certainly felt this onslaught. They suffered discrimination and abuse, and Christian members of the community were forced to make choices on how to behave toward them.

On April 25, 1933, the Reich Sports Commissar decreed the exclusion of "non-Aryans" from sports clubs. The Oberbrechen TSG (*Turn- und-Sportgemeinschaft*) complied. Paul, Max, and Moritz Stern were removed from the board, and other, non-Jewish board members left as well.[71] During the same month, SA men stood in front of the Altmanns' shop to enforce a boycott.[72] The cattle-trading businesses of Siegfried Stern and Siegfried Lichtenstein suffered, and both men feared that their licenses would be revoked.[73] Customers began to stay away from Jewish-owned businesses. Nevertheless, despite growing social isolation, Moses Stern remained a sought-after participant in the card games played in the village pubs, and Gertrud Marx stayed on as the maid in the Altmann's house (due to her age, the Nuremberg Laws' prohibition on Jews hiring domestic servants under 45 could not touch her).[74]

In records of what happened at the village school, we can investigate how a place that was key to the Nazis' attempts to win the hearts and minds of youth was at the same time a place of ruthless assaults on Jewish children. Teachers Hermann Müller, who lived in Niederbrechen, Gutberleb—remembered as "a 200 percent" Nazi—and, most notoriously, Bruno Semrau, who was transferred from Berlin to Oberbrechen in the summer of 1935, actively indoctrinated students.[75] Semrau is remembered

---

70 See Michael Wildt, *Hitler's Volksgemeinschaft and the Dynamics of Racial Exclusion: Violence against Jews in Provincial Germany* (New York: Berghahn, 2012).

71 Directive regarding the exclusion of Jewish gymnasts and athletes issued by Reich Sports Commissar, April 25, 1933, reprinted in *Das Sonderrecht für die Juden im NS-Staat: Eine Sammlung der gesetzlichen Maßnahmen und Richtlinien*, ed. Joseph Walk (Heidelberg: Müller, 1981), 18; Chronicle of TSG 1899 Oberbrechen, entry 1933, last accessed March 6, 2023, https://web.tsgoberbrechen.de/berichte/chronik.

72 Frederic J. Hacker and Klaus D. Hoppe, Medical opinion for submission to the *Wiedergutmachung* authorities and courts of the Federal Republic of Germany, March 1966, HHStAW, 518, 53361, vol. 1, compensation file Selma Altman née Stern, 116–144, here 118 (see Part II, Document 19 in this book).

73 Affidavit of Siegfried Lichtenstein, Buenos Aires, January 11, 1954, HHStAW, 518, 22333, vol. 1, compensation file Siegfried Lichtenstein, 8.

74 Letter from Dora and Moses Stern, Oberbrechen, to Herman Stern in Valley City, North Dakota, December 31, 1933, University of North Dakota, Department of Special Collections, Chester Fritz Library, Herman Stern Papers, OLGMC 217, Series I, Box 9, Folder 51 (see Document 2); Letter from Gertrud Marx, Oberbrechen, to the Compensation Office in Wiesbaden, July 1, 1961, HHStAW, 518, 53361, vol. 1, compensation file Selma Altman, née Stern, 18 (see Document 17).

75 On Gutberleb, see Provisional minutes of a conversation on the subject "Catholic resistance against the Hitler Youth," July 30, 1984, Estate of Eugen Caspary, 2.

by Jews and non-Jews alike as a rabid antisemite who never tired of inciting his pupils against Jews.[76] For the non-Jews, putting the blame on Semrau alone, a man who came from the outside and left Oberbrechen again in October 1938, was surely convenient, not least when it came to escaping one of the most uncomfortable questions in the social history of the Holocaust: how did non-Jewish children behave toward Jews? Eugen Caspary testified that he was among the young Oberbrecheners who harassed Moses Stern. Classmates abused and threw ink at Irene Lichtenstein for whom, in the words of her father, "going to school was an ordeal."[77] She and her younger brother Kurt were the only, and in fact also the last, Jewish children in the village school, where Jewish and Christian children had studied side by side since 1817/19.[78]

Initiatives to strengthen the Jewish school system as an alternative gathered momentum, and by 1937 there were over 160 Jewish schools in Germany, in which 60 percent of Jewish children of compulsory school age were enrolled (23,670). The orthodox Samson-Raphael-Hirsch-School in Frankfurt am Main, founded in the 1850s, became one of these "safe havens."[79] Kurt Lichtenstein was a pupil there from early 1935 until the family's escape from Germany in the spring of 1937. At the young age of nine, he lived apart from his family. For a monthly fee of 150 RM, he could stay at "Beit Neorim" at 10 Hölderlinstraße. Also among the children getting board and lodging there was the 13-year-old Manfred Moses, who had also escaped antisemitic discrimination in the school of his hometown, Alsfeld in Hesse. He described the relief that he felt in the big city: "I was able to wander the streets without being attacked or called names. I visited museums, galleries, the theater, and the opera without any obstruction. In school, I was very happy. . . . With Nazi ideology absent, I enjoyed studying History and German. For the first time, gym class was not a torture."[80]

---

76 Letter Siegfried Lichtenstein to Eugen Caspary, May 1975, quoted in: Caspary, "Jüdische Mitbürger," 199. See also letter from Flora Lichtenstein to "Maria," Colonia Avigdor, December 11, 1955, HHStAW, 518, 82816, compensation file Kurt Lichtenstein, 3.

77 Caspary, "Jüdische Mitbürger," 218; Letter from Carl Reifert, Oberbrechen, to the Compensation Office in Wiesbaden, April 30, 1960, HHStAW 518, 81953, Compensation file Irene Lenkiewicz née Lichtenstein, 26 (see Part II, Document 15); Sworn statement of Siegfried Lichtenstein, November 25, 1958, ibid., 14.

78 Caspary, "Jüdische Mitbürger," 176.

79 Kaplan, *Between Dignity and Despair*, 94, 103.

80 Testimony Manfred Moses, quoted in: Monica Kingreen, "'Ihr in Frankfurt habt's gut! Ihr habt Euch gegenseitig. Wir auf dem Land sind allein': Jüdische Menschen aus dem weiten Umland suchten Zuflucht in Frankfurt am Main," in *"Und keiner hat für uns Kaddisch gesagt . . . " Deportationen aus Frankfurt am Main 1941 bis 1945*, ed. Martin Liepach (Frankfurt am Main: Stroemfeld, 2004), 51–77, here 63. On Kurt's education in Frankfurt, see sworn statement of Kurt Lichtenstein, Buenos Aires, September 2, 1957, HHStAW, 518, 82816, Compensation file Kurt Lichtenstein, 15. See also Kaplan, *Between Dignity and Despair*, 101.

When the regime officially turned Jews into second-class citizens through the promulgation of the Nuremberg Laws on September 15, 1935, Nazi activists all over Germany were emboldened to intensify their campaign of antisemitic terror. Representatives of Jewish welfare organizations visiting the rural communities in Hesse made alarming reports. They observed that Nazi orders not to do business with Jews, the establishment of "Jew-free" markets, and the prohibitions on Jews entering certain localities had led to drastic losses of earnings and shortages in food provisions.[81] Oberbrechen was no exception. SA-men stormed into the house of the Altmanns and held Max, Selma, and her mother Rosa at gunpoint. Local Jewish businesses suffered as Christian customers avoided them, either as a deliberate antisemitic boycott or due to social pressure not to buy from Jews. Siegfried Lichtenstein had to close down his cattle-trading business as early as 1935, three years before Jews were officially banned from engaging in this activity nationwide. Cilly Strauss née Stern reported that "the few Jewish families of Oberbrechen were exposed to enormous hostilities. Constantly, they threatened to kill us and this is why I decided to emigrate." In the years 1935–1936 Jewish rural communities shrank at an accelerating rate.[82]

YOUTH ORGANIZATIONS UNDER NAZISM

On Palm Sunday, March 21, 1937, the papal encyclical *Mit brennender Sorge* ("With deep anxiety") was read in almost all Catholic churches.[83] It warned against a state-organized national youth movement "hostile to the Church and Christianity," defended religious education in schools, and called upon parents to make sure that their children were brought up in the Catholic faith.[84] The encyclical came at a critical time. In 1936–1937, the

---

81 Report on a visit of Jewish communities in the Schlüchtern and Gelnhausen districts, August 19, 1935, United States Holocaust Memorial Museum (USHMM), RG-11.00 IM, Reel 99 721, quoted in: Kingreen, "Jüdische Menschen," 57.

82 Sworn statement of Cäcilie "Cilly" Strauss née Stern, New York, July 7, 1955, HHStAW, 518, 81140, Compensation file Cäcilie Strauss née Stern, 5. See also sworn statement of Siegfried Lichtenstein, Buenos Aires, January 11, 1954, HHStAW, 518, 22333, Compensation file Siegfried Lichtenstein, 8; Hacker and Hoppe, Medical opinion, HHStAW 518, 53361, vol. 1, Compensation file Selma Altman née Stern, 119 (see Part II, Document 19); Herbert A. Strauss, "Jewish Emigration from Germany: Nazi Policies and Jewish Responses (I)," *Leo Baeck Institute Year Book* 25 (1980), 313–361, here 326.

83 Hans Günter Hockerts, "Die Goebbels-Tagebücher 1932–1941: Eine neue Hauptquelle zur Erforschung der nationalsozialistischen Kirchenpolitik," in *Politik und Konfession: Festschrift für Konrad Repgen zum 60. Geburtstag*, ed. Dieter Albrecht (Berlin: Duncker und Humboldt, 1983), 359–392, here 377; Gailus, *Gläubige Zeiten*, 41–43.

84 *Mit brennender Sorge*, encyclical of Pope Pius XI on the Church and the German Reich to the venerable brethren the archbishops and bishops of Germany and other ordinaries in peace and communion with the apostolic See the Vatican, March 14, 1937, sections 16, 33, 39, last accessed December 30, 2022, https://www.vatican.va/content/pius-xi/en/encyclicals/documents/hf_p-xi_enc_14031937_mit-brennender-sorge.html.

battle between an aggressively recruiting Hitler Youth (HJ) and Catholic youth groups was at its height. The HJ aimed to become a state organization in which every child from the age of ten would have to be enrolled. The Law on the Hitler Youth, issued on December 1, 1936, required all boys between the ages of ten and fourteen to be members of the German *Jungvolk* and girls in the same age group were required to join the Young Girls' League (*Jungmädelbund*). Likewise, those aged between fourteen and eighteen had to be in the Hitler Youth (for boys) or the League of German Girls (*Bund Deutscher Mädel*).[85]

The Catholic Church made it a high priority to fend off these attempts at total indoctrination and to form instead a young generation firmly rooted in the Christian faith. In 1933, about one-and-a-half million German boys and girls were organized in Catholic youth groups. The largest of these groups, with a following of some 470,800, was the *Jungmännerverband* (JMV), subdivided into *Jungschar* (to the age of fourteen), *Jungenschaft* (ages fourteen to eighteen), and *Jungmannschaft* (for those over eighteen).[86] Catholic youth groups continued to exist after the introduction of the Hitler Youth Law. They thus retained a special status in comparison to all the other organizations that Reich Youth Leader Baldur von Schirach had dissolved or integrated into the Hitler Youth by the winter of 1933–1934. Counting barely more than 100,000 members on January 30, 1933, the Hitler Youth grew to almost 2.3 million by the end of that year and to 7,728,259 in early 1939.[87]

In his efforts to curtail Catholic influence over Oberbrechen's youth, Bruno Semrau, mentioned earlier, denounced Chaplain Franz Pabst to the Gestapo in Frankfurt am Main in late November 1936, citing the children's loyalty to him as a threat.[88] Ordained in December 1935, the 26-year-old Pabst took up his first position in Oberbrechen early in the following year. He had come straight out of the theological seminar Sankt Georgen in

---

85   Law on the Hitler Youth (December 1, 1936), in: United States Chief Counsel for the Prosecution of Axis Criminality, Nazi Conspiracy and Aggression. Washington, D.C.: United States Government Printing Office, 1946. Volume 3, Document 001-PS—Document 1406-PS. Document 1392-PS, 972–73, available online at: German History in Documents and Images, German Historical Institute, Washington, D.C. (hereafter GHDI), last accessed December 31, 2022, https://germanhistorydocs.ghi-dc.org/sub_document.cfm?document_id=1564&language=english. On the formations of the Hitler Youth, see Armin Nolzen, "Vom 'Jugendgenossen' zum 'Parteigenossen:' Die Aufnahme von Angehörigen der Hitler-Jugend in die NSDAP," in *Wie wurde man Parteigenosse? Die NSDAP und ihre Mitglieder*, ed. Wolfgang Benz (Frankfurt am Main: Fischer Taschenbuch, 2009), 123–150.

86   Lawrence D. Walker, *Hitler Youth and Catholic Youth 1933–1936: A Study in Totalitarian Conquest* (Washington, D.C.: The Catholic University of America Press, 1970), 26, 28.

87   Ibid., 147; Nolzen, "Vom 'Jugendgenossen' zum 'Parteigenossen,'" 126, 132–133.

88   Letter Bruno Semrau to Frankfurt am Main Gestapo, end of November 1936, HHStAW, 411/3060.

Frankfurt am Main, and his talents as an educator were rated positively.[89] No sooner had he arrived in the village than he was faced with the local Nazis' dispute with the church and their relentless attempts to recruit boys and girls for the Hitler Youth. A report from Constable Heinrich Rettinghaus to the *Landrat* on April 13, 1937, led to the withdrawal of Chaplain Franz Pabst's teaching permission in the village school.[90] In 1939, Pabst moved on to serve as chaplain in Eltville.[91]

Led by Father Kunz, the pilgrimage of forty young men to Altötting in the fall of 1937 attested to the strong bond between Oberbrechen's youth and the Catholic Church. Gestapo interrogations were initiated after this remarkable event.[92] The pilgrimage had been a response to the dissolution of the JMV in the Limburg diocese on November 27, 1937.[93] At the time of its dissolution, the JMV had 120 members in Oberbrechen.[94] On February 6, 1939, the Gestapo disbanded the JMV nationwide, only days before the death of Pope Pius XI, its "great protector."[95] As the only institutions that retained at least some degree of autonomy in an otherwise fully coordinated totalitarian state, both the Catholic and Protestant Christian churches failed to condemn Nazi persecution and the murder of the Jews. A deafening institutional silence prevailed in the Catholic Church, under both Pius XI and his successor, Pius XII (in office from March 1939), whose indifference toward Jewish suffering weighs even more heavily in light of the atrocities of the Holocaust.[96]

WAR, HOLOCAUST, AND RESCUE

Anti-Jewish violence reached an unprecedented scale in November 1938. The Kurhesse Gau was among the areas in Germany where Nazi activists started attacking Jews as soon as the news broke about Herschel Grynszpan's attempt on the life of the German diplomat Ernst vom Rath

---

89 Judgment of head of theological college leaders on Franz Pabst, undated [c. 1935], personal file Franz Pabst, Diözesanarchiv Limburg.

90 Record of interrogation of Franz Pabst, Oberbrechen police station, December 31, 1936; Statement of Alois Kunz, undated [c. 1936/37], both in personal file of Franz Pabst, Diözesanarchiv Limburg.

91 Letter Franz Pabst to the Limburg Episcopal Ordinariate, March 8, 1978, personal file Franz Pabst, Diözesanarchiv Limburg.

92 Gensicke and Schmidt, "Die Kirche," 144.

93 Walker, *Hitler Youth*, 151.

94 Gensicke and Schmidt, "Die Kirche," 144.

95 Walker, *Hitler Youth*, 151.

96 Gailus, *Gläubige Zeiten*, 105. See also 97. On Pope Pius XII, see Michael Phayer, *The Catholic Church and the Holocaust, 1930–1965* (Bloomington: Indiana University Press, 2000); Friedländer, *Years of Extermination*, 72–75, 184–187, 463–467.

in Paris. Antisemitic assaults took place in Kassel and two other localities on the evening of November 7 and continued on the following day.[97] After vom Rath's death, a nationwide pogrom was launched on the evening of November 9. The SS and SA, aided by the Hitler Youth and other party organizations, set synagogues on fire, vandalized Jewish-owned shops and offices, and forced their way into private houses and apartments to mistreat Jews, destroy furniture, and steal valuables (see Map 5). The Nazis euphemistically called this horrific event *Kristallnacht*—"the night of broken glass." In actuality, it was a pogrom. The Gestapo leadership ordered that Jewish men should be taken into "protective custody" (*Schutzhaft*). With an estimated 36,000 arrests and the deportation of more than 26,000 men to the concentration camps of Buchenwald, Dachau, and Sachsenhausen, virtually every Jewish family in Nazi Germany—which included the annexed territories of Austria and the Sudetenland—was affected.[98]

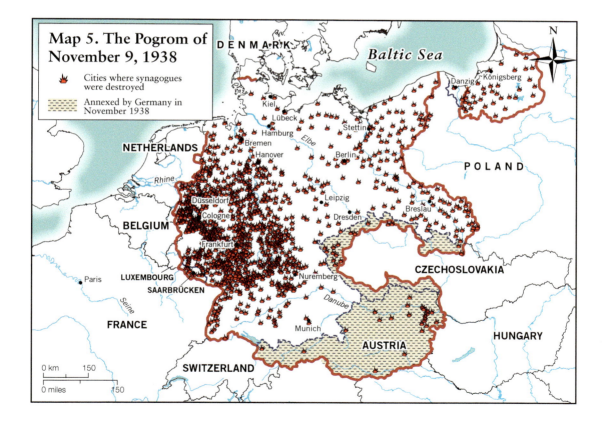

97 Junge, "Niemand mehr da," 90–91. See also Wolfgang Benz, "Der November Pogrom 1938," in *Juden in Deutschland, 1933–1945*, ed. id., 499–544; Friedländer, *Years of Persecution*, 267–305; Alan E. Steinweis, *Kristallnacht 1938* (Cambridge, MA: Harvard University Press, 2009).

98 Wünschmann, *Before Auschwitz*, 197–203.

In Oberbrechen, policemen arrested Max Altmann and Siegfried Stern, who were imprisoned in Buchenwald's notorious "special camp"—five jerry-built barracks made of "wooden boards provisionally nailed together which let the wind and rain in through their many cracks and gaps."[99] Some 2,000 men were crammed together in each of these emergency shelters. They had to endure the violence of SS guards who, mostly during the night, raided the barracks and beat up the terrified inmates. When Max Altmann returned from Buchenwald around Christmastime in 1938, his wife found him looking "ragged, filthy, and completely distraught. He seemed dazed and told her only that he was constantly beaten." In the wake of the pogrom, Selma had meanwhile fled to Limburg to stay with her sister and cousin. There, the women had been arrested and publicly harassed.

The Altmanns did not ever return to live in Oberbrechen after the November Pogrom. Max, who had to report to the police daily after his release from Buchenwald, made the journey from Limburg. With great difficulty, the couple managed to obtain emigration papers to escape Germany in mid-February 1939.[100] By May 1939, Moses Stern, the couple Siegfried and Sophie Stern, and Siegfried's sister Jette were the only Jews still living in Oberbrechen. The Nazis had ousted 71 percent of the Limburg county's pre-1930s Jewish population.[101] For the German Reich as a whole (taking its borders as those existing before the territorial expansions of 1938), approximately half of the roughly 500,000 Jews registered in 1933 had fled the country by 1939.

FLIGHT AND RESCUE

Throughout the 1930s German policy toward Jews led to a gradual deprivation of civil rights, economic expulsion, and dehumanization. Hitler's rise to power in 1933, the Nuremberg Laws of 1935, the *Anschluss* (annexation of Austria), and the 1938 November pogroms were only the key milestones among the hundreds of laws, decrees, and actions designed to humiliate and drive Germany's Jewish population away. Each new outrage increased the number of Jewish refugees from Germany desperately looking for a new home.

---

99 Julius Meyer, *Buchenwald, 1940*, Wiener Holocaust Library London, P.II.d.No. 77, 77–79, 51.

100 Hacker and Hoppe, Medical opinion, HHStAW 518/53361, vol. 1, compensation file Selma Altman née Stern, 120 (see Part II, Document 19).

101 Kingreen, "Jüdische Menschen," 68. The first ones to leave Oberbrechen after the Nazi seizure of power were Selma's twin brother, Max Stern, who escaped to the Netherlands, and Moritz (later Maurice) Stern, who left for Paris. Émigrés of the early phase often left Germany for neighboring European countries, as did Gustave Stern and his wife and son, who escaped from Duisburg to Paris in August 1933, and Flora Lichtenstein's sister, Irma Hess, who fled to Belgium. In 1936, Kurt, Paul, Cilly, and Ida Stern left Oberbrechen for the United States, followed in the next year by the four-person Lichtenstein family who fled to Argentina. In February 1939, Selma and Max Altman emigrated to the United Kingdom but moved on from there to the United States.

German Jews with family members abroad asked for their help in getting one of these life-saving visas.[102] As early as July 1933, Herman Stern, in the United States, received an alarming letter from a family member, who—fearing immediate persecution—signed the letter as "the Chammer"[103] to conceal their identity from authorities. This relative wrote the letter from Venlo in the Netherlands to report that the Jews in Germany were in mortal danger, and that help from abroad was needed to save their lives. From the time that he received this news, Herman Stern did everything humanly possible to rescue family members in need.

The situation was particularly hard for elderly and poorer Jews who were exposed to antisemitic violence and lacked the physical strength and economic means to find refuge abroad. We know from letters from Moses and Dora Stern to their brother Herman in the United States that they considered emigration as early as 1933. After some reflection, Dora decided that making such a new start was not really feasible because of their lack of money, her old age, and her declining health. She explained to her brother Herman that "things concerning Palestine are not so easy. Everywhere you hear that people who aren't able to take any money along have to work hard.... Skilled craftsmen are among the professions sought after..... I'd rather go to America. [But t]here they won't have much use for old aunts."[104] While waiting for opportunities to escape the country, Jews from rural areas often first looked to move to bigger cities within Germany, where the anonymity of urban life offered some protection from antisemitic harassments. As many Jewish families in Hesse had lived in their villages and small towns for generations and felt attached to their "homeland," this was not an easy choice. And yet, over 10,000 Jews eventually gave in to the pressure and fled to Frankfurt in the hope of finding relief from insufferable persecution. A good number of them hoped to move on from there to safe places of exile outside Germany.[105] Jewish

---

102 Mark Wischnitzer, "Jewish Emigration from Germany 1933–1938," *Jewish Social Studies* 2, no. 1 (1940): 23–44, here 29.

103 The word *Chammer* comes from Yiddish and means donkey. It can also refer to a stubborn person or a simple person who does not know a lot; see Heidi Stern, *Wörterbuch zum jiddischen Lehnwortschatz in den deutschen Dialekten*, Reprint 2012 (Berlin: De Gruyter, 2013), 71.

104 Letter from Dora and Moses Stern to Herman Stern (see Part II, Document 2). On immigration to British Mandatory Palestine and the different categories, see Juliane Wetzel, "Auswanderung aus Deutschland," in *Die Juden in Deutschland 1933–1945: Leben unter nationalsozialistischer Herrschaft*, ed. Wolfgang Benz (Munich: Beck, 1988), 412–498, here 451–453.

105 Max Hermann Maier, "Auswanderungsberatung in Frankfurt/M 1936–1938: Geschrieben 1961," in *Dokumente zur Geschichte der Frankfurter Juden 1933–1945*, ed. Kommission zur Erforschung der Geschichte der Frankfurter Juden (Frankfurt am Main: Waldemar Kramer, 1963), 382–398, here 385, 392. See also Kingreen, "Jüdische Menschen," 60–61, 69.

communities and relief organizations and consulates in urban areas provided help and support with arranging emigration.[106]

At the same time that the ruthless emigration policy of the Nazis made it harder for Jews to escape Germany, other countries were also growing increasingly more reluctant to accept refugees. As a result, it became more difficult by the day to obtain a visa from a country outside of Europe. Countries that continued to accept refugees did so only on the condition that the involuntary migrants would have sufficient financial means for their social and economic integration. As many refugees from Nazi Germany were heading for the United States, the Roosevelt administration feared that growing masses would arrive to pound at the doors. The United States had introduced a quota system regulating the number of immigrants from each country in 1924 and agreed to fully accept, but not extend the German quota. The situation became particularly dire after the annexation of Austria in March 1938, which dramatically increased the number of political and Jewish refugees. Around 130,000 Jews had managed to leave the country already before the catastrophic events of the year 1938.[107] In order to address the growing refugee crisis, Roosevelt had called for a conference at the French Spa Evian, inviting representatives from thirty-one nations, and its own administration. At this historic gathering, the U.S. delegation confirmed that "no preferential treatment may be accorded to so-called political refugees, as such, as distinguished from other immigrants."[108] In addition, the Roosevelt administration bluntly stated that it would not spend any money from taxes on the rescue of Jews.[109] It was only after the explosion of antisemitic violence during the November Pogrom of 1938 that consulates of the United States received directions to loosen visa restrictions for refugees from Germany. Jewish men who were incarcerated in concentration camps during and in the days after the pogrom could only be released if they were able to present immigration papers to the Nazi authorities. In the following year, the Roosevelt administration fully, and only once, exhausted the annual quota for German and Austrian refugees, that was 27,370.[110]

---

106   Avraham Barkai, "Jüdisches Leben unter der Verfolgung," in *Deutsch-Jüdische Geschichte in der Neuzeit, Vol. IV: Aufbruch und Zerstörung, 1918–1945*, ed. Avraham Barkai, Paul Mendes-Flohr, and Steven M. Lowenstein (Munich: Beck, 1997), 228.

107   Ibid., 227.

108   Intergovernmental Committee, Technical Sub-Committee, Statement of Details regarding the number and the type of immigrants which the government of the United States is prepared to receive under its existing laws and practices, Evian, July 8, 1938, p. 4, 840.48 Refugees/586, General Records of the State Department, RG 59, National Archives at College Park, MD.

109   Deborah E. Lipstadt, *Beyond Belief: The American Press and the Coming of the Holocaust, 1933–1945* (New York: Free Press, 1986), 89.

110   Avraham Barkai, "Selbsthilfe im Dilemma 'Gehen oder Bleiben,'" in *Deutsch-Jüdische Geschichte IV*, ed. Barkai, Mendes-Flohr, and Lowenstein, 316.

Those who decided to leave the homes they loved faced numerous obstacles. Not only did the lack of places to escape deter Jews from emigrating, but also the seizure of their property if they did so. The Reich Flight Tax (*Reichsfluchtsteuer*), "Aryanization" (the transfer of Jewish-owned property into non-Jewish hands at throwaway prices), theft, and expensive immigration visas were only a few of the additional barriers that lay in the way. Jewish newspapers relayed how helpless Jewish organizations felt in trying to assist: "This misery is rooted in circumstances beyond the influence of Jewish organizations and people. This is especially true for difficulties in transferring money. Even for well-to-do Jewish emigrants, it is impossible to take their money with them."[111] Most Jews left Germany penniless. In 1938 the German foreign ministry congratulated itself in an internal communication: it counted the policy as a success because "the poorer the Jew leaves Germany, and therefore burdensome, the bigger charge he will be for the host country."[112] To add insult to injury, potential receiving countries responded to the refugee crisis with the introduction of or restricted access to visas, working permits, and quota numbers. Often people had to wait several years before their quota number came up.

German Jews with family in the United States desperately asked them for help with obtaining a visa for the country. Refugees needed to provide extensive personal and financial documentation and affidavits of financial support from a citizen or permanent resident of the United States to prove that they would not become a public burden. It required a lot of patience, financial means, and personal support to secure the precious document. For the American Jews who helped relatives in Germany, it meant exposing themselves to arduous bureaucratic processes that were full of unforeseeable obstacles. From 1934 onward, Herman Stern selflessly signed affidavit after affidavit on behalf of his family members and relatives, and incessantly wrote to political leaders in Washington and consuls overseas to break through the "wall of bureaucracy" created by the U.S. administration.[113] He also helped arrange transportation for those who were lucky enough to receive a visa, paying their fares. His niece, Klara Stern, was the first family member he rescued. Once these refugees arrived in the United States, "Uncle Herman," as he was

---

111 Quoted in Michael Schäbitz, "Flucht und Vertreibung der deutschen Juden, 1933–41," in *Juden in Berlin, 1938–45*, ed. Beate Meyer and Herman Simon (Berlin: Philo Verlag, 2000), 55.

112 Quoted in Wetzel, "Auswanderung aus Deutschland," 426.

113 We kindly acknowledge support from Treva Walsh, Collection Project Manager, Museum of Jewish Heritage, New York, who shared exhibition texts and installation images of "Against the Odds: American Jews and the Rescue of Europe's Refugees, 1933–1941," presented at the Museum of Jewish Heritage, May 21, 2013–February 15, 2015.

lovingly called, helped them get settled in Fargo, North Dakota, or elsewhere. Stern often found himself advising these newcomers to the United States on how to build up a business and adapt culturally to American life and manners. Thanks to his relentless determination with the often sluggish U.S. consuls and bureaucracy, he helped his brother Adolf Stern and his family to get out of German-controlled France as late as 1942. At that point, the Nazis had already set in motion the deportation of Europe's Jewry to death camps.

South America was another important place of refuge. More than 90,000 Jews from Germany and Austria fled to its various countries, with Argentina taking in the largest share—over 30,000 men, women, and children.[114] While Argentina's immigration policies became increasingly restrictive throughout the 1930s, refugees whose professional background enabled them to work on agricultural settlements were still allowed in. The Jewish Colonization Association (ICA), founded by Baron Maurice de Hirsch in 1891, assisted them in starting new lives as farmers and cowboys in colonies established in the provinces of Entre Rios, Buenos Aires, La Pampa, Santa Fé, and Santiago del Estero. In 1935, a first group of such "Gauchos Jeckes" rescued from Nazi Germany were settled into the newly founded Colonia Avigdor, some 700 kilometers away from Buenos Aires in the Entre Rios province, north of the capital. This settlement differed from others since it was populated almost exclusively by German Jews, among them the Lichtenstein family, who arrived in mid-1937. Living conditions were harsh and cultivating the land was a near-Sisyphean task, with regular plagues of locusts ruining the harvest. The Avigdor community nonetheless developed a rich religious and cultural life. The colony had a central synagogue and three smaller temples, and its residents frequently put on events in the fields of education, sports, theater, dance, and music. Some colonists had brought Thora Scrolls from their German communities.[115]

---

114 *Heimat und Exil: Emigration der deutschen Juden nach 1933*, ed. by Stiftung Jüdisches Museum Berlin und Stiftung Haus der Geschichte der Bundesrepublik Deutschland (Frankfurt am Main: Jüdischer Verlag im Suhrkamp Verlag, 2006), 143–154; Herbert A. Strauss, "Jewish Emigration from Germany: Nazi Policies and Jewish Responses (II)," *Leo Baeck Institute Year Book* 26 (1981), 343–409, here 363–382.

115 Alfredo José Schwarcz, *Trotz allem . . . Die deutschsprachigen Juden in Argentinien*, trans. from the original Spanish by Bernardo and Inge Schwarcz (Vienna: Böhlau, 1995), 106–107, 116–117, 186, 190–196. From the second half of the 1940s, settlers started to leave the colony and move to the cities. Kurt Lichtenstein, his wife, and daughter left Avigdor in 1957 for Buenos Aires. His parents Siegfried and Flora followed in 1958. See also Strauss, "Jewish Emigration," 370–371.

DISPOSSESSION

Expulsion came with dispossession. In the 1930s, it was the regime's policy not only to drive as many Jews as possible out of Germany, but also to ensure that they should leave behind as much of their wealth and property as possible. The Ordinance on the use of Jewish Property of December 3, 1938, for example, forced Jews, among other things, to hand over valuables, works of art, and precious metals. Among the objects Max Altmann had to deliver to a state-run pawn shop were an antique silver *Chanukkia* chandelier, a large silver plate for *Mazze*, two silver *Kiddush* cups, and a golden wedding ring.[116] Whoever sought refuge abroad had to pass a complicated, costly, and distressing bureaucratic obstacle course for which the rules and responsibilities constantly changed.[117] Apart from the police, it was mainly the fiscal authorities who organized what can only be considered a large-scale theft. They did so with the help of local administrative bodies, banks, insurance and shipping companies, and other institutions and individuals supporting the regime. But the role of ordinary people in the dispossession of Germany's Jews should not be underestimated. A large number of "national comrades" eager to enrich themselves already benefited from "Aryanizations" even before new legislation to oust Jews from the German economy was introduced in 1938. Research for Hesse has found that "[i]t was first in the countryside and later in the cities that a dynamic of boycott, 'Aryanizations,' and flight developed that could only be set in motion with the keen participation of the local population."[118]

Once again, our microhistorical study of Oberbrechen helps show who was involved in the dispossession of Jews, how it worked in practice, and how it intertwined with longstanding neighborly relations—even friendly ones. As in other rural Jewish communities, the assets of Oberbrechen's Jews were mainly bound to the ownership of houses and land, cultivated and farmed so that they could make a living and do business. In Siegfried Lichtenstein's case, the mayor withdrew the plots of land Lichtenstein had leased from the municipality to grow food to sustain the family and provide fodder for his animals. This put his livelihood as well as his cattle trade into immediate danger.[119] As traders, Jews often also held assets in the form of

---

116 Affidavit of Max Altman, Los Angeles, December 12, 1963, HHStAW, 460, FN 1828, restitution file Max Altman, 2–3.

117 Arthur Prinz, "Die Gestapo als Feind und Foerderer juedischer Auswanderung," The Wiener Holocaust Library London, P.II.f.No.792. See also Bettina Leder, Christoph Schneider, and Katharina Stengel, *Ausgeplündert und verwaltet: Geschichten vom legalisierten Raub an den Juden in Hessen* (Berlin: Hentrich & Hentrich, 2018), 16.

118 Leder, Schneider, and Stengel, *Ausgeplündert und verwaltet*, 13.

119 Siegfried Lichtenstein mentions "5 Morgen Land" on which he grew potatoes, grass, and clover. Compensation file Siegfried Lichtenstein, HHStAW 518, 22333.

credit on goods. Before his flight to France in August 1933, Moritz (later Maurice) Stern, whose family business dealt with tobacco, entrusted receivables to the amount of 12,000 Reichsmark (RM) to a lawyer in Limburg who promised to collect them. But Stern was never shown any account statement and a mere 4,000 RM was paid out to his mother. So long as it was possible, she transferred a monthly allowance of 200 RM to him.[120]

Siegfried Stern's neighbor Johann Ricker, who sought to expand his business in fertilizer, fodder, fruit, and other goods, had cast an eye on the Stern family's house: "When the affair with the Jews started and it became clear that the Jews had to go away one day, I went to my neighbor Siegfried Stern and complained about [my] confined space and I asked him to sell me his property, which bordered my property. For 45 years we had lived peacefully next to each other, and he promised me that I would get his property, but that he would sell only if he was forced to leave . . . ."[121] This statement, which was made after the Holocaust, reveals the self-interest of the non-Jewish businessman wanting to buy Stern's house. Ricker invokes the long years of good relations to express entitlement to the property rather than to suggest solidarity with a neighbor in distress. Interestingly, Ricker's plans were thwarted by Hugo Trost, who pressured Stern to sell his property to the Oberbrechen municipality instead. The fact that this sale was only authorized in 1941, the year that Siegfried, Sophie, and Jette Stern were forced to leave the village, testifies to a remarkable resistance on the part of the Jewish merchant.

Moses Stern, the last of the eight Stern siblings still living in Oberbrechen, had to sell the family house at 14 Lange Straße as early as 1936. He was unable to maintain it in his precarious economic circumstances. Albert and Maria Schmidt bought the house, and Moses continued to live in the house as their tenant until he had to leave Oberbrechen in 1940.[122] There can be no doubt as to the forced nature of the sale, or the old man's dependency on help in a time of growing isolation.

DEPORTATIONS AND MURDER

The sources do not reveal more about the circumstances under which Moses Stern departed from the village or how he got by in Frankfurt am Main. We find his name and his last address, the Jewish hospital at 36 Gagernstraße, on the list of the seventh transport that left the city on August 18, 1942, from the Großmarkthalle assembly via the rail station

---

120 Sworn statement of Maurice Stern, November 1955, HHStAW 518, 81104, Compensation file Maurice Stern.
121 Compensation file Johann Ricker, claim undated (c. March 1950), HHStAW 518/48154.
122 Caspary, "Jüdische Mitbürger," 216.

Ostbahnhof. This was a "transport of elderly people" (*Alterstransport*), which deported slightly more than 1,000 Jews to the Theresienstadt ghetto in German-occupied Czechoslovakia; among them were 678 Jews from Frankfurt's old-age homes and the hospital. Julius Lichtenstein, Siegfried's father, was on this transport, too. He was killed in the Treblinka death camp a few weeks later. The mortality rate was as brutal as that on the other transports leaving Frankfurt between 1941 and 1945: only 17 people survived it. All in all, more than 10,000 Jews were deported from Frankfurt am Main to ghettos and killing sites in German-controlled Eastern Europe. Moses Stern died in Theresienstadt on October 9, 1942, aged 70.[123]

Siegfried, Sophie, and Jette Stern—the other three Oberbrecheners who spent the last months of their lives in Frankfurt—lived close to the Ostbahnhof at 4 Schichaustraße. They maintained some ties with Oberbrechen. Mathilde Roth, née Schickel, remembers visiting the Sterns, who lived in poor conditions, when she was doing an apprenticeship in Frankfurt. She brought them food and clothes from Oberbrechen and surely also delivered news about the former neighbors in the village community.[124] The International Tracing Service of the Red Cross records that Siegfried and his wife Sophie Stern were "deported from Frankfurt/Main to [the] east on 5.1942." The Nazis used the phrase "to the east" as a euphemism for transports sent directly to the death camps, for which they often did not keep registers. Two transports to Izbica left Frankfurt am Main in May 1942, and the deportees were murdered in Sobibor. We may assume that Siegfried and Sophie Stern were on one of these transports.[125] Jette Stern, Siegfried's sister, is registered as having lost her life at the killing site of Maly Trostinec, most likely in a mass shooting perpetrated by men subordinated to the Commanding

---

123 List of 1,010 Jews deported on transport no. XII/1 from Frankfurt am Main to the Theresienstadt ghetto, August 19, 1942, Yad Vashem Archives, O.64—Theresienstadt Collection, File no. 262, last accessed March 27, 2023, https://documents.yadvashem.org/index.html?language=en&search=global&strSearch=3733312&GridItemId=3733312; Bundesarchiv Gedenkbuch, entries "Moses Stern" (born February 28, 1872) and "Julius Lichtentein" (born May 22, 1864); Result form Datenbank Gedenkstätte Neuer Börneplatz, Email Heike Drummer to Kim Wünschmann, August 19, 2021; Monica Kingreen, "Gewaltsam verschleppt aus Frankfurt: Die Deportationen der Juden in den Jahren 1941–1945," in: id. (ed.), *Nach der "Kristallnacht:" Jüdisches Leben und antijüdische Politik in Frankfurt am Main 1938–1945* (Frankfurt am Main/New York: campus, 1999), 357–402, here 375–377, 389.

124 Doris Hecker, summary of interview conducted with Mathilde Roth on October 31, 2020, Email Doris Hecker to Kim Wünschmann, November 3, 2020.

125 ITS records for Siegfried Stern (born October 25, 1879) and Sophie Stern (born September 27, 1889), Letter ICRC Archives Geneva to Kurt Stern, July 5, 1985, private archive of Susan Mayerowitz; Email Cornelia Shati-Geißler, Yad Vashem, to Kim Wünschmann, December 15, 2019.

Officer of the security police and the SD, the security service of the SS, (KdS) Minsk.[126]

On June 22, 1941, the Wehrmacht attacked the Soviet Union, to start a "war of annihilation," which brought about not only an ideological radicalization but also a shift in Nazi anti-Jewish policies from expulsion to extermination. In October, the regime banned Jews from emigrating from Germany and targeted those who had remained in the *Altreich* (Germany within the pre-1938 borders)—some 163,000 men, women, and children—with systematic deportation to their deaths. The Eleventh Decree of the Law on the Citizenship of the Reich, promulgated on November 25, 1941, rendered stateless both those who had escaped abroad and those who had been deported. Their property became forfeit to the German state, which redistributed parts of this massive haul of loot to "ordinary Germans" via auctions or re-housing promises. In Oberbrechen, by 1941 all five houses in which Jewish families had lived were owned by non-Jewish villagers or the municipality. Jewish life in this community had come to an end.

JUSTICE?

Reparation claims and practices of denazification as experienced by Jews and Christians from Oberbrechen raise larger questions about perpetration and victimhood. While the war was still being fought, the Allies already started making plans to prosecute Nazi crimes and restore justice for the victims. But what was meant by justice, and how was it to be implemented? What forms did restoration and reckoning take, how did morality and politics interact, and how can we explore attempts to address and repair past injustices in everyday life?

HOLOCAUST RESTITUTION AND COMPENSATION

In many ways, the reparations program implemented in Germany after 1945 was without historical precedent. While postwar reparations had traditionally been settled at the political level between states, Jewish successor organizations dedicated to tracing and recovering Jewish property now assumed the legal status that entitled them to engage in negotiations and act as treaty partners. These organizations were eventually merged into the

---

126 Bundesarchiv Gedenkbuch. Another way of killing deportees at Maly Trostinec was by the use of gas wagons. See Petra Rentrop, *Tatorte der "Endlösung:" Das Ghetto Minks und die Vernichtungsstätte Maly Trostinez* (Berlin: Metropol, 2011), 208. On the KdS, see Christian Schmittwilken, *Zentralen des Terrors: Die Dienststellen der Kommandeure der Sicherheitspolizei und des SD im Reichskommissariat Ukraine* (Munich: De Gruyter Oldenbourg, 2024).

newly founded Conference on Jewish Material Claims Against Germany (JCC).[127] In the three zones occupied by the Western powers after the war, legislation to regulate compensation for personal injuries and the restitution of confiscated property started as early as 1946/1947. The occupying powers implemented these measures together with German administrators at the local and regional level. After the establishment of the Federal Republic of Germany (FRG) in May 1949, these laws and regulations were standardized by the federal government.[128] Jewish claims, whether voiced at individual or collective levels, were always troubled by the moral question of how suffering and murder could in any way be monetarily quantified, let alone compensated for. The Hebrew term *shilumim*, with its biblical roots relating to "recompense," carries a meaning very different from that of the reconciliatory German word *Wiedergutmachung*—literally "making good again"—which is overwhelmingly rejected by the Jewish side.[129]

Broadly speaking, there were two strands of victim reparation: restitution and compensation. Restitution mostly addressed deprivation of property, while compensation was mostly for personal injuries, which the Federal Compensation Act (BEG) of 1956 defined as including loss of life, damage to limb or health, deprivation of liberty, damage to assets, damage to professional careers, and damage to business.[130] While restitution took the form of a one-time payment, compensation resulted in lifelong pension payments. Another significant difference between the two strands of reparation was that restitution claims could be brought not only against the state, but also against private individuals who had obtained property owned by Jews. These private individuals had to respond to claims

---

127 Regula Ludi, *Reparations for Nazi Victims in Postwar Europe* (Cambridge: Cambridge University Press, 2012), 90, 111–113; Constantin Goschler, *Wiedergutmachung: Westdeutschland und die Verfolgten des Nationalsozialismus (1945–1954)* (Munich: Oldenbourg, 1992); Jürgen Lillteicher, *Raub, Recht und Restitution: Die Rückerstattung jüdischen Eigentums in der frühen Bundesrepublik* (Göttingen: Wallstein, 2007); id., "Who Is a Victim of Nazism? West Germany and Its Approach to Private Participation in the Aryanization Policy of the Nazi Era," in *The Post-War Restitution of Property Rights in Europe: Comparative Perspectives*, ed. Wouter Veraart amd Larens Winkel (Amsterdam: RVP Press, 2011), 79–93.

128 Ludi, *Reparations*, 112.

129 José Brunner, Nobert Frei, and Constantin Goschler, "Komplizierte Lernprozesse: Zur Geschichte und Aktualität der Wiedergutmachung," in id. (eds.), *Die Praxis der Wiedergutmachung: Geschichte, Erfahrung und Wirkung in Deutschland und Israel* (Göttingen: Wallstein, 2009), 9–25, here 18–19. For the biblical references, see Deuteronomy 32:35 and Isaiah 34:8.

130 German Federal Ministry of Finance, *Compensation for National Socialist Injustice Indemnification Provision* (Berlin: BMF, 2011), 48 (henceforth BMF, *Compensation*), 5–7, 44. The *Bundesentschädigungsgesetz* (BEG) of 1956 amended the 1953 *Bundesergänzungsgesetz zur Entschädigung für Opfer der nationalsozialistischen Verfolgung*, the Additional Federal Compensation Act (BErgG). See Ludi, *Reparations*, 93; Lillteicher, *Raub*, 13; BMF, *Compensation*, 27–31.

and could face charges, payments, or an obligation to return property. Restitution thus forced individuals to confront their behavior during the Nazi dictatorship in the most urgent way. The direct confrontation between Jewish claimants and non-Jewish beneficiaries of property transfers that were enabled by the Holocaust turned restitution cases into particularly intense forms of post-genocidal reengagement at grassroots level. In the case of compensation, by contrast, private individuals might be called upon as witnesses or evaluators, but it was the state alone, at *Länder*—or regional—level, that paid out indemnification.

NEGOTIATING VICTIM REPARATION AT THE LOCAL LEVEL

With the proclamation of OMGUS law no. 59 on November 10, 1947, restitution legislation was introduced by military decree in the U.S.-American occupation zone.[131] Oberbrecheners living in houses that had belonged to Jews were required to report on these properties. Albert and Maria Schmidt, for example, were asked to provide details of the house at 14 Lange Straße and how it had been acquired from the Stern family. The authorities found that the "property changed hands under duress," and on April 23, 1948, the Schmidts were given notice that the house was "declared to be under the control of the Land Civilian Agency Head pursuant to the provisions of the Blocking and Control of Property Law (No. 52)."[132] A custodian was appointed to report on the monthly income and expenses relating to the property.

At this point, the Schmidts contacted Herman Stern in North Dakota and asked for a peaceful settlement.[133] Father Alois Kunz supported the plea not to place any claims against the Schmidts by stressing that their "purchase of the property at the time was done in a thoroughly legal way. No kind of pressure was in any way exerted by the buyer."[134] Endorsements by respected authority figures, in this case the village's priest, allowed people to create narratives that reframed sales under duress as orderly transactions. Research has shown that many buyers of Jewish-owned property, when faced with restitution claims after the war, invoked the "legality of the purchase agreement."[135] In his deliberations on whether to

---

131 Ludi, *Reparations*, 87. The acronym OMGUS stands for Office of Military Government, United States.

132 Report of Property Taken under Control, April 23, 1938, Notice of Custody issued by the Land Civilian Agency Head (LCHA), Limburg an der Lahn, Apr. 23, 1948, HHStAW 519V/3109–259.

133 Letter from Albert Schmidt, Oberbrechen, to Herman Stern, Valley City, July, 20 1948, Herman Stern Collection OLGMC 217, Series 1, SubA, Box 9, Folder 3 (see Document 12).

134 Letter from Alois Kunz to Herman Stern, ibid.

135 Lillteicher, *Raub*, 504.

claim restitution, Herman Stern decided to settle for something that meant more to him than money. As we know from the letters sent to him from Oberbrechen, he asked the Schmidts to look after his ancestors' graves in the Jewish cemetery in Weyer instead of laying claim to the family home. In late September 1948, the authorities ordered the release of the property, because "the restitutee has irrevocably waived by waiver, notarized on 19.8.48, all claims due to him under the Restitution Law."[136]

Other reparation cases in Oberbrechen similarly reveal how Christian villagers downplayed anti-Jewish persecution. In the case of Siegfried Lichtenstein, who filed for damages to his cattle-trading business, members of the local population, along with the mayor, Josef Keuler, understated the value of his business. The narratives constructed around the expulsion of Siegfried, Sophie, and Jette Stern from Oberbrechen in 1941 were especially trivializing. When the children of the Sterns, Kurt and Ilse/Isabella, claimed restitution of the family home at 2 Lange Straße, the local police questioned the mayor and the villagers in 1959—about a decade after the case was first opened. Keuler stated that "nothing was confiscated" and that the Sterns "could freely sell all of their household goods." The house, which was bought by the Oberbrechen municipality, was reported to have been completely empty when the Sterns were driven out. However, nobody, including former mayor Hugo Trost, could remember who it was that might have bought the family's belongings.[137]

There was also a legal dispute between the Lichtenstein and Deisel families over the restitution of the property at 17 Frankfurter Straße. The sources do not reveal whether there was much direct contact between Siegfried and Flora Lichtenstein in Argentina and Josef and Maria Deisel in Oberbrechen, and how the two sides tried to negotiate the past. What we do know is that an attempt to reach an amicable settlement fell through in 1953. It took until 1956 for the case to end in a court settlement which ruled that the Deisel family would pay 1,000 DM to the Lichtensteins and henceforth be registered as the owners of the property.[138] This silence when it comes to personal exchanges and expressions of motivation or feeling is

---

136 Declaration of property release by LCAH, 27.9.1948, HHStAW 519V/3109–259; Waiver by Herman Stern, ibid.; Letters Albert and Maria Schmidt to Herman Stern, Herman Stern Papers, Correspondence German.

137 Statement of Oberbrechen mayor Josef Keuler, June, 26, 1959 and Report of Polizeiobermeister Otto Schmidt, July 29, 1959, HHStAW, 519/6 Nr. 13575 N, 16, 21. The restitution claims of Kurt and Isabella lasted from 1948 to 1960. On May 16, 1960, the Landesamt für Vermögenskontrolle und Wiedergutmachung in Hesse ruled that the German state, represented through the Oberfinanzdirektion Frankfurt, must pay 1,500 DM "due to the confiscation of precious metals and household goods," p. 44. The sources do not tell us what happened to the Sterns' house and the gardens.

138 HHStAW, (Z)460/1 Wik. 244 + 245; HHStAW, 519/A, Nr. 25491.

typical of the reparation files. The language and logic of restitution and compensation—its civil law discourse—left little or no room for recognition of the suffering caused by Nazi persecution. At the same time, there was much at stake in the reparation processes that could set emotions running high. In fact, reparation legislation was all about interpreting historic injustices perpetrated within the context of a regime whose ideology and rule required everybody to take a stand. But who held the power to interpret this history of violence? Victims-turned-claimants had to learn to translate their ordeal into technical bureaucratic terms. They were forced to engage in "endless and humiliating" disputes that have led historians to describe postwar reparation as a form of "second persecution."[139]

THE IMPOSSIBLE BURDEN OF PROOF

Risks of being traumatized all over again could be high when Jewish victims of Nazi policies claimed compensation for impaired health. They had to go through an arduous process that involved medical examinations, which often probed into the most intimate spheres of personal life.[140] To determine whether the physical or psychological suffering of survivors fell into the classes of disabilities qualifying claimants for pension payments, the compensation offices relied on the opinions of medical experts. These experts' decisions were, in turn, influenced by the particular academic discourses within which they worked. In countries outside Germany, medical schools began researching a specific Holocaust "survivor pathology" from the late 1940s onward. The dominant approach in Germany, however, was to apply the traditional compensation scheme for war victims whose underlying doctrine focused on physical disabilities. Mental health conditions did not count as compensable injuries, and "healthy human organisms were said to be capable of recovering from even the most serious experiences of psychological stress in a relatively short time."[141]

We can observe a clash of these two very different schools in the interpretation of Holocaust survivors' impaired health in the case of Selma Altman, discussed in 1966. Klaus Hoppe was a psychiatrist of German origin who treated many Holocaust survivors during his thirty years of service at the Hacker Clinic in Beverly Hills, California. He clearly attested that

---

139   Ralph Giordano, *Die zweite Schuld: Oder: Von der Last, Deutscher zu sein* (Hamburg, Zurich: Rasch u. Röhring, 1987). See also Christian Pross, *Wiedergutmachung: Der Kleinkrieg gegen die Opfer* (Frankfurt am Main: Athenäum, 1988); Lillteicher, *Raub*, 24; Brunner et al., "Lernprozesse," 28.

140   Ludi, *Reparations*, 122.

141   Svenja Goltermann, "Kausalitätsfragen: Psychisches Leid und psychiatrisches Wissen in der Entschädigung," in: Brunner et al., *Praxis*, 427–451, here 432. On the survivor pathology, see Ludi, *Reparations*, 122.

Selma's suffering "was caused by the events and experiences made during the years 1933 to 1939 and has existed since then."[142] However, the psychiatrist tasked with reviewing the case for the German compensation office, Nikolaus Petrilowitsch of the University of Mainz, did not accept his colleague's opinion. In a highly conservative judgment, Petrilowitsch argued that "in Mrs. A.'s case no illness in the psychiatric-neurological context exists that stands in causal connection to the persecution she suffered." Only concentration camp imprisonment, he claimed, would cause "severe long-term stress." Instead, he suspected that Selma Altman's illness had organic causes.[143] Although medical examiners, like Petrilowitsch, who worked for the compensation offices rarely examined the claimants they were assessing, basing their opinions entirely on written documents, their judgments had powerful effects. As a study of the Bavarian compensation office has shown, they overruled the medical opinions of their American counterparts in 60 percent of cases and those of Israeli physicians in 80 percent.[144]

German victim reparations of the postwar era have left a complicated and difficult legacy. Reparations never had strong official backing and, in contrast to other forms of coming to terms with the past, the scheme was accompanied by "little discourse."[145] To satisfy the wider public, politicians and lawmakers frequently used the rhetoric of "closing the matter for good." Populist talk about the supposedly alarming burden victim reparations put on the state budget, however, does not merit serious examination.[146] Most victims of Nazi persecution never received any restitution or compensation at all. What is more, the expense of reparations to Jewish victims was, up to the 1990s, considerably less than that of compensation paid to other groups. Until then, far larger compensations had been paid to Germans and ethnic Germans expelled from the eastern territories under the equalization of burdens legislation (*Lastenausgleich*), as well as to public service personnel discharged in the denazification process.[147]

---

142 Hacker and Hoppe, Medical opinion, HHStAW 518/53361, vol. 1, compensation file Selma Altman née Stern, 143. As the report was written in German, we can assume that Hoppe is the sole author, although both psychiatrists signed it and may have examined Selma Stern. On Hoppe, see obituary in the *Los Angeles Times*, March 26, 2006.

143 Nikolaus Petrilowitsch, Psychiatric opinion submitted to Landgericht, 7. Zivilkammer Wiesbaden, July 4, 1966, HHStAW 518/53361, vol. 1, Compensation file Selma Altman née Stern, 148–161, at 156–7, 159–61; U. H. Peters, "In memoriam Nikolaus Petrilowitsch," *Psychiatria Clinica* 4, no. 4 (1971), 194–199.

144 Anke Schmeling, *Nicht Wieder Gut Zu Machen: Die bundesdeutsche Entschädigung psychischer Folgeschäden von NS-Verfolgten* (Herbolzheim: Centaurus Verlag, 2000). See also Ludi, *Reparations*, 122.

145 Brunner et al., "Lernprozesse," 15, 19.

146 Ibid., 14.

147 Ludi, *Reparations*, 104.

The displacement of German nationals and ethnic Germans (*Volksdeutsche*) from territories east of the Oder-Neiße border affected millions of people. Due to the fragmentary source base, it is difficult to arrive at accurate numbers. Current research estimates that about 14 million people were expelled from eastern provinces of the German Reich and from settlement areas of ethnic Germans in Eastern Europe. More than 600,000 of them did not survive the expulsion. The fates of hundreds of thousands can no longer be determined. Some 8.5 million were resettled in the territories that became the Federal Republic (see Map 6), and around 720,000 of these arrived in Hesse.[148] Oberbrechen absorbed some 250 people, including families with children. They arrived mostly without means and confronted the task of building new lives for themselves in a war-torn and defeated society preoccupied with its own troubles. With housing, food, employment, and other basic goods in short supply, the newcomers' arrival did not pass without conflicts. Franziska Deisel, who lived in the Lichtenstein family's old house, tried to resist an order from the Oberbrechen mayor to take in the four-person Leimpeck family expelled from Győrsövényház in Hungary. Deisel's husband was still interned in a French POW camp and was kept there until 1947.[149] By the summer of that year, 93,508 former Wehrmacht soldiers from Hesse who had been captured by the Allies had still not returned home. Some, particularly those in Soviet internment, had to wait for repatriation until the mid-1950s. Others never returned, among them 101 men from Oberbrechen who had died in action or who remained missing.[150]

During the tenure of Konrad Adenauer, West Germany's first postwar chancellor (1949–1963), narratives of German victimhood took shape that allowed those formerly living as 'national comrades' (*Volksgenossen*) in the Nazi 'people's community' to shift responsibility for exclusion, dispossession, expulsion, and murder onto the Nazi leaders—first and foremost onto Hitler himself. Christian faith provided comfort for those who mourned the war dead: in Oberbrechen in 1955, a large cross was erected in their memory on a hill overlooking the village. Nationwide, there were

---

148 Email Nils Köhler, Documentation Centre for Displacement, Expulsion, Reconciliation in Berlin to Kim Wünschmann, January 23, 2024. See also Ian Connor, *Refugees and Expellees in Post-war Germany* (Manchester: Manchester University Press, 2007), 18–19; Mathias Beer, *Flucht und Vertreibung der Deutschen* (Munich: Beck, 2011); Ludi, *Reparations*, 100.

149 List of expellees that came to Oberbrechen after the Second World War, in: *Geschichte von Oberbrechen*, 480–485, here 482. Interview with Philomena Höhler née Deisel, conducted by Kim Wünschmann, Oberbrechen, August 13, 2021.

150 List of soldiers killed in action or missing, in *Geschichte von Oberbrechen*, 477–479; Kropat, *Hessen*, 218; Bob Moore, *Prisoners of War: Europe: 1939–1956* (Oxford: Oxford University Press, 2022), 464–474.

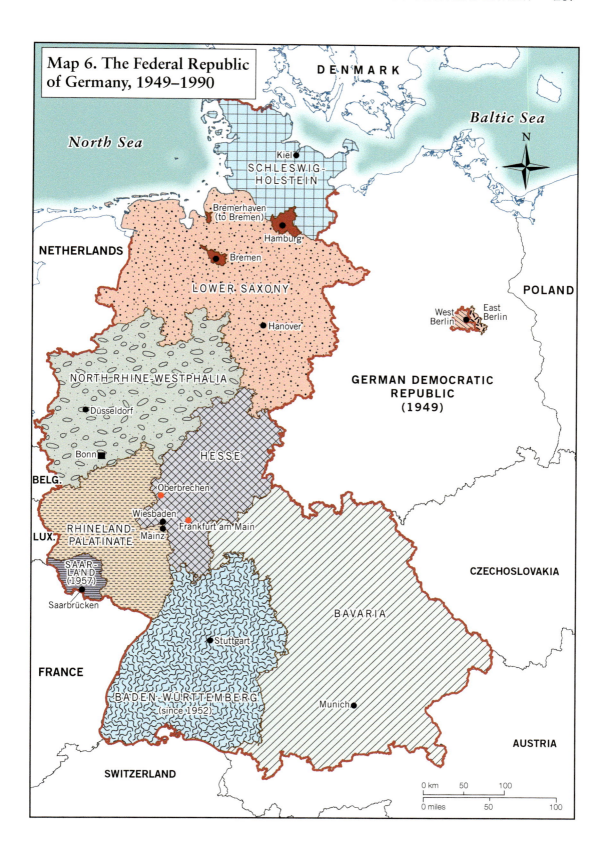

more aggressive expressions of lament and indignation at how Germans themselves had been treated. As historian Regula Ludi observes, these likened "the fate of the Germans to Jewish suffering under Nazi rule." The result was an "erosion of moral distinctions [that] turned perpetrators into victims."[151]

DENAZIFICATION

Demands to finally "draw a line under the past" and return to "normality" were widespread in West German postwar society. In 1953, a survey conducted in Hesse found that the overwhelming majority of the population did not agree with the policy of denazification initiated by the Allies.[152] As an exercise in large-scale political cleansing, denazification affected millions of Germans. With the Law for Liberation from National Socialism and Militarism, promulgated in the U.S. occupation zone on March 5, 1946, the Americans, though retaining overall supervision, transferred the responsibility of screening former *Volksgenossen* to the German authorities. Boards of Germans were to assess how implicated their compatriots had been in the Nazi dictatorship. Behavior under Nazi rule was to be classified according to five categories ranked in decreasing order of incrimination: I. major offender, II. offender, III. lesser offender, IV. follower, and V. exonerated.[153] Everyone over the age of 18 had to complete a questionnaire to provide detailed information about their membership in Nazi and other organizations, as well as their activities and assets. Denazification boards (*Spruchkammern*), set up specifically for this purpose, then processed the cases to determine which category each citizen fell in. If they decided that someone appeared guilty, investigations followed. Depending on their outcome, a statement of claim placed the person in question in one of the categories and suggested appropriate sanctions. Sanctions imposed on major offenders included confiscation of assets, loss of pensions and core civil rights, and sentencing to hard labor for up to ten years or a prohibition on working in certain professions for the same duration. For lesser offenders

---

151 Ludi, *Reparations*, 99–100.

152 Allensbach Institute survey 1953, quoted in: Armin Schuster, *Die Entnazifizierung in Hessen 1945–1954: Vergangenheitspolitik in der Nachkriegszeit* (Wiesbaden: Historische Kommission für Nassau, 1999), 424. See also Norbert Frei, *Vergangenheitspolitik: Die Anfänge der Bundesrepublik und die NS-Vergangenheit* (Munich: Beck, 2012), 88; Hanne Leßau, *Entnazifizierungsgeschichten: Die Auseinandersetzung mit der eigenen NS-Vergangenheit in der frühen Nachkriegszeit* (Göttingen: Wallstein, 2020).

153 Law for Liberation from National Socialism and Militarism, March 5, 1946. For a definition of the categories and the sanctions to be imposed, see Lisa Klages, "'Ich bitte heute nicht um Gnade': Zur Entnazifizierung der Alten Garde im Gau Hessen-Nassau," in Jürgen W. Falter et al., *"Wie ich den Weg zum Führer fand": Beitrittsmotive und Entlastungsstrategien von NSDAP-Mitgliedern* (Frankfurt am Main: Campus, 2022), 362–408, here 374–375.

this sentence was five years and involved only a partial confiscation of property.¹⁵⁴

In contrast to regular criminal law proceedings in which a person is deemed innocent until proven guilty, the denazification boards operated with the burden of proof laid on those who had been summoned to hearings. The accused then had to offer evidence to refute a presumption of their guilt, though they could seek legal assistance. However, research has found that this reversal in proceedings did not, in practice, actually work to the disadvantage of the "defendants." On the contrary, "in the implementation of the paralegal *Spruchkammer* proceedings, denazification and rehabilitation were melted together in the same process."¹⁵⁵ Although the population was encouraged to testify against the defendant, reporting Nazi behavior, very few did. Instead, a whole mass of witnesses tended to come forward to support the defense. As a result, it was the rule rather than an exception that the defendant left with an exculpatory certificate. These certificates were nicknamed *Persilscheine* after the Persil laundry detergent that claimed to "wash whiter than white." Of the 143,923 hearings conducted in Hesse up to April 15, 1948, some 109,975 ended with classifications of the accused into category IV—follower—and this was by far the largest group. Some 24,448 of those who appeared were categorized as lesser offenders (III), and 4,917 were exonerated (V). Only 4,252 were found to be offenders (II), and 331 major offenders (I).¹⁵⁶

The case of the former Oberbrechen mayor Hugo Trost was still pending when the denazification boards began to wind down and the rulings became milder over time. Despite this, when eventually brought to one of the boards, Trost was still categorized as an offender (II) in June 1948. However, the appeals commission canceled this ruling in December 1949 and, referring to the amnesty for returning POWs, closed his case.¹⁵⁷ He was not the only Oberbrechener to benefit from the amnesties being issued. The "Christmas amnesty," announced in December 1946 and effective from February 5, 1947, applied to people on lower incomes while the

---

154 Klages, "Entnazifizierung," 374–375; Clemens Vollnhals, *Entnazifizierung: Politische Säuberung und Rehabilitierung in den vier Besatzungszonen 1945–1949* (Munich: dtv, 1991), 18; Mikkel Dack, *Everyday Denazification in Postwar Germany: The Fragebogen and Political Screening during the Allied Occupation* (Cambridge: Cambridge University Press, 2023).

155 Vollnhals, *Entnazifizierung*, 20. See also Schuster, *Entnazifizierung*, 301.

156 Schuster, *Entnazifizierung*, 168. By April 15, 1948, a total number of 894,568 men and women had been affected by denazification in Hesse.

157 HHStAW, Spruchkammer Trost, Ruling of Wiesbaden Appeals Court, December 13, 1949, 104 (see Document 13). On the amnesty for repatriated POWs (*Heimkehreramnestie*) of April 15, 1948, see Klages, "Entnazifizierung," 376.

"youth amnesty" of August 6, 1946 exempted all those born after 1919 from denazification hearings.¹⁵⁸ Among those exempted by the "youth amnesty" was Josef Kramm, who had joined the Nazi Party on the mass entry date for his age cohort, April 20, 1944. Confronted with denazification procedures, he claimed that his membership was initiated automatically and without his knowledge when he was transferred from the Hitler Youth to the Nazi Party. Many people in his generation nourished this same exculpatory narrative. The latest research has largely rebutted this claim: pressure on adolescents may indeed have been high, but "[t]here was never an automatism, as a young person could, at all times, decide against joining the party." Membership applications had to be signed personally.¹⁵⁹

What is perhaps surprising, considering its own suppression under Nazism, is the Catholic Church's criticism of, if not outright opposition to, denazification measures. Not only did many Nazi functionaries, such as the press officer and treasurer of the party's local group in Oberbrechen, present themselves as "devout Catholics" and "only nominal members [of the Nazi Party]," but they could rely on the support of the clergy. Just as he had intervened in favor of Hugo Trost, his former antagonist, Father Kunz issued countless certificates whitewashing compromised villagers.¹⁶⁰ In other places, too, the Catholic Church spoke out against denazification, with petitions and memoranda addressed to the highest levels in the U.S. military government. These campaigns by the church were not only driven by religious motives and the hope of winning those who had gone astray back to their congregations, but also had an important political dimension. The Catholic Church was strongly anti-Communist and feared that those staffing the boards—among them a significant number adhering to the political left—would dominate Germany's new postwar order.¹⁶¹ Debates on the church's own responsibility and guilt culminated in the mid-1960s, when the role of Pope Pius XII was critically discussed in Rolf Hochhuth's play *The Deputy* (1963) and the Second Vatican Council convened in October 1965 reformulated the Catholic Church's relationship

---

158   Vollnhals, *Entnazifizierung*, 21; Klages, "Entnazifizierung," 367.

159   Statement of Josef Kramm, June 28, 1948, Family archive Kramm-Abendroth and Wünschmann; Nolzen, "Vom 'Jugendgenossen' zum 'Parteigenossen,'" 132. See also 147–148.

160   HHStAW, Spruchkammerakte Franz Rettinghaus; Alois Kunz, Attestation in the denazification case of Hugo Trost.

161   Mark Edward Ruff, "Katholische Kirche und Entnazifizierung," in: Christoph Kösters and id. (eds.), *Die katholische Kirche im Dritten Reich: Eine Einführung* (Freiburg: Herder, 2011), 142–153, here 145, 149.

to Jews by officially condemning antisemitism in the declaration *Nostra aetate* ("In our time").[162]

Researchers disagree on the extent to which the Allies' policies in postwar West Germany were effective and had a lasting impact. To "undo" Nazism, the Allies set out to prosecute those responsible for Nazi crimes, re-educate Germans in the ways of democracy, launch reparation payments for victims, and implement a denazification program vetting much of the population for complicity in the late regime's injustices. Scholars mostly come to sobering, if not negative, assessments of this approach to denazification.[163] New research argues that denazification—and we could add reparation—confronted millions of Germans with their own past and made them explain to themselves, not just to the authorities, what their participation in the dictatorship had been. Even though such reflection on personal behavior often ended in justification narratives and a yearning for closure, it did at least raise important questions of individual accountability and agency.[164] In Oberbrechen, questions about the injustices committed during the Nazi era were negotiated in various ways: narratives took shape, coalitions to fend off claims were forged, measures were used and abused in the pursuit of private interests. No matter how flawed these strategies may have been, the villagers ultimately had to face their own accountability.

THE "ORANGE BOOK," OR LOCAL ATTEMPTS AT *WIEDERGUTMACHUNG*

In the 1970s, when the village chronicle (widely called the "Orange Book" because of its cover) was being drafted, Eugen Caspary and Josef Kramm, then mayor of Oberbrechen, contacted a number of former Jewish residents of the village. This outreach project evolved into a long-lasting written and then also personal exchange at a time when many non-Jewish Germans wanted to forget the Nazi past altogether. In postwar Germany, the general sentiment remained antisemitic, even if it was frequently disguised in "philosemitic" terms, such as when the absence of the many Jewish Nobel Prize

---

162 Rolf Hochhuth, *The Deputy* (Baltimore: Johns Hopkins University Press, 1997 [1963]). See also Karl-Joseph Hummel, "Umgang mit der Vergangenheit: Die Schulddiskussion," in *Die Katholiken und das Dritte Reich: Kontroversen und Debatten*, 2nd edition, ed. by id. and Michael Kißner (Paderborn: Schöningh, 2010), 217–235, here 225–229.

163 Lutz Niethammer, *Die Mitläuferfabrik: Die Entnazifizierung am Beispiel Bayerns* (Berlin, Bonn: Dietz, 1982).

164 Leßau, *Entnazifizierungsgeschichten*, 53, 437–443, 487–489; Dack, *Everyday Denazification*, 250–252.

winners, musicians, and artists was felt to be a cultural loss to Germany.[165] Eventually, these encounters set in motion an ambitious, but fraught, social process of coming to terms with the past in Oberbrechen and in the surrounding Goldener Grund region.

Some of the Jews Eugen Caspary corresponded with eventually dared to come back and visit Oberbrechen. For many of them, it was the first time they had set foot on German soil after having escaped Nazism. For others, however, it was not: they had returned on their own initiative long before Eugen Caspary and Josef Kramm reached out to them.[166] Those who had come before, like Selma Altman and Maurice (formerly Moritz) Stern, often chose not to engage with non-Jewish villagers. For many Jews, it seemed that the only way of bearing the inner conflict involved in visiting the "country of the murderers" was to avoid or repress any contact with locals. By ignoring non-Jewish Germans and referring to the "beauty of the German countryside," they expressed both speechlessness at the crimes committed and a longing for their lost homeland.[167]

Herman Stern was one of these early visitors. Some sources suggest that he returned to reconnect with the region he grew up in and loved dearly; others imply that it was the family graves in the Jewish cemetery at Weyer that motivated his visit to Oberbrechen.[168] These gravesites offered an emotional refuge for those who mourned the dead—places where they could direct their feelings of loss. Many German Jews who had fled the country traveled to Europe to visit the graves of their deceased parents—and they often came into contact with locals even if they tried to avoid them.[169]

---

165 Frank Stern, *Im Anfang war Auschwitz: Antisemitismus und Philosemitismus im Deutschen Nachkrieg* (Gerlingen: Bleicher, 1991).

166 See also Helmut Walser Smith, "It Takes a Village to Create a Nation's Memory: Returning Jews and Local Communities Worked Together to Lead Germany Toward Historical Reckoning," in *Zócalo* last accessed March 1, 2021, https://www.zocalopublicsquare.org/2021/01/11/post-war-germany-jewish-return-memory-national-reckoning/ideas/essay, January 11, 2021.

167 Walter and Dr. Lotte Grünwald, "Stuttgart—Chile—Mallorca—Neustadt/Weinstraße," in Franz J. Jürgens, *"Wir Waren Ja Eigentlich Deutsche": Juden Berichten von Emigration und Rückkehr* (Berlin: Aufbau Taschenbuch Verlag, 1997), 204–226, here 211; Jack Kugelmass, "Strange Encounters: Expat and Refugee Polish-Jewish Journalists in Poland and Germany Shortly after World War II," *Juden und Nichtjuden nach der Shoah: Begegnungen in Deutschland*, ed. Stefanie Fischer, Nathanael Riemer, and Stefanie Schüler-Springorum (Berlin: De Gruyter Oldenbourg, 2019), 31–48, 41.

168 Travel Report of Adeline Stern, April 12–17, 1972, in University of North Dakota, Department of Special Collections, Herman Stern Papers, OLGMC 217, Series 4, SubB, Box 20, Folder 1, 1–9.

169 Stefanie Fischer, "Jewish Mourning in the Aftermath of the Holocaust: Tending Individual Graves in Occupied Germany, 1945–1949," in Kerry Wallach and Aya Elyada (eds.), *German Jewish Studies. Next Generations* (New York: Berghahn Books, 2023), 211–228, here 213.

For Kurt Lichtenstein, his sister Irene Lenkiewicz, and Herman Stern's nephew, Gustave Stern, their trips to Oberbrechen were the result of their correspondence with Eugen and Josef. While the case of Oberbrechen has some unique features, we should also appreciate these visits in the context of other German communities that officially invited displaced Jewish residents to visit. This trend began in 1969, when West Berlin—on the initiative of Hans Steinitz, chief editor of the weekly newspaper *Aufbau/Reconstruction*—started a visiting program for Jews from Berlin who had escaped Nazism.[170] In the following years, more and more German cities followed the Berlin initiative and invited surviving Jews back.

In the countryside, procedures were rather different. Visits of émigré German Jews to small towns and villages were often initiated and organized by lay people rather than by officials. If municipalities from rural towns offered no public funds to offset these costs, it was common to collect private money to cover the visitors' travel expenses. In some instances, however, the Jewish émigrés themselves initiated and paid for their visits. In Oberbrechen, arrangements varied. After exchanging letters with Eugen over several months, Gustave Stern proposed coming to Oberbrechen to conduct a concert on the occasion of the 1,200th anniversary of the village's foundation. Under the leadership of Mayor Josef Kramm, the municipality compensated Gustave Stern for his travel expenses, as he had asked for an honorarium for his performance. However, other former Oberbrecheners who made the trip back did not receive any reimbursement for their travel expenses. The journeys could be expensive, and Jewish visitors often made sure that returning to their place of origin was not the only object of their trips. Like many who came over from the United States, Herman and Adeline Stern combined their visit to Oberbrechen with an extended stay in Israel. Gustave Stern asked Eugen Caspary to send him a Neckermann[171] travel catalog so that he too could arrange a trip to Israel on leaving Oberbrechen.

Financial considerations certainly impacted decisions about traveling to Germany. Invitations from German communities, like those extended by Mayor Josef Kramm, often provided refugee German Jews with a welcome, if problematic, opportunity to travel to Germany, which, if self-organized, would have been difficult to arrange and fund. Some survivors said that they had accepted an official invitation only so that they could

---

170 Lina Nikou, "Vollständige Angaben sind unbedingt nötig," Berlins Einladungen an im Nationalsozialismus verfolgte ehemalige Bürgerinnen und Bürger, in *Juden und Nicht-Juden nach der Shoah*, ed. Fischer, Riemer, and Schüler-Springorum, 141–156, here 145.

171 At the time, Neckermann Reisen was a reputed, well-known travel agency in West Germany.

say a Kaddish at their parents' graves.[172] A number of those who accepted invitations only spent a minimum amount of time in their former hometowns and were sure not to stay there overnight, preferring to check into a hotel in a nearby city or, if possible, one across the border in France or Switzerland.[173] The trauma of being attacked when they were off their guard was by no means forgotten. Other Jewish survivors felt unable to face the emotional challenge of returning to their former hometowns, after it had taken them decades to recover their health, mental stability, and financial resources following their flight from Nazism. They declined all invitations and kept their vows never to set foot on German soil again (although, much later, some of them relented).[174]

Inequalities characterized the encounters that took place when survivors returned to visit the places they had once called home. Jews and non-Jews did not meet as equal partners, but rather in an asymmetrical relationship in which the Jewish visitors found themselves reliant on the generosity of the German community representatives.[175] Despite such disparities, the towns' and private initiatives toward reconciliation could still lead to exchanges in which Jews and non-Jews confronted their shared history together, as was the case between Gustave Stern and Eugen Caspary, and Kurt Lichtenstein and Josef Kramm.

As in these two cases, it naturally made a difference whether hosts and visitors had known one another before 1933 or were meeting after the war without having any prior experiences in common. For example, it seems that Gustave and Gertrude Stern felt more comfortable engaging with the villagers of Oberbrechen than with people from Duisburg, where Gertrude was from and where the couple had experienced Nazi terror firsthand.[176] As Gustave did not live in Oberbrechen during the Nazi years, his memories of the village were only of a childhood when he played with other children in the Emsbach Creek. His feelings were quite different from those of Kurt Lichtenstein, who had lived in Oberbrechen during the 1930s.

---

172 See Wolfgang Benz, "Rückkehr auf Zeit: Erfahrungen deutsch-jüdischer Emigranten mit Einladungen in ihre ehemaligen Heimatstädte," in *Das Exil der kleinen Leute: Alltagserfahrungen deutscher Juden in der Emigration*, ed. Wolfgang Benz (Munich: Beck, 1991), 332–340.

173 Kenneth Wald, "Revenge, Reconciliation, and Responsibility," in קולות, *Voices of Conservative/Masorti Judaism*, Summer 2010/5770, Vol. 3, No. 4, 14–16, here 16.

174 Stefanie Fischer, "Mit gemischten Gefühlen. Besuche von Holocaust-Überlebenden in ihren ehemaligen Heimatgemeinden," *Einsicht: Bulletin des Fritz Bauer Instituts* Vol. 10, No. 19 (2018), 78–85.

175 Lilach Naishtat-Bornstein, "'I Am Their Jew': Karla Raveh's Testimony in Germany and in Israel," *History and Memory* 32, No. 2 (Fall/Winter 2020), 110–145.

176 Gertrude Stern to Eugen Caspary, Seattle, April 13, 1977, Estate of Eugen Caspary.

Even if, there was no secret formula for successful encounters between Jews and non-Jews after the Holocaust, the case of Oberbrechen shows that gender and social background influenced how they progressed. Gustave and Eugen were connected through a German middle-class male culture that did a lot to help them overcome their differences. Such configurations sometimes led to the development of resilient, long-term relationships, but this familiarity only rarely extended to the women who accompanied their husbands during these encounters: in many cases they were excluded. In the very rare cases in which Jews received support from non-Jews during the years of persecution, people tended to remain in contact after 1945, as was the case with Selma Altman and Gertrud Marx.

GERMAN FANTASIES OF *WIEDERGUTMACHUNG*

Eugen Caspary and Josef Kramm gained recognition from refugee German Jews for their reconciliation efforts as they organized the visits of Oberbrechen's displaced Jews to their hometown. And they benefited in other ways as well. As these exchanges provided a glimpse into German-Jewish diasporas in the United States, Argentina, and Israel, Eugen in particular was able to add a sense of cosmopolitanism and exoticism to his life as a high school teacher in provincial Germany.[177] This exoticism was coupled with a certain familiarity arising from shared childhood experiences with Jews from the village. Jewish visitors were often "well-behaved" and appreciative toward those who gave them hospitality, which left their German hosts reassured in their endeavors.

As German-born Jews, the visitors knew how to conduct themselves in a German setting. They acted like locals, spoke the local dialects, and performed, read, and understood the cultural codes. They acknowledged the non-Jewish Germans' endeavors to unearth their communities' Jewish pasts. Many of them did not claim anything back—although moral questions around stolen Jewish property remained subtly present even after the late 1970s, when most judicial restitution and compensation claims had been officially settled. While the Jewish guests did not stay, but tended to depart after a couple of days,[178] their visits might leave their hosts—who

---

177 See also Geneviève Zubrzycki, "Nationalism, 'Philosemitism,' and Symbolic Boundary-Making in Contemporary Poland," *Comparative Studies in Society and History* 58, no 1 (2016), 66–98, here 91.

178 Frances Henry recounts how people from a German village reacted to the proposal of a former Jewish villager to resettle there after the war; see Frances Henry, *Victims and Neighbours: A Small Town in Nazi Germany Remembered* (South Hadley, MA: Bergin & Garvey, 1984), 125.

had once oppressed them or connived in this oppression—feeling a sense of relief, perhaps even of redemption.[179]

In postwar encounters, however, both sides, Jews and non-Jews, tended to focus mainly on what unified them, often sidelining the dreadful events and actions that had caused division. The survivors of persecution, now scattered across the globe, would return to Oberbrechen and other places of origin with memories that were "like a wonderful gift and a relentless curse. This curse—what the poet Paul Celan called 'black milk'—nourishes and nauseates, repels and attracts, seduces and disgusts."[180] Among the non-Jewish Germans, conflicted feelings of shame and a desire to put the past behind them contributed to unrealistic fantasies about instant personal and emotional reconciliation (*Wiedergutmachungsfantasien*) and thus a Christian understanding of atonement (*Versöhnung*) with Jews.

Over the years, Josef Kramm repeatedly expressed his strong wish to present "the new Germany" to the outside world. By this, he meant to present a country that had learned salutary lessons from the past. During Gustave and Gertrude Stern's first visit to Oberbrechen, he asked the Jewish guests to tell their friends in America about the "new Germany" they experienced during their visit.[181] However, the calls they made for a "new, more humane and friendly Germany in spite of everything" can also be understood as calls for atonement (*Versöhnung*) with the Nazi past.[182] In general, many local historians wished for some sort of *Versöhnung* when they addressed the suffering of Jews in their communities. In their encounters with Jewish visitors, they sought to overcome their own feelings of guilt concerning Germany's Nazi past and their personal involvement in Nazism. They often expressed public contrition in symbolic gestures or oblations in which they sought such atonement. This is reflected in Josef Kramm's framing of Gustave Stern's concert as an attempt at *Wiedergutmachung* or "making it alright again," recounted in Chapter 5 of the Graphic History.[183] The call for *Wiedergutmachung* can be understood as a request for forgiveness

---

179 Michael Meng, *Shattered Spaces: Encountering Jewish Ruins in Postwar Germany and Poland* (Berlin: De Gruyter, 2011), 214.

180 Ibid., 221–222.

181 Sch., "Gustave Stern gab sich die Ehre, und die Brechener waren dankbar. Der Gast aus Seattle demonstrierte sein großes musikalisches Können in einem Konzert," in *Weilburger Tageblatt*, September 7, 1976, no page number.

182 See Draft response from Eugen Caspary to Gustave Stern's letter of June 27, 1974, Estate of Eugen Caspary; see also Eugen Caspary to Kim Wünschmann, Bad Camberg-Erbach, July 3, 2013, Family Archive Wünschmann and Kramm-Abendroth (see Part II, Document 30).

183 Notice title "Bitte um Veröffentlichung," no date, Estate of Eugen Caspary. After publication of the "Orange Book," Josef Kramm donated a copy to Yad Vashem, referring to it as a gesture of "*Wiedergutmachung*"; see Mayor Josef Kramm, Mayor of Brechen, to Ms. Alcalay, library of Yad Vashem, Brechen, March 10, 1978, Estate of Eugen Caspary.

addressed to Jews—and indeed to the world at large. Invited Jewish partners were asked to participate in this social process under the terms of their non-Jewish hosts, who paid no regard to any Jewish understanding of forgiveness.

By reaching out to refugee German Jews, lay historians like Eugen Caspary positioned themselves alongside those liberal Germans who openly condemned the Nazi past. This appeal, however, tells us little about Josef Kramm's political preferences, nor those of Eugen Caspary, and how these preferences may have shaped their reconciliation efforts. As the historian Helmut Walser Smith points out, it remains hard to pin down the politics of those initiating, hosting, and funding the visits of former Jewish residents. Some of those who reached out to refugee Jews supported conservative parties like the Bavarian Christian Social Union (CSU).[184] As mayor, Josef Kramm was an independent, and we know little about Eugen Caspary's political views, though people say that he did not support the center-left Social Democrats.

NARRATIVES OF THE "NOT SO EVIL NAZI"

Other Christian Germans dealt with their feelings differently when encountering Jews after 1945. They pinned all blame on Nazism or they came out with a torrent of stories about their own suffering during and after the war, portraying themselves as victims—in a perverse reversal of the perpetrator–victim relationship that had actually existed.[185] The majority of Germans refused to engage emotionally with the sufferings of others, much less admit their involvement in Nazism and accept a share of moral responsibility for the Holocaust.

It was common for lay historians to shy away from naming local Nazi perpetrators, bystanders, and beneficiaries in the villages or towns they studied.[186] Memories of the Nazi past were quickly sanitized from local involvement in the exclusion of Jews from the town. After the war's end, like members of small communities elsewhere, Oberbrecheners quickly created a narrative of Hugo Trost, their former Nazi mayor, as a "not so evil Nazi." Not only was Trost granted amnesty by the Wiesbaden appeals commission in his denazification case, but people from the village chose to remember him as a man not implicated in Nazi crimes. Those who turned a blind eye in this way included many who had seen incriminating events at first hand and even those who were later keen to engage with Jewish

---

184 Walser Smith, "It takes a village."

185 See also Hannah Arendt, "The Aftermath of Nazi Rule. Report from Germany," *Commentary* (October 1950), 342–353, here 342.

186 Adelheid von Saldern, "Stadtgedächtnis und Geschichtswerkstätten," *Werkstatt Geschichte*, Nr. 50 (2009), 54–68, here 60.

survivors. Josef Kramm, for example, had only good words to say in the obituary for Trost he wrote for the local newspaper when the former mayor died in August 1977. Keeping silent about Trost's involvement in Nazism, Kramm wrote: "During [the Nazi years], he [Trost] selflessly advocated for the needs of the community. The deceased is most sincerely thanked for his work for the people [of Oberbrechen]."[187] Kramm himself indulged in a narrative of Catholic reluctance to participate in Nazi organizations like the Hitler Youth and kept quiet about the Nazi Party membership he acquired at the age of seventeen. In his dealings with the denazification authorities after the war, he had turned to Hugo Trost to help clear his name. The myth of Hugo Trost as the Nazi mayor "selflessly advocating for the needs of the community" was deeply inscribed in Oberbrechen's postwar narrative. Trost continued to serve on the municipality council from the mid-1950s to the late 1960s.[188] When a documented "history of the Third Reich" in Oberbrechen was discussed during a local colloquium in January 1982, the participants agreed that "the research findings and documents should be preserved in the archive and by no means be made available to the public. This would prevent persons who are still living and were closely associated with the Third Reich from experiencing any disadvantages."[189] We have no sources to indicate how Jewish survivors felt about this cover-up of Hugo Trost's and other villagers' Nazi past.

Just how biased and conflicted Oberbrecheners were about researching the village's Jewish history is also evident in Eugen Caspary's choice of title for the chapter he wrote for the "Orange Book." He called the chapter *Jüdische Mitbürger in Oberbrechen, 1711–1941: Eine Bestandsaufnahme* ("Jewish Fellow Citizens in Oberbrechen, 1711–1941: A Survey"). By referring to Jews as *Mitbürger*, he emphasized that Jews were full citizens (*Mitbürger*) of Oberbrechen. Since democracies usually do not differentiate between citizens of different origins, it smacks of "othering" when he talks about "Jewish fellow citizens." This phrasing suggests that Jews were not a fully integrated part of the village and implies a demarcation separating Jewish from Christian villagers.[190] By othering one segment of

---

187   Josef Kramm, Obituary Hugo Trost, *Inform*, August 31, 1977.

188   Minutes of the municipal council (*Gemeindevertretung*) dated December 7, 1956; October 10, 1958; November 18. 1960; December 9, 1960; and May 27, 1966. We thank Georg Beinrucker for this information. See also *Journal of the Municipality of Oberbrechen* (Heft Gemeinde Oberbrechen), March 1958, p. 3, in Frankfurt Box No 6, Estate of Eugen Caspary.

189   Minutes of the Colloquium, January 24, 1981, at Emstalhalle Brechen, district of Oberbrechen, 4, Estate of Eugen Caspary.

190   Yael Kupferberg, "Philosemitismus im Kontext der deutschen Nachkriegszeit," in Julius H. Schoeps (ed.), *Leben im Land der Täter. Juden im Nachkriegsdeutschland (1945–1952)* (Berlin: Jüdische Verlagsanstalt, 2001), 267–283, here 276.

the population in this way, Oberbrecheners indicated who, in their eyes, belonged to the village community—those who were protected by an exculpatory postwar narrative from accountability for their involvement in Nazism. The victims—those they had wronged—were hangers-on, or merely visitors. In the process, boundaries were established that, in many cases, were never crossed. It was common practice to appease former Nazi leaders while, at the same time, seeking rapport with exiled Jews.[191]

Moreover, contact with both non-Jewish and Jewish refugees was not always welcomed or appreciated by the wider community. The ambiguities of Eugen Caspary and Josef Kramm's engagement with former Jewish Oberbrecheners are reflected in the critical statements delivered by some fellow villagers, who looked with suspicion on the two men's efforts to unveil the Jewish history of their community. Sources refer to villagers openly criticizing the mayor for making contact with exiled Jews and hosting them.[192]

But Eugen also felt a pervasive indifference from others when he was researching the history of Jews in Oberbrechen. Colleagues and academics alike snubbed him. Egon Eichhorn, co-editor of the "Orange Book," openly raised concerns about his undertaking. In a letter to Mayor Kramm, Eichhorn questioned whether any sources about the village's Jews were available at all. He wrote: "about such a small population group as Jews in a Catholic village.... 2–3 pages appended to the big chapter on church and parish history are enough for us when it comes to the [history of the] Jewish religious community."[193] But Eugen Caspary persevered. In the end, due to his meticulous research, the chapter on Oberbrechen's Jews became the longest in the village chronicle, taking up 75 pages of the 542-page book. To the end of his life, however, Eugen Caspary received little recognition from academia for unearthing Jewish history from the region. In contrast, he received tremendous acclaim from Jewish survivors and public institutions alike. Even today, many Jewish families originating from Oberbrechen keep a copy of the "Orange Book" on their shelves. International research institutions, such as the Leo Baeck Institute in New York and Yad Vashem in Israel, have copies of his work in their collections. In 1999, the Leo Baeck Institute even commissioned a translation of excerpts from Eugen's chapter into English, choosing passages focusing on Jewish genealogy but leaving aside Eugen's accusatory interpretation

---

191 See also von Saldern, "Stadtgedächtnis," 64.

192 Eugen Caspary to Kim Wünschmann, Bad Camberg-Erbach, July 3, 2013, private collection of Kim Wünschmann (see Part II, Document 30).

193 Egon Eichhorn to Josef Kramm, Wiesbaden, November 4, 1973, in Estate of Eugen Caspary.

of Nazism as a "machinery of death."[194] As the greatest honor of all, in 1982 Eugen was awarded Germany's highest federal decoration, the *Bundesverdienstkreuz (Verdienstkreuz am Bande)*.[195] Typical for its time, the document explaining the award does not mention his activity in unearthing the Jewish history of his home community; it confines its praise to Eugen's expertise, engagement, and publications in local history.[196]

Decorations and awards reflect a society's social, cultural, and political values. It is therefore remarkable that until the present day (see Map 7), no German institution has acknowledged Herman Stern's rescue and reconciliation efforts during and after the Second World War. He rescued more than one hundred German Jews during the Holocaust. In the 1970s, on the occasion of Herman's ninetieth birthday, Gustave Stern proposed to Eugen Caspary and Josef Kramm that an honorary citizenship of Oberbrechen should be bestowed on this tireless champion. The Brechen municipality, to which the village belongs, declined to honor him.[197] This starkly contrasts with the honorary citizenship bestowed on Father Alois Kunz on the fortieth anniversary of his ordination, October 3, 1954.[198] At present, all *Ehrenbürger* (honorary citizens) of the municipality are men and Christians.[199] The global dimensions and implications of Oberbrechen's local history and that of its inhabitants, whether Jewish, Catholic, or neither, are still waiting to be recognized by the town's representatives.

This micro-study of Oberbrechen has looked at encounters between Jews and non-Jews, and has brought out Jewish participation in the social process of coming to terms with the aftermath of the Holocaust. It has shown that surviving Jews were not outside figures in the internal debate on Germans' "collective guilt," but that they actively participated in it.[200] Only recently have the efforts and achievements in unearthing Jewish

---

194 Eugen Caspary and Justin J. Mueller, *Jewish Citizens in Oberbrechen 1711–1941* (Manchester, Vermont: no publisher, 1999).

195 Head of the Office of the Federal President to the Hessian Minister-President, Bonn, October 13, 1980, in Federal Archives, Bundesarchiv (BArch), B122_83545 VL-Nr_150-80.

196 Document titled "Eugen Caspary, born June 21, 1929, occupation: high school teacher [. . .]", in BArch B122_83545 VL-Nr_150-80.

197 Gustave Stern to Eugen Caspary, Seattle, April 17, 1976, and Gustave Stern to Eugen Caspary, Seattle, May 14, 1976, Estate of Eugen Caspary.

198 *Nassauer Bote*, October 5, 1954, Diocesan Archives Limburg.

199 See Gemeinde Brechen, "Brechener Persönlichkeiten," last accessed October 18, 2022, https://www.gemeinde-brechen.de/gemeinde/arbeitskreis-historisches-brechen/brechener-persoenlichkeiten.

200 Atina Grossmann, *Jews, Germans, and Allies: Close Encounters in Occupied Germany* (Princeton, NJ: Princeton University Press, 2007), 6; on the relationship between general history and Jewish history, see Mathias Berek, Kirsten Heinsohn, David Jünger, and Achim Rohde, "Vom Erfolg ins Abseits? Jüdische Geschichte als Geschichte der 'Anderen'. Ein Gespräch," *Medaon* [November 20, 2017] 1–17.

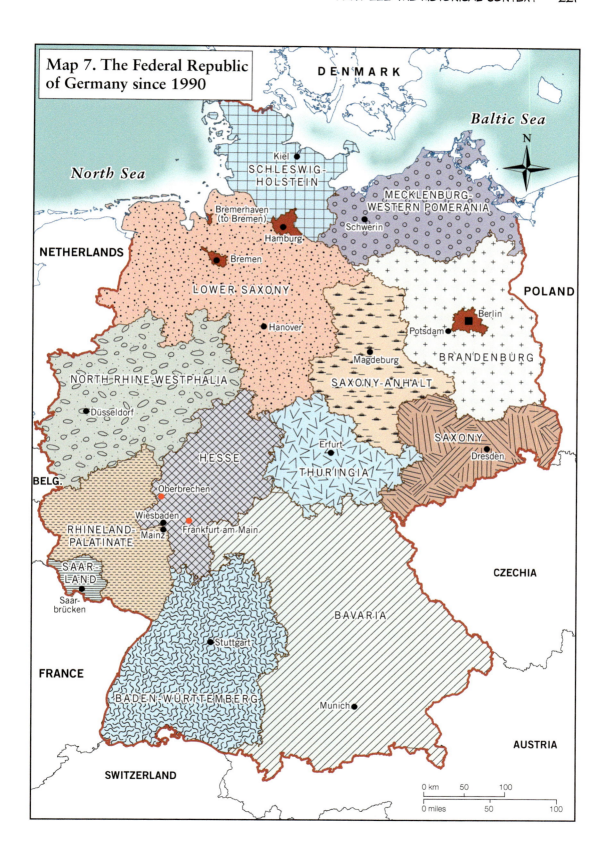

history of local historians and politicians like Eugen Caspary and Josef Kramm been taken up in "official" historical scholarship.[201] These lay historians brought Jewish aspects of local history into a new focus and, in doing so, engaged in a dialogue with refugee German Jews that has greatly contributed to a broadening of perspectives by integrating Jewish voices into our understanding of the past. Most importantly, they have contributed to the social process of *Vergangenheitsbewältigung* (coming to terms with the past) that has been so important to Jews and non-Jews across the globe in the aftermath of the tragedy of the Holocaust.

---

201   See Jenny Wüstenberg, *Civil Society and Memory in Postwar Germany* (Cambridge: Cambridge University Press, 2017); and Susan Neiman, *Learning from the Germans: Race and the Memory of Evil* (New York: Farrar, Straus & Giroux, 2019). Helmut Walser Smith is working on a research project titled "Facing the Past in Small-Town Germany, 1945–2000."

PART IV
THE MAKING OF OBERBRECHEN

A CONVERSATION BETWEEN STEFANIE FISCHER AND KIM WÜNSCHMANN WITH JAY H. GELLER AND DEBORAH POMERANZ

STEFANIE FISCHER AND KIM WÜNSCHMANN: Thank you very much, Debby and Jay, for taking part in this discussion on how we composed the Graphic History *Oberbrechen: A German Village Confronts Its Nazi Past*. In this section of the book, we want to reflect with you on the making of *Oberbrechen* and think critically about the creative process of writing and drawing this history, the decisions we made, and the challenges we faced. Both of your perspectives are extremely valuable, and you are very well placed to be part of this exchange, given, in Debby's case, your contribution to the project as a research assistant, and in Jay's case, your expertise as a scholar of German-Jewish history and culture.

JAY H. GELLER: I wonder if I could start with a question to Kim. Kim, growing up in Oberbrechen in the 1970s and 1980s, what was your awareness of the former Jewish presence in the town? And, either related to that or separately, was there any discussion of the town's history under National Socialism or during the late Weimar era?

KIM WÜNSCHMANN: As a child, I witnessed the visits of the Jewish former Oberbrecheners coming to the village and to our house. I was born in 1977 and grew up in a four-generation household with my parents, grandparents, and great-grandparents. My grandfather Josef Kramm—he was known as "Jupp" or "Kramm Jupp"—was very active in communal life. Between 1972 and 1980, he served as the independent mayor, initially of Oberbrechen, and then, after the administrative-territorial reform of 1974, of the Brechen municipality, encompassing the villages of Oberbrechen, Niederbrechen, and Werschau. Our home was a public place and we had many visitors, including from abroad.

My grandfather had a passion for history. The Nazi era was of particular interest to him as it coincided with his coming of age. He was born in 1925. The dominant narratives in the village were those of low election results for the Nazi Party and ongoing Catholic life under Nazi rule, often framed as resistance. In this selective way of communicating about the past, not much was said about neighbors who had been Nazis. The experiences of Jewish Oberbrecheners were marginalized. Although I witnessed their visits, neither the historical context nor their symbolic meaning was discussed much. Why were we hosting them? Why was this important to my grandfather? What did it mean to the visitors to return to their former homes in Oberbrechen, a place that had become tainted by its history of violence?

JAY H. GELLER: But, ultimately, an exception to that is Eugen Caspary. And in many towns and villages across Germany, there were Eugen Casparys who either helped bring the story to light or took the lead in some sort of *Vergangenheitsbewältigung* (working through the past). What was your experience of knowing Eugen Caspary?

THE RESEARCH PROCESS

KIM WÜNSCHMANN: I knew Eugen Caspary, who was born in 1929, as a very close friend of my grandfather's. They shared a passion for history, and in particular for local history. My grandfather helped to found the local history workshop, and his initiatives were also important in establishing the municipality archives. Both men had a talent for writing. Josef Kramm started a local newspaper called *Inform*, which was published between 1974 and 2001. Today, it is an important source for researching Oberbrechen's history. For this paper, he chronicled many events of village life past and present, including the visits of the Jewish former Oberbrecheners, complete with photographs that he took. Eugen Caspary authored numerous studies on local and regional history. I think Eugen and Josef took pride in their historical work. It was something that connected them.

When, in 2013, Stefanie and I started discussing the phenomenon of Jews visiting their places of origin in rural post-Holocaust Germany, it was clear to me that the person I should turn to in order to find out more was Eugen Caspary. My grandfather had passed away by then. He died in 2004. So, I wrote a letter to Eugen. I knew that he had been involved in reestablishing contact with the Jewish families from Oberbrechen—he was often present in our house when the visitors

Figure 1. Gustave Stern, Josef Kramm, Marcia Smith (Gustave's partner), and Eugen Caspary during Gustave's last visit to Oberbrechen in September 1989, Kramm family home. Credit: Ursula Königstein.

came—but I had only a vague idea of how this had come about, and I was not aware of the key role he played in these initiatives to reconnect (see Figures 1 and 2).

JAY H. GELLER: Well, a remarkable aspect of the story is the way that the Jewish former Oberbrecheners and the Christian Oberbrecheners related to each other. And they related to each other as Oberbrecheners, or even as Germans. But in the book, we see very little discussion of the former Oberbrecheners' Jewishness. Do you think that aspect of their identity was pushed aside or simply ignored during their visits? And if so, what do you make of that?

KIM WÜNSCHMANN: For the visits of the 1970s, we can say that, at that time, many Germans perceived Jewish life as a historical phenomenon only, in particular in the countryside. In the Federal Republic, Jewish communities in the larger cities were smaller and much less visible or diverse than today. Their

Figure 2. Josef Kramm, Eugen Caspary, and Kurt Lichtenstein during a visit in Oberbrechen, Kramm family home, early 1980s. Credit: Family Archive Wünschmann/Kramm-Abendroth.

members did not amount to more than 30,000 in total.[1] Many Christians did not know Jews personally, let alone share a daily life with them. There was no practiced form of social interaction. Addressing the matter of "Jewishness," in many instances, referred back to Nazi persecution and ordinary Germans' complicity in the regime's measures of exclusion.

In Oberbrechen, Catholicism, as the dominant religion that also shapes people's identities, informed these re-encounters between Jews and Christians, which take place in a distinct village space marked by the presence or absence of religion. It is a place that had never had a synagogue. The Jews of Oberbrechen used to pray in synagogues in the neighboring towns and villages. There is no Jewish cemetery in Oberbrechen. Both synagogue and cemetery would be spatial markers of practiced Judaism in a small town. From Stefanie's research we can learn about the cattle trade as a sign of Jewishness in rural areas.

STEFANIE FISCHER: I agree that the Jewishness of the visitors was sidelined or even ignored by their Christian hosts. By doing this, Oberbrechen presented

---

1 Constantin Goschler and Anthony Kauders, "The Jewish Community," in *A History of Jews in Germany Since 1945: Politics, Culture and Society*, ed. Michael Brenner, transl. Kenneth Kronenberg (Bloomington: Indiana University Press, 2018), 289–324, here 290.

itself as a typical 1970s West German town in which white Christian men dominated politics and historiography. In this cultural setting we can see an "absence of the Jews as *Jews*" in daily life, but also in historiography.² In such a setting, non-Jewish Germans would often emphasize how "normal" and "decent" (*anständig*) and—above all—how "German" the Jews who had once lived in their town were.

Given the context of the history of Jewish emancipation in German lands, it is not surprising that belonging to German culture and "being German" stand out in these encounters. Often, emphasizing how *German* Jews were, rather than focusing on their *Jewishness*, went hand in hand with silencing Jewish experiences of the Holocaust. While the Holocaust was recognized in West Germany, it was, until the 1990s, largely portrayed as a tyranny imposed on the Jews by a machinery of terror and death. The narrative of an anonymous killing machine devoid of individual German agency (for or against) was often set out alongside lengthy elaborations about German war losses and trauma: the Allied bombing of German cities, the rape of German women by Soviet soldiers, the expulsion of Germans from the lost territories in the East, and so on.

Still, Jewishness was present during the visits to Oberbrechen. Jewish spaces, such as the Jewish cemetery in the neighboring village of Weyer, were an integral part of the visits by the expelled Jewish Oberbrecheners (Figure 3). At the Jewish cemetery, the Jewish visitors would recite a *Kaddish* at their parents' grave and place a rock on top of the gravestone (an ancient Jewish tradition). After the Holocaust, mourning the dead became a symbol of both cultural belonging and Jewishness. Thus, these visits were also an expression of Jewishness and were about mourning both the dead and cultural losses.

JAY H. GELLER: Kim mentioned that for most Germans in the 1970s, Jewish life was solely a historical phenomenon. That's certainly true. The majority of Germans living in the so-called Bonn Republic didn't know any Jews personally and had no first-hand knowledge of Jewish culture. If they knew anything about Jews, it was likely from books, and probably books about the Holocaust, where the Jews were depicted as victims. But many older West Germans had known Jews before 1938 or 1933. They personally knew individuals who had suffered, and, though it was far in the past, they had had some exposure to Jewish practices. Did that affect how various Oberbrecheners responded to the visitors? Did these different age cohorts treat them differently?

---

2 Sharon Gillerman, *Germans into Jews: Remaking the Jewish Social Body in the Weimar Republic* (Stanford, CA: Stanford University Press, 2009), 9.

Figure 3. Gertrude Stern at the Jewish cemetery in Weyer during a visit to Oberbrechen in the 1970s. Credit: Department of Special Collections, Chester Fritz Library, University of North Dakota. Herman Stern Papers.

STEFANIE FISCHER: The Jewishness of the visitors was indeed negotiated differently by the Christians born before 1933 and those born after 1945. The generation born before 1933—like Josef Kramm and Eugen Caspary—had experienced Jewish religion, culture, and everyday life as children. They grew up with Jews living next door. They knew, for example, what *challah* was and were aware that it was baked for the Sabbath, just as they knew about

Jewish holidays. As children, they watched Jewish neighbors preparing their homes for Jewish holidays, setting up a *sukkah* or lighting the *Chanukkah* candles. Some of them had worked for Jewish households or even acted as a *Shabbes Goy*, a non-Jew who performs a certain type of work for a Jew on Sabbath (when such work is prohibited by Jewish law). Eugen grew up next door to the family of Siegfried Stern. Josef Kramm went to school with Kurt Lichtenstein, whose parents kept a kosher household and whose father was a cattle trader, a typical occupation for German Jews.

But even though Eugen and Josef's generation experienced Jewish daily life and Jewish customs during their childhood years, this did not necessarily mean that they had a nonbiased sense of cultural and religious differences. The harm inflicted on Jews as a result of a centuries-long historic discrimination by Christians only slowly started to be recognized within German society in the 1970s and 1980s. We can also see no critical reflection on their own dominant Christian view among non-Jewish Germans. This becomes apparent in their use of Christian rites and symbols in encounters with Jews. For example, Josef Kramm suggested to Herman Stern that he should donate money for the celebration of Mass in the local church as a way of expressing his gratitude for the publication of the so-called Orange Book (the village chronicle published on the occasion of the 1,200-year anniversary of Oberbrechen, as discussed in Chapter 5 of the Graphic History). It seems that Kramm did not see the cultural dynamics at work in encounters with Jewish Oberbrecheners and what it meant to ask a Jew to give money for the celebration of Mass.

The Christians' lack of awareness of the cultural and religious differences present in these encounters also comes to light when we look at how Oberbrecheners sent annual Christmas and Easter cards to Jewish former Oberbrecheners. The Jewish former Oberbrecheners, in turn, regularly sent seasonal greetings to Oberbrecheners on Christian holidays, but we found no evidence of Oberbrecheners sending holiday greetings on Jewish holidays. So, while the Christian hosts welcomed the Jews from Oberbrechen with warm-hearted hospitality, they did so with a lack of religious and cultural sensitivity.

JAY H. GELLER: Before I heard Stefanie speak about her research and her own experience, I did have a number of thoughts, but I'm not sure, now, that any of them are quite right. I wondered, for example, whether the non-Jewish Oberbrecheners didn't know how to interact with their Jewish visitors on the level of their Jewishness, or if perhaps they didn't want to interact on that level. And thinking too about Kim's point (and again, this is before I heard Stefanie's explanation), I wondered whether maybe Jewishness or Jewish identity was never really the basis of their rapport. Because the synagogue and the cemetery were in another village, I wondered whether these interactions were shaped by the fact that Jewish Oberbrecheners had been living the most visibly Jewish component of their identity in another locale. But Stefanie's point about their lived Jewishness being visible and understandable to the older generation has made me rethink that.

So, when the visitors come, there's a spatial dimension, but there's also a kind of chronological dimension at work in that they're making a journey to the past. And maybe it makes sense, therefore, that at least in their initial contacts, these two groups are relating to each other on the basis of the past, on the basis of a shared history. That's their common ground. And that experience is both extremely uncomfortable and diverges radically when you get to the National Socialist era or the postwar era. Perhaps they didn't quite know how to talk to each other about that, even if they were inclined to do so. That takes us to the issue of the friendships as well. The Jewish former Oberbrecheners came back, and we see some friendships developed, but there were no reciprocal visits to the United States or Argentina. Why do you think this is the case? Was it simply the culture of the era (not least because of the prohibitive cost of travel), or was there something about the nature of the rapport between these two groups that meant they couldn't take their friendship or their connection to another level?

STEFANIE FISCHER: Let me start with some thoughts about the basis of their rapport and how it stemmed from being German. After emigrating to the United States, Herman and Gustave Stern, even if somewhat differently, remained rooted in and sustained their ties to German culture and language for the rest of their lives. In an interview, Gustave's son Michel Stern recalled about his father: "[Gustave] was a real German. I mean, had he not been Jewish, there was no question he was German. His temperament was very, very German."[3] In his newly established bonds with Oberbrecheners, Gustave was able to reconnect to his life before coming to the United States. Eugen's letters opened a gate for Gustave to get in touch with his "German side," in a way he could not do in the United States. Gustave's pride in German *Bildung* comes to light in his relationships to his students. (The German term *Bildung* can be translated as education. However, its meaning transcends the meaning of (academic) education; it also encompasses a person's moral education and character formation.) While teaching music at Seattle University, he sent several of his students to study opera singing in Germany. To Eugen, Gustave Stern outspokenly praised German

---

3 Michel Stern, interviewed by Steve Adler, Seattle, WA, November 7, 2001, University of North Dakota, Department of Special Collections, Chester Fritz Library, Herman Stern Papers, OLGMC 217, Series 8, SubA, Box 16, Folder 52.

Bildungskultur (a culture of *Bildung*), which was the foundation of Jewish Weimar culture before the Nazis came to power and destroyed it.[4] Gustave and Eugen were connected through a German-bourgeois culture that helped them enter into a new dialogue. Such configurations sometimes led to the development of resilient and long-term relationships.

Jewish–non-Jewish rapport could also foreground other themes, like sports. Kurt Lichtenstein and Josef Kramm bonded over their deep love of soccer. In the 1970s this constituted a fundamental part of (German) male and mostly nonbourgeois bonding culture. Though it is still true that the encounters remained within a German context, locally and culturally. Neither Josef nor Eugen ever returned the visits to Herman, Gustave, or Kurt. The in-person encounters took place solely in and around the village of Oberbrechen.

JAY H. GELLER: I think that when Jews and non-Jewish Germans become acquainted, the issue of the Holocaust is almost always in the background. They have to decide either to ignore the issue or to address it at some point and then move on. But if their connection is exclusively about the legacy of the Holocaust, or if their relationship remains in the shadow of the Holocaust, it's very hard to develop a friendship on a personal basis that has real substance to it.

When considering the Jewish visitors to Oberbrechen, I could not help but think of the German-born Israeli philosopher and historian Gershom Scholem, his brothers, and their return trips to Germany. The second brother, Erich, had a very negative experience when he visited Germany in 1960 and never returned, though he did have one or two good encounters with former friends from Berlin DDP circles and his visit was centered on Berlin.[5] The oldest brother, Reinhold, had a better experience, though I don't think he met old friends in Berlin. And despite Gershom's tremendous skepticism and his public persona, he returned quite frequently in the 1960s and 1970s. But he noted that he was visiting Germany as a Jew or as an Israeli, not as a former German. At most, he might concede that he was returning as a former Berliner, and Berlin specifically had a special hold on him.[6] So we can see that the local is important to German Jewish émigrés

---

4 See also Ismar Schorsch, "German Judaism: From Confession to Culture," in *The Jews in Nazi Germany, 1933–1943*, ed. Arnold Paucker (Tübingen: Mohr, 1986), 67–74. According to George L. Mosse, German *Bildungskultur* had become the very heart of German Jewishness; see: George L. Mosse, *German Jews beyond Judaism* (Bloomington: Indiana University Press, 1985).

5 The abbreviation DDP stands for *Deutsche Demokratische Partei*, the center-left liberal German Democratic Party of the Weimar era.

6 See Jay Howard Geller, *The Scholems: A Story of the German Jewish Bourgeoisie from Emancipation to Destruction* (Ithaca, NY: Cornell University Press, 2019), 196.

KIM WÜNSCHMANN: Reflection on the experience of visiting Germany after the Holocaust is certainly a trope that features in many accounts—from those accounts of Jews with rural backgrounds to those of intellectuals like Gershom Scholem, Hannah Arendt, Fritz Stern, or Peter Gay. The last-named describes "uncomfortable days" during a visit of Germany in the summer of 1961 that felt like an "ordeal." A high "level of tension" set in the very moment he and his wife Ruth crossed the French–German border. Traveling on to Berlin, they "did not get on with each other, whether in the car or our hotel room; at one point we even discussed turning back. We snapped at each other, bickered in unaccustomed ways. We had had words before and would have words again, but never for a reason so obviously imposed from the outside. It is pointless to assign blame: the provocation of Germany all around us was simply too strong, for Ruth as a newcomer, American-born but from a Jewish Eastern European family, as much as for me, the returning native. Contemporary history raw and ugly had caught up with us."[7] How do you deal with the tension and the acute emotional stress? What do you talk about—among your fellow visitors, but also with those non-Jewish Germans you encounter as history is still "raw and ugly"?

In the case of Oberbrechen, we observe that Jewish visitors and Christian hosts often conversed about what can be interpreted as surrogate topics—culture and sports—as a way of avoiding difficult conversations. How could you deal with the perpetrator people after the Holocaust? How could you speak to them at all? Sharing a passion for sports or culture enabled Jews and non-Jews to rebuild relations. This way they could establish the trust needed for the Jewish participants to face otherwise unsettling encounters that could easily trigger, as Peter Gay observed, projections as well as feelings of hatred, which "left no doubt in my mind: murderous anti-Semitism was alive and flourishing in my native land."[8] The German language was also important, and through conversations in the local dialect, the *Oberbrechen platt*, a shared heritage and a common ground could be conjured up.

STEFANIE FISCHER: As Jay said, the Holocaust was almost always in the background. In all these encounters, questions of moral responsibility for the crimes committed and how to continue living after them were consciously and

---

7 Peter Gay, *My German Question: Growing Up in Nazi Berlin* (New Haven, CT: Yale University Press, 1998), 7.

8 Ibid., 5.

unconsciously negotiated. Even though each of their encounters with non-Jewish Germans represented a unique experience for Jews, there were nevertheless commonalities: grief for the murdered and anger at the murderers, the shame of their own survival, the speechlessness at the atrocity—all this resonated in the encounters with non-Jewish Germans, who stood in for "the perpetrators." In this context, therefore, Eugen's openly articulated regrets about Nazi crimes helped Jews to enter into conversations with non-Jewish Oberbrecheners. Early on, Eugen identified himself as one of the children who mocked the elderly Moses Stern (Herman Stern's brother and Gustave Stern's uncle). These postwar encounters can therefore be understood as a form of grief work in which a symbolic connection between the past and the present was produced.

KIM WÜNSCHMANN: As we have already noted, Christian Oberbrecheners almost never traveled to see the new homes of their Jewish friends, although they were invited to do so numerous times. To be sure, class and generation play a role in explaining this. In Eugen's and my grandfather Jupp's generation, Germans from rural backgrounds were not used to international travel in the way that would become normal for those from younger generations and upper-middle-class, urban backgrounds. Those whose careers had allowed them to climb the social ladder were a little different in this respect. Karl Jung from Oberbrechen, for example, who became a high-ranking official in the West German state bureaucracy and apparently helped Kurt Lichtenstein re-acquire German citizenship, did travel to Los Angeles in the 1960s to visit Selma and Max Altman. Karl was born in 1930 into the family of Peter Jung, the village baker, whose shop was next door to the Altmans' house. And we know of Eugen's nephew Helmuth, who visited Gustave Stern in Seattle and was warmly welcomed.

DEBORAH POMERANZ: I remember being really struck by the intensity of Gustave and Eugen's friendship when I read their letters to one another. It was something I didn't see in others. It's not necessarily the content of what they talked about, because I agree that this was definitely focused on the past, and within that on the commonalities rather than the differences in their experiences. Rather, it was the way that, if they didn't hear from one another for a couple of weeks, they would get so hurt and have this really wounded response, "Do you not care about me anymore?" So, there was an emotional intensity, at least in that one relationship, that was really striking to me. I think that it points to at least the possibility of a genuinely two-sided relationship between Jewish and non-Jewish Oberbrecheners.

JAY H. GELLER: To return to something Stefanie said, one thought I had is that the German Jews who had emigrated to places like the United States, Palestine, and Argentina were a minority within the Jewish world. The majority Jewish culture that they encountered in these places was derived from Eastern Europe. It wasn't German-Jewish, and they were out of place in their new Jewish communities. But in Oberbrechen or on return trips to Germany, they could be German once again. In Oberbrechen, they could be Hessians once again. They could speak their dialect. They could eat the foods of their childhood, which already differentiated them from other Germans, but also, notably, differentiated them from other Jews living in places like Palestine and America. This was a unique and probably special experience for them.

STEFANIE FISCHER: During these visits German-Jewish refugees privately mourned the loss of their home, but also the loss of their cultural bonds—bonds for which the societies in the countries that received them provided no space. The United States, in particular, offered no room for mourning the loss of German culture. On the contrary, U.S. society demanded a swift adaptation to an American lifestyle, along with a profound gratitude to the United States for having allowed German-Jewish refugees to settle there. Many American Jews with an Eastern European background openly condemned any pro-German feelings or sentiments. In their encounters with non-Jewish Germans in postwar Germany, returning Jews might experience a space for mourning their cultural losses, alongside their feelings of grief and anger and the other emotions that we have already touched on.

We can also see generational differences in the response of the Jewish families to Germany. For Jewish visitors who had been born in Germany and had grown up there, it seems that these visits were crucial for allowing them to deal with their German roots and with their experience of Nazi violence. After their first and surely most difficult visit to Oberbrechen, some of them returned several times, even though none of them ever thought about permanently returning to Germany.

However, it seems that many German Jews who returned to visit after the war stayed silent about their experiences, not sharing their experiences and feelings even with their own children or grandchildren. The inner conflict which accompanied making contact with Germany was so great that it was not uncommon for parents to conceal that they maintained connections to Germany from their own children—and later, it happened the other way around.[9] The preservation of German heritage and culture, as well as relationships with non-Jews in Germany, was often met with complete

---

9 The German-Israeli co-production *The Flat*, הדירה, *Die Wohnung* (2011), directed and produced by Arnon Goldfinger, explores how German-Jewish refugees dealt with encounters with non-Jewish Germans and questions of their cultural heritage after the end of the war.

incomprehension from one's own family or the wider community.[10] For many German Jews, it remained a lifelong question—which connections to Germany and to German culture they should keep and which they should sever.[11] Even when some individuals found a satisfying answer for themselves, this remained precarious and could change quickly, for example, if they had a bad experience with a non-Jewish German, which was not uncommon. For some, their first visit to Germany after the war could also be their last.

JAY H. GELLER: I don't know if their children or grandchildren would have understood this. Perhaps their grandchildren, or great-grandchildren, were a bit incredulous about their older family members wanting to have a continued connection to Germany after what Germany had done to them. But it was the country of their birth. Germany was part of them, and perhaps they understood Germany differently.

DEBORAH POMERANZ: It seems that Selma Altman experienced this conflict in her family even within the same generation. When she visited in 1965, she almost went on her own. Her husband and her sister stayed in the United States, though in the end she was accompanied by a cousin who lived in France. Later, she chose not to have an ongoing correspondence with Eugen when he was compiling the village chronicle. She sent one brief and polite letter to the mayor, and that was it.[12] We were speaking earlier about how relationships between Jewish and non-Jewish Oberbrecheners largely took place on the terms of the latter. Nonetheless, the Jewish Oberbrecheners did have a choice about whether or not to engage at all. Some, like Selma, kept their distance. Kurt Stern answered letters from Oberbrechen angrily. So, for those who did build these relationships, or even visit, it was clearly something they wanted, and something they chose, I guess, for the variety of reasons we've been talking about.

KIM WÜNSCHMANN: This also makes me think of Walter Stern, who fled Nazi persecution to Palestine in 1936. His father Joseph was from Oberbrechen and was murdered. Walter Stern never wanted to set foot on German soil again. It is important that our project makes these reactions visible, too. During our research, we constantly struggled with the positive narrative of

---

10   Anna Cichopek-Gajraj, *Beyond Violence: Jewish Survivors in Poland and Slovakia, 1944–48* (Cambridge: Cambridge University Press, 2014), 73.

11   Kateřina Čapková and David Rechter, "Germans or Jews? German-Speaking Jews in Post-War Europe: An Introduction," *The Leo Baeck Institute Year Book* 62 (2017), 69–74, here 73.

12   The letter is reproduced as Document 20 in Part II of this book.

reconciliation that was constructed by my grandfather and Eugen. That's why it was so important to recover these other narratives—narratives of reluctance, refusal, or outright anger that confronted the Christians with a violent past and with a responsibility for crimes that had not gone away.

I should say here that it troubles me that I did not know much about Selma Altman before I started this project. She is such an important person in this history. It was one of the biggest revelations for me to discover her story, and with it this whole other dimension that Debby just described—that of people who chose not to engage and instead reminded non-Jewish Germans of their complicity, collaboration, or acquiescence.

DEBORAH POMERANZ: Selma Altman is indeed a very important person in this story, and her testimony of persecution as recorded in her compensation file is such an important source for us. On the other hand, this file is also a record of all the rejections—all the times she was told by the officials, "No, you didn't suffer harm under the Nazis, we reject your compensation claims." And then she would have to go to another doctor and explain again all the worst things that had happened to her, and try and quantify her trauma in a way the German officials would recognize. So this file also raises ethical questions for us because Selma only created these extensive records of her distress in order to have her persecution recognized by the authorities. We have to ask ourselves, how do we deal with sensitive sources like psychiatric reports? Can we really say they represent Selma's perspective? What perspectives on her life are missing? Who is benefiting from this? And in what ways might we be doing the same thing as the officials deciding on victim reparations, that is to say, forcing Selma to disclose a trauma that, if she had had the choice, maybe she would not have spoken about in this way, or at all?

KIM WÜNSCHMANN: As historians we have a responsibility to deal in an ethical way with sources created within the highly problematic processes of restitution and compensation. Our research exposes Selma. We were very hesitant to use this source, the medical report. How much intimate detail should we bring into the narrative? On the other hand, Selma's testimony is vital in reconstructing the history of violence in Oberbrechen. It also remains a mediated third-person account. As Selma is being examined and it is the (male) psychiatrist who recounts her experiences in a professional, clinical voice, there is also a gender aspect to take into account. This source required particularly careful treatment. What remains is a certain sense of unease. Did we treat Selma's story in a respectful way? Did we give her a self-determined voice and secure as well as commemorate her place in history? Or did we perpetuate her victimization?

STEFANIE FISCHER: As Kim said, sources from postwar compensation and restitution files are highly relevant for Holocaust research. Importantly, female voices are included along with those of the male family members, and the perspectives span multiple generations. The files include testimonies by (non-Jewish) neighbors, customers, and employees of Jewish claimants that help to reconstruct daily life before, during, and after the Holocaust. The personal voices documented in these files offer vital insights that underscore the emotional trauma Holocaust survivors dealt with for the rest of their lives. As in the case of Selma Altman, medical and psychiatric documents provide details about a very intimate world of encounters between Jews and non-Jews, and survivors' mental health. The psychiatric report required particularly careful consideration by us as researchers. The question of which (private) details to include in the historical narrative, and which to leave out in order to protect her privacy, had to be discussed over and over again.

KIM WÜNSCHMANN: Selma Altman's case is also a telling example of how historical narrative at the community level can change. It is remarkable that her story was literally on the stage when Brechen celebrated its 1250th anniversary in 2022. A theater performance produced by the Brechen Municipality, with a cast of dozens of amateur actors, dancers, and musicians, included scenes dealing with the persecution of Oberbrechen's Jews. For Cara Basquitt, who directed the play, it was important to represent Jewish voices and Jewish experiences. The project included Selma's story and with it the village's history of violence that we had discovered (see Figure 4).

REFLECTIONS ON METHODOLOGY

JAY H. GELLER: To turn things around: For many historians, the professional is also very personal. You're non-Jewish Germans of a different generation. What did the story mean to you, or how did this journey, which is both professional/scholarly and personal, shape your views?

KIM WÜNSCHMANN: For me, this project has been unlike any other project I'd done before. Researching a history that is, to such a great extent, also family history is challenging in many ways. As historians, we may be aware of why we do what we do, how our biographies and world views shape our profession, and what draws us to work on a certain topic or to apply a particular approach. But projects that involve family history make these questions unavoidable. The confrontation with the personal is of an intensity that we seldom experience in any other work.

Figure 4. Scene from the theater performance *Dorfgeschichte(n)—Fragmente aus 1250 Jahren Niederbrechen und Oberbrechen* (Village History/ies: Fragments from 1250 Years of Niederbrechen and Oberbrechen), directed by Cara Basquitt, showing Selma and Max Altmann with Gertrud Marx (standing), Oberbrechen, July 2022. Credit: Zettner Fotoprojekte.

In academic writing, particularly in the German tradition, the personal dimension is mostly suppressed in the interest of adhering to a scientific ideal of "objectivity."[13] With our study we seek to strengthen one critical claim in particular: the personal in history writing is not a constraint, let alone an epistemological impediment. On the contrary, inserting the personal into history writing means being true to scholarly requirements of source-criticism, transparency, and (self-)reflexivity. Working collaboratively with Stefanie and Debby, the project made me realize how important it is to address the personal with all its intellectual and emotional implications. At the same time, the disclosure of family history and of my own

---

13 Lorraine Daston and Peter Galison, *Objectivity* (New York: Zone, 2010).

biography makes me feel uncomfortable and anxious. Which blind spots did I fail to identify?

For example, a decision that we made—and that we discussed at great length in the context of our own possible biases—was to represent both Jewish and Catholic experiences of Nazism in the narrative. By narrating this simultaneity of living under Nazi rule, we wanted to create a multiperspectivity and analyze how the lives, attitudes, and behaviors of Catholics and Jews intersected in the village microcosm. This helps to counter exonerating narratives constructed in non-Jewish families which postulate that "Grandpa was not a Nazi" or underestimate the degree to which "ordinary Germans," including practicing Christians, were implicated in and supported the regime.[14] In stark contrast to their Jewish neighbors, Catholic Oberbrecheners, whose religious and social life was deeply affected by Nazism, were not driven from their homes, robbed, and threatened with systematic physical annihilation. On the one hand, Nazi oppression of Catholicism did not result in solidarity with those neighbors affected by antisemitic discrimination. On the other, these experiences shaped a postwar narrative of victimhood and resilience among the Catholic Oberbrecheners, including my grandfather.

STEFANIE FISCHER: We discussed the question of the personal in the professional over and over again. The genre of the Graphic History has allowed us to collaboratively reflect both on our authorship and on our biographical background. Kim and I share a similar upbringing. We both grew up in a small-town, Catholic, and West German milieu, although in different regions. Kim comes from Hesse, and I am from Central Franconia, a Protestant region in Bavaria. As Kim said, the German academic setting in which we work does not encourage discussion of the personal motivations behind one's research agenda. Rather, it expects the author to remain invisible to the reader.

Working with Kim on *Oberbrechen* provoked questions about my own family history, in particular about Catholicism during Nazism and my grandparents' agency during Nazism. Even though I have found no

---

14 Harald Welzer, Sabine Moller, and Karoline Tschuggnall, *"Opa war kein Nazi:" Nationalsozialismus und Holocaust im Familiengedächtnis* (Frankfurt am Main: Fischer Taschenbuch, 2002). The 2020 MEMO Study III, conducted at Bielefeld University, found that more than a third of Germans interviewed (35.8 percent) stated that there were victims of National Socialism in their families. And 32.2 percent said that their ancestors had helped Nazi victims. Only 39.7 percent categorized their ancestors as *Mitläufer* ("fellow travelers") of Nazism. Institut für interdisziplinäre Konflikt- und Gewaltforschung, Universität Bielefeld, *MEMO: Multidimensionaler Erinnerungsmotor. Studie III (2020)*, 16, last accessed February 25, 2023, https://www.stiftung-evz.de/assets/4_Service/Infothek/Publikationen/EVZ_Studie_MEMO_2020_dt_Endfassung.pdf

evidence that my grandparents were part of the Nazi Party, questions around their involvement in Nazism have resonated with me for years. Above all, I have wondered whether my grandfather, who was drafted into the *Wehrmacht* (German army), participated in war crimes against Jews, Soviet POWs, or other targeted groups. You did not have to be part of the Nazi Party to harm Jews or others. The questions of guilt, shame, and responsibility for Nazi crimes work on me. One lesson I took away from this project is that, as historians, but also as *Menschen* (humans), we need to understand how the past relates to us and how it continues to shape our lives today—or, in the case of *Oberbrechen*, how our biographical background sometimes shapes the questions we ask about history.

As historians, we are not only asked to document historical events, but also to interpret them. In researching and writing *Oberbrechen* we had to navigate our roles as granddaughters who found themselves critically judging their grandparents' choices and actions. We waded through the sources of *Oberbrechen*, trying to be neither supercritical (which would have meant seeing fierce Nazi perpetrators in our grandparents) nor apologetic (which would have led us to excuse their actions or nonactions during Nazism). At the same time, we were afraid of misinterpreting the Jewish actors in our story whose sources often lacked a critical account on their visits to Oberbrechen. It would, therefore, be preposterous not to raise questions about our biographical biases when writing history.

One of these questions was undoubtedly which role Catholicism played in the formation of the so-called *Volksgemeinschaft* (the "people's community") and the exclusion of Jews from it. In the 1980s, the role of Christian milieus and their participation in Nazism were the subjects of heated debates among West German historians. And then, with the fall of the Iron Curtain, these debates ended almost abruptly in favor of debates about belonging to the so-called *Volksgemeinschaft*. There is no doubt that our grandparents experienced Nazism as a brutal disruption of Catholic religious and social life (witness the ban on Catholic youth groups). At the same time, antisemitism and anti-Judaism are indisputably deeply rooted in Catholicism. The experience of Catholic Oberbrecheners, like Eugen and Josef, challenged us to present this history alongside the experience of Jews during Nazism and to show how these histories sometimes collapse into, and at other times pull apart from, one another.

JAY H. GELLER: Many non-Jewish Germans experienced the prewar years of the "Third Reich" as a rupture of their social networks. Others experienced those years as a time of stability and prosperity after the tumultuous final years of the Weimar Republic. And for many people, it was ultimately both. Maybe your grandparents had such a dual experience. But for the

Jews of Germany, the rupture was more pervasive, and there was no potential place for them in the *Volksgemeinschaft* or in the National Socialist economy. That is what fundamentally differentiates those two persecuted communities.

For historians, it's hard to achieve a critical distance when there is a personal connection to the history under examination. Given that difficulty, maybe we shouldn't insist on utter neutrality. But perhaps thinking about how the past has shaped our own sphere and our own experiences might be a way both to make the past usable and to navigate the challenge of scholarly objectivity.

STEFANIE FISCHER: This brings me to a second point: Working on *Oberbrechen* made me reflect on the question of why Kim and I have devoted our careers to working on Jewish history and the history of the Holocaust. Part of my experience growing up in West Germany was being taught by teachers who were very outspoken about the "failures" of our grandparents' generation, urging us to someday represent a new Germany. Eugen could have been one of them. These teachers would take us on excursions to former concentration camps, like Dachau, and encourage us to commemorate the past (although, of course, there were also teachers who would say, "Why do we need this?").

Another important impact on our upbringing occurred with the creation and expansion of the European Union, which accelerated after the fall of the Iron Curtain in the 1990s. The introduction of the Schengen Agreement made traveling ever easier. Both Kim and I volunteered in a kibbutz in Israel. We both started our undergraduate education in Germany, focusing on Jewish topics as well as on the history of the Holocaust, and we continued moving and studying abroad. Researching the Holocaust and Jewish history and working with colleagues in Israel, the United States, and the United Kingdom introduced me to new perspectives about history. This experience has clearly shown me that the environment we work in and in which we write history shapes our scholarship and that different perspectives and exchange across academic cultures are crucial for writing history.

JAY H. GELLER: Can I ask about the research process? How did you do your research about the Jewish Oberbrecheners, and where are the sources on them located?

KIM WÜNSCHMANN: We started in 2013 with Eugen Caspary's private archive. Eugen was eighty-four when I contacted him, and he supported our project from the start, answered our many questions, and gave us access to his collection of letters, postcards, newspaper clippings, and pictures, as well as to the notes and materials for his research on Oberbrechen's Jewish history. As a historian, he had worked on many areas of local and regional history, but I felt from the start that this subject was special for him. He immediately responded to my first letter, and soon we were corresponding regularly. I also visited him in his home. In his eighties, Eugen still had a sharp memory, and he was the only witness from this generation whom we could still speak with.

We then established contact with the Jewish families from Oberbrechen, who openly shared their private archives and memories. Mostly second-generation, the members of the Stern and Lichtenstein families in Argentina, Israel, and the United States trusted us with this project and its rather unconventional Graphic History approach.

Our project is therefore very much community-based. We were also provided with many additional sources, as well as extensive research assistance, by members of the Brechen history workshop (*Arbeitskreis Historisches Brechen*). They put us in touch with local residents like the family of Gertrud Marx, who hosted Selma Altman when she visited Oberbrechen in the 1960s, or the Höhler family, who live in the house that formerly belonged to the Lichtensteins.

STEFANIE FISCHER: As Kim said, Eugen's letters were the starting point of our project, and by "Eugen's letters" I mean the letters Eugen received from Jewish Oberbrecheners now living abroad. We were impressed by his initiative to research the town's Jewish history in the early 1970s and by the huge number of letters exchanged between him and the Jews from Oberbrechen. We hired a research assistant, Deborah Pomeranz, and Debby supported us in researching primary sources from Jewish families in the United States. Debby—along with Mason Reck—also helped us to unearth Herman Stern's papers at the University of North Dakota. This filled a huge gap: while Eugen's collection included the letters he received from Jewish Oberbrecheners, it often did not include copies of the letters he sent out. In Herman Stern's collection we were able to uncover some of Eugen's letters, and we also found the names of others whom we then contacted.

JAY H. GELLER: Do you think that the letters sent to Eugen were completely forthcoming, perhaps even cathartic, or was there a hidden layer? Did the Jewish Oberbrecheners hold something back in telling their stories to Eugen? You've seen the letters, and they form a starting point for constructing or reconstructing the story of the Jewish Oberbrecheners. But they're telling their story to someone who is not Jewish, who had a different experience of those years in Oberbrechen, and who also did not experience the trauma of displacement in emigration. So, when they tell Eugen their story, I wonder, do they tell the whole story, or do they hold something back, or do they tell the story in a certain way, knowing who their reader is?

STEFANIE FISCHER: Gustave's first response to Eugen was very composed, written in a very formal tone. In one of his early letters, Gustave outspokenly explained that he never wanted to set foot on German soil again, and he held back from telling Eugen about his wartime trauma. Still, Gustave seemed to be impressed by Eugen's openness about Nazi crimes and how he addressed and condemned the Holocaust. After exchanging a handful of letters, Gustave himself suggested visiting Oberbrechen on the occasion of the town's anniversary. Gustave—also in the name of Herman Stern—wanted to acknowledge the town's efforts in commemorating the history of Oberbrechen's Jews in what came to be known among the survivors as "the Orange Book" (that is, the village chronicle, published in 1975). Others, like Max Altman or Kurt Stern, were more reluctant to personally engage with non-Jewish Oberbrecheners and never returned.

As for Kurt Lichtenstein, he didn't write much about the pain and hardships he endured *in Oberbrechen*—although, interestingly, he did speak about this in his interview with the USC Shoah Foundation in 1996. But during his visit to Oberbrechen, he repeatedly spoke about the hardships his family was experiencing *in Argentina*. The Lichtensteins migrated into poverty. In Germany they had belonged to the rural middle class. When Kurt's father, Siegfried Lichtenstein, had to undergo surgery in Buenos Aires, they had difficulty paying for his operation.

DEBORAH POMERANZ: The first letter Eugen sent out to everyone was basically the same. He had his list of questions, what he thought would be helpful or relevant for his chronicle chapter, so: Who was your family? What did your parents do for work? Where did you live? This means that even if the Jewish Oberbrecheners weren't holding anything back per se, we would still end up with sources that were direct responses to the questions Eugen felt were most important, that reflected his priorities. I think that fits in really well with what we were talking about, reflecting on the role of historians: even our sources are constructed through the questions authors choose to ask.

KIM WÜNSCHMANN: I think a breakthrough moment in the relationship to the Christian Oberbrecheners was when the Jewish families received "the Orange Book." We are reminded of the importance of *Yizkor* books for the surviving members of Jewish communities destroyed in the Holocaust. "The Orange Book" served as a genealogical record of their ancestors and an account of Jewish life and persecution in the place they had called home. This enabled commemoration and communication across the generations.

The book could be given to children and grandchildren. We know from Lotte Ullmann's testimony that her mother Jette learned about the fate of her brothers Moses and Julius Stern through Eugen's research. When I visited Yossi Shachar in North Israel, he showed me "the Orange Book," which he had inherited from his father, Walter Stern. The book was and is of value for the families. For us, it embodies the hermeneutic struggle this project has presented us with: valuing genuine attempts at reconnection, but remaining critical about non-Jewish agendas of reconciliation and the desire to "overcome the past."

JAY H. GELLER: I'd like to ask, how have the descendants of the Jewish Oberbrecheners responded to you? By that, I mean how did you make contact with these Jewish families, and how have they reflected on or received your work since then? I'm particularly interested in their emotional and intellectual reception of your work, given that it was done by one outsider and one semi-outsider to their story.

STEFANIE FISCHER: The reception was overwhelmingly positive. We experienced great interest and trust in our work from descendants of the Lichtenstein and Stern families in Argentina, Israel, and the United States. We experienced great curiosity, particularly about the choice to present our research as a Graphic History. I feel it was so easy to connect with the descendants of the Jewish Oberbrecheners because of the experiences they had had with Josef Kramm and Eugen Caspary. We were able to build on their existing relationships. In a metaphorical sense, Kim and I walked over the bridges Eugen and Josef had built in the 1970s. While we were working on this book, a new dialogue started between the third or maybe even the fourth generations of Jews and non-Jews from Oberbrechen.

DEBORAH POMERANZ: Our sources really drove the focus of the project. At first, we had all this exciting archival material from Eugen, and so he became the default main character. But then, once we went looking for other sources compiled by other people and with other emphases, we were able to tell a much fuller story. One of the things I learned from this project, as well as from my current work in provenance research, is that you never know what's out there until you look. And it's often easier than people assume to find sources from different perspectives, from nondominant perspectives.

Part of that is thanks to the amazing digitization work that's happening in a lot of archives and historical institutions. That really helped us, based in Germany, to find sources to work with, find the oral history interview with Kurt Lichtenstein in the Visual History Archives of the USC Shoah Foundation, and find the Herman Stern papers. Then, when we got in contact with the children and grandchildren of the Jewish Oberbrecheners, we were looking mostly for letters from Eugen or for other archival material from that generation. And I don't think we ever found that. But they told us their own stories. That's how we found out, for example, that Herman Stern brought his grandson Rick with him to visit Oberbrechen. And Rick Stern then sent us photos from the trip.

Establishing these relationships was also such an important part of the project for me personally. When we were trying to find the Lichtenstein family in Argentina, I was looking online, trying to figure out who their children were, where they are now, how to get in contact with them. In the process, I figured out that an old family friend of mine from my childhood synagogue, Margot Stern, was their cousin. So she was able to give us the contact information for Kurt's and Irene's children, whose oral history interview adds so much to the book. But more than that, reaching out to her in the context of this project created a new relationship between us and an opportunity for her to talk to me about her experience of fleeing Germany in 1941, as well as about her life in general. So I got to know this person I had known my whole life, and I got to know her in a different way, because I had never spoken to her about her story and her history before. This relationship has been so meaningful for me, and I hope for her as well.

USING THE GRAPHIC HISTORY MEDIUM

JAY H. GELLER: Can you say something about the medium you chose for presenting your research? Why a Graphic History?

STEFANIE FISCHER: I was introduced to the Graphic History genre in 2014, when I was a fellow at the Oxford Centre for Hebrew and Jewish Studies in the United Kingdom. While I was there, two colleagues were working on Graphic Histories. Ronald Schechter had just finished his book *Mendoza the Jew* (OUP, 2014), and Nina Caputo had started working on *Debating the Truth* (OUP, 2016). I was fascinated by the many different modes this genre provides for interpreting primary sources, and how it provokes new methodological questions about historical storytelling. The collaborative nature of art-based research allows historians and artists to unfold complexly woven stories and to rethink the interpretation of sources.

When I told Kim about the genre, she, too, was fascinated, and we quickly decided to present *Oberbrechen* as a Graphic History. After receiving a grant from the German Volkswagen Foundation, we researched the sources, drafted the script, and then pitched it to Charles Cavaliere at Oxford University Press. We were convinced that OUP's Graphic History

Series would be a perfect fit for our project because it combines graphics with material on the historical context as well as a selection of primary sources. Discussions with Charles encouraged us to shift our focus from Eugen to the village of Oberbrechen. Charles took on the project, and we quickly decided to work with illustrator Liz Clarke. We were impressed by her artwork. As novel as her style might be for graphics about the Holocaust, we felt that it would allow us to unveil the different layers of our story for a younger audience perfectly. Liz then visually presented our research. We provided as many historical images as possible that Liz could work with. We had to make sure that the graphics would authentically reflect the landscapes, architecture, and fashion of the time, as well as the historical actors (see Figures 5 and 6). Unlike writing a historical

Figure 5. An early draft shows Father Alois Kunz wearing a chasuble while collecting money for a new church building, Oberbrechen, 1933. Credit: Liz Clarke.

Figure 6. After Professor Matthias Theodor Kloft from the museum of the Limburg diocese explained that priests do not wear a chasuble when collecting money, we asked Liz Clarke to remove it from the picture. In the revised version, the priest only wears the alb, a white garment girdled with a cincture. Credit: Liz Clarke.

text, composing a script for a Graphic History requires making decisions about body language, interactions between actors, gender roles, and—of course—the use of Nazi symbols, and much more. All of this provokes reactions and engages the reader so that they can interpret the story. There was no shortage of images of historical actors and events. In particular, we had the collection of about 1,500 photographs that Chaplain Franz Pabst took between 1936 and 1939, which provided captivating insights into everyday life in a Catholic village—a remarkable example of vernacular photography.

Liz used these documents as templates, creating new images which—of course—use some artistic freedom. The process of artistic presentation and interpretation was new and unfamiliar to us as historians. At first, it seemed unscholarly to us. This concern led us to engage in serious reflections between the two of us and in intellectual debates with colleagues and friends. In its final form, our Graphic History includes scripted scenes and dialogues based on our research. In the beginning, we used strictly verbatim quotes from primary sources which we would then translate into English. However, this resulted in clumsy and hard-to-read dialogues. As historians, we were reluctant to create dialogues, but we soon realized that moving away from direct quotes from German sources toward realistic dialogues made the narrative of our book much stronger. This allowed us to add another level of analytical reflection.

KIM WÜNSCHMANN: Comics is a unique medium for constructing history, but it also shares a basic commonality with other forms of mediation: the past is gone and we can only approach it, study it, imagine it from the vantage point of the present and with our hindsight knowledge. With its specific structure of frames and gutters, comics constantly shuttles between presence and absence. The gutter—that is, the space between the panels—hints at the voids and ruptures that are so characteristic of modern German-Jewish history and the history of the Holocaust.

We chose the comics medium precisely because of its potential to express traumatic histories. In comics, past, present, and future are conflated as readers see whole pages at once and can choose where to turn their attention first. The medium thus challenges, as Hillary Chute stresses, conventional historiography and "place[s] pressure on traditional notions of chronology, linearity, and causality—as well as the idea that 'history' can ever be a closed discourse, or simply a progressive one."[15] Our Graphic History utilizes a number of visual techniques to analyze the difficulty, if not impossibility, of "coming to terms" with the Nazi past. We chose four different time periods for our narrative, all of which have distinct graphic schemes developed by Liz. Perhaps most striking is the black-and-white representation of Nazism and the Holocaust. This might appear somewhat distancing, but visual breakthroughs in the form of flashbacks defy all attempts to keep the Nazi era at a distance. The Graphic History helps us to show how experiences of what had happened then affected lives and events at later times. In visualizing their disruptive power, we negate any form of closure and underline the long-term impact of this history of violence.

---

15 Hillary L. Chute, *Disaster Drawn: Visual Witness, Comics, and Documentary Form* (Cambridge, MA: The Belknap Press of Harvard University Press, 2016).

Persecution and murder become transgenerational trauma in the case of many survivor families, including those from Oberbrechen.

The comics genre also allows us to address conspicuous gaps in the sources. Remarkably, not one photograph among the hundreds taken by Chaplain Franz Pabst shows the exclusion of Oberbrechen's Jews during these violent years between 1936 and 1939. A history that would rely solely on these visual sources would thus miss the most decisive events. By overwriting Pabst's photographs with depictions of anti-Jewish persecution, we create images that do show this violent history (see Figures 7 and 8). The panel at the end of Chapter 1, for example, depicts an adult Kurt Lichtenstein sitting at the desk of the village school pictured by Pabst in the 1930s. The figure of Kurt, drawn in color, is superimposed on the otherwise black-and-white image of the classroom with the large swastika flag on the wall. According to non-Jewish sources, Kurt did not discuss the harassment he and his sister suffered at school during his visits to the village. His memory of this traumatic experience, however, was strong, and he testified to it in other contexts.

Figure 7. Students attending the *Volkschule* Oberbrechen, the village's local school, shown in a photograph taken by Chaplain Franz Pabst between 1936 and 1939. Credit: Hessisches Hauptstaatsarchiv Wiesbaden.

Figure 8. Drawing by Liz Clarke showing Kurt Lichtenstein as an adult at *Volksschule* Oberbrechen, 1930s: Credit: Liz Clarke/Hessisches Hauptstaatsarchiv Wiesbaden.

DEBORAH POMERANZ: Even so, a lot of the dialogue in the book is translated from the letters. So, in some way, it's people's own words, but in other ways, those words are very much mediated. In particular, they are mediated by me as the translator. I remember working on the translations at the time, and I was like, "Oh, gosh, how did people talk in the 1970s?" And I just kind of wrote them the way my grandparents write letters, which is probably not the way they would have spoken. I think the images raise a similar contradiction. A drawing of a photo, or a drawing based on a photo—what is that? Is it "fiction" or "history"? I think one of the things that makes the graphic form so powerful is that it highlights this contradiction, this appearance of an "authentic" or unmediated access to the past that, in reality, is anything but.

KIM WÜNSCHMANN: Drawing history does indeed raise fundamental questions of representation, particularly when it comes to aesthetic and visual representations of the Holocaust. How do we deal with artistic expressions of painful histories? What is an adequate and dignified form for speaking about violent events and the ongoing trauma that outlives them? Take the debates about filmic representations of Holocaust history shuttling perhaps most vividly between the polar opposites of Steven Spielberg's *Schindler's List*, which stages so much violent history, and Claude Lanzmann's *Shoah*, which strictly abstains from reproducing historic images and remains in the present and in the abstract. Decades earlier, Alain Resnais's *Night and Fog* took another approach and combined historic black-and-white images of concentration camps produced by the Nazis or the Allies with colored shots of the same places after liberation. These different forms of visual and artistic representation of Holocaust history guided our work and provoked constant methodological reflection.

Scholarly representations of the Holocaust can face a moral dilemma when, as Saul Friedländer feared, "postmodern thought's rejection of the possibility of identifying some stable reality or truth beyond the constant polysemy and self-referentiality of linguistic constructs challenges the need to establish the realities and the truths of the Holocaust."[16] The constructed nature of history is very obvious in comics, and you can't escape these questions of representation. Chute says that comics works "risk representation." Precisely because it is "a form that is constantly aware of its own mediation," comics enables multiperspectivity and the expression of ambivalences and ambiguities.[17] Graphic History combines scholarly and artistic methods to visualize events and processes that have previously been dealt with in the more abstract written or oral forms. This is why comics is such a suitable medium to research and represent the history of Oberbrechen.

STEFANIE FISCHER: The collaborative nature of our project brought together a diverse group of people, from survivors to artists, archivists, and local historians, as well as ourselves and our families. It has been a rewarding experience to see how this project started a new dialogue around the history of Oberbrechen, but also about microhistory and the writing of history.

JAY H. GELLER: When I think about the Graphic History aspect of this project, in some ways I think about it as operating on two planes. The first facilitates the storytelling and the transmission of the story in a way that a text-only book could not. And this is exactly what Kim's just been talking about. But there's also something challenging about it in that you wrote the text, and the artist had to bring it to life visually. So, how did you collaborate

---

16 Saul Friedlander, "Introduction," in *Probing the Limits of Representation: Nazism and the "Final Solution"* (Cambridge, MA: Harvard University Press, 1992), 1–21, here 4–5.
17 Chute, *Disaster Drawn*, 17–18.

so that Liz could give representation to your narrative in the way that you envisioned it? You have the skill set of the words, but she has the skill set of the pictures, and she's bringing your book, your story, your narrative to life. So these are the two challenges, the two tracks that I've been thinking about when reflecting on doing a Graphic History.

KIM WÜNSCHMANN: I've always described it as a magic moment: we sent Liz a written text trying to describe what a scene should look like, and what came back were images that were so astonishingly close to what we imagined—a breathtaking transformation from written to visual history. The impact that a Graphic History has on the reader is different from that of a regular, written history book. The images have a powerful effect. They invite you to really *look* at this history and bear the sight. You might not have words but understand emotionally, feeling empathy or anger.

STEFANIE FISCHER: Working on a Graphic History also requires reflections about the use of images that may trigger national, religious, or gender stereotypes. We carefully looked at the illustrations, and we wondered if any of our historical actors, either Jewish or non-Jewish, men or women, were portrayed in a biased, cliché-like style. One of the scenes we discussed at length was the panel that shows children openly mocking the elderly Moses Stern in the village (Part I, Chapter 2). A reader raised concerns about this scene. He said that the children in these pictures are presented as stereotypical "evil-looking Germans," like those often portrayed in Blockbuster movies.

KIM WÜNSCHMANN: I would like to add that, given our attention to the representation of female experiences in history, we also discussed how women should be depicted in a graphic narrative. Selma Altman's graphic alter ego is a case in point. We know from the sources that Nazi persecution negatively impacted her physical and mental health. But should she be portrayed as a frail, vulnerable woman in need of support from her husband? Visual storytelling can easily reproduce the gendered stereotypes we carefully strive to avoid when writing history. Working on a Graphic History demands constant close reading and rereading of imagery because as a text, it transports so many messages beyond the lettered lines.

JAY H. GELLER: I think the visual aspect heightens the emotional experience for the reader. Of course, to some degree, it takes something away in that it fills in the blanks and gives visual representation where, before, a reader might only have been able to imagine—although I think that's more of an issue in fiction than in nonfiction. For me, for example, to see the Jewish former Oberbrecheners at the cemetery and to have the very mediated experience of entering that space and what for them is a very, very personal moment was very touching.

DEBORAH POMERANZ: I knew the story well and had worked on the material quite intensely. I'd read most of the sources and a lot of the drafts of the manuscript, but I hadn't seen it illustrated. And then reading the illustrated manuscript for the first time. . . . It was very moving! It brought a new level of emotion to the story that I hadn't expected, given how well I knew its text-based aspects.

JAY H. GELLER: And there are also comical moments in the story that come out too, and I think that if this were purely a text, that aspect wouldn't be present. Something that was extremely interesting for me, and important for this project, is the presence of both of you in the book, and I'd like to know more about the genesis of that. You are in the book. You, as historians, are present, reflecting on the story at the beginning, as you drive across the desert in America in your rental car, and at the end, as you walk through Berlin, talking about what you have accomplished and where it might go next. And of course, Kim is also present in the story as a character as well.

KIM WÜNSCHMANN: Coming back to what we discussed before about the complexities of the personal and the professional, the scholarly and the emotional, I think the graphic genre helps me to address these issues. Experimenting with researching family history as contemporary history and becoming very personal in my scholarly work were possible because we chose the method of visual storytelling. In an illustrated history you need clearly identifiable places and people. This allows you to draw yourself into the narrative, to literally be present in this history and to be vulnerable. We talked a lot about our personae in the comic and how we have become literary figures. To me, it was liberating to realize that I am a character in a narrative, but the character is not necessarily the co-author of this book, which is, of course, a cultural product composed in a particular historical time and place. We needed this distance between "real" Stefanie and Kim and our comic alter egos. And, of course, Debby is in the comic, too. The comics medium allows us to creatively bring the reflexive practice into history writing and to find new ways to discuss scholarly objectivity, as we said before.

STEFANIE FISCHER: It was an enlightening moment when we realized that we had become characters in the book who differ from us as real people. This only developed over time. We first drafted the scene where we were driving through the desert in the rental car in 2019, although this scene actually took place in 2013. And as the attentive reader of this book will realize when reading Eugen's first letter to Kim in the source section, we had already spoken about the topic before we even embarked on the road trip, although we then had the chance to delve into the complexities of it during the long conversations we had on our journey. We close the book with us walking along the river Spree in Berlin reflecting on our collaboration in 2021. This scene is invented. That walk never took place (though maybe it will one day in the future), but the dialogue is real and mirrors our discussions as researchers.

JAY H. GELLER: There's something comical about two German historians driving across the American desert, discussing *Vergangenheitsbewältigung.*

STEFANIE FISCHER: It is comical in a way, but it also stands for our generation, who travel so much. Today, access to global travel is no longer limited to an educated or economic elite. It simply would not have occurred to the Eugens and Josefs of this world to take such a trip. In a metaphorical sense, they met the world in their village, but they would not engage with "the world" outside their village. This more limited mobility is also reflected in the use of language. Kurt, Gustave, Josef, and Eugen communicated in their mother tongue, German. All their encounters took place in Oberbrechen and the surrounding villages. As a result of Nazi persecution, the history of Jews from Oberbrechen, however, continued outside Germany, in Buenos Aires, Valley City, Seattle, New York, and in Nahariya or Haifa, Israel. Through our project, we approached the village's history beyond Oberbrechen. Our study presents the global dimension of Oberbrechen's history, but also more generally the global dimension of local history, as well as the history of the Holocaust. By publishing in English, we present the history of Oberbrechen to a global readership and invite them to engage with it. Our decision to use English as the primary language of our study gives the second and third generations of survivors access to our research. This is particularly important because the history of their parents is part of their own lives, yet they often do not speak German anymore. But we can say, not only in Oberbrechen, but also more widely, that the history of the Holocaust is not yet over. It is still part of our lives, and it will be so for the rest of our lives.

DEBORAH POMERANZ: Yes, especially since, as we said earlier, language is such an important space in the story. Gustave shows his belonging by using the Oberbrechen dialect. And then, a couple of months into his correspondence with Eugen, he suggests that they say *du*, the familiar "you," to one another, rather than *Sie*, the formal "you," as a sign of their friendship.

On the one hand, this represents the recognition and formalization of an intimate relationship as peers, rather than as researcher and subject, or as older and younger man. On the other hand, it shows Gustave's adoption of American mores, as it was uncommon for adults to use *du* with one another in Germany, and in particular in the West German Federal Republic at the time, even if they knew each other well.

Gustave is aware that after more than thirty years in the United States, he no longer speaks German quite like a native speaker, and he is self-conscious about errors in his letters. Kurt Stern, on the other hand, had no interest in writing grammatically correct German. He didn't use any punctuation. He didn't use any capitalization. He wrote a very American-English inflected German, which showed, I guess, a kind of assimilation or chosen assimilation—certainly a rejection of Germanness. Still, he had to use German in order to communicate, and this is another aspect of the power dynamics of these relationships: the meetings were not only in Germany, but also only in German.

Gustave and Kurt's German expresses so much, but it posed a challenge for me as a translator. How do I show the ways their German was inflected by English, both intentionally and unintentionally, when writing in English? I really struggled with those translations. But through them, we can move the story out of a space where you can only access it via German.

KIM WÜNSCHMANN: With time, "the Orange Book" has aged, too. Now, fifty years later, the third and fourth generations of the families probably won't be able to read it without translation. Our project enables a new engagement with this history.

STEFANIE FISCHER: Yes. We need to leave our cultural comfort zone in order to engage with the outside world.

JAY H. GELLER: This book is the story of Oberbrechen and Oberbrecheners, but it's the story of telling the story of Oberbrechen and the Oberbrecheners as well. There's a meta level at work here: layers of the onion that are peeled away, and they're all fascinating in their own right.

DEBORAH POMERANZ: That's one of the things that I really love and find fascinating about this project—that it's the story of telling the story of telling the story. Seeing intergenerational attempts at telling and retelling the story, and the relationships that build across time and place as a result, has really impacted how I understand what history is, its importance, and how we can approach it, especially in the context of the Holocaust.

KIM WÜNSCHMANN: Every generation poses new questions to history and, in particular, to the history of the Holocaust. And that's why it is so meaningful for Stefanie and me to work with Debby, who is of a younger generation and comes from a different background. Debby brought new perspectives to the project, and she questioned our approach.

DEBORAH POMERANZ: I started working on this project soon after I graduated college, and I learned so much about historical research, what it takes to go from an idea to a book, or to an article or something else. I think the reader can have a similar experience, because we see the research process in the book, the steps the project went through from start to finish. So, the message to the reader is that you can do this too.

CONTRIBUTORS

Jay Howard Geller is the Samuel Rosenthal Professor of Judaic Studies at Case Western Reserve University in Cleveland, Ohio. His research focuses on the history of the Jews in modern Germany. He is the author of *Jews in Post-Holocaust Germany* and *The Scholems: A Story of the German Jewish Bourgeoisie from Emancipation to Destruction* and co-editor of *Rebuilding Jewish Life in Germany* and *Three-Way Street: Jews, Germans, and the Transnational*.

Deborah Pomeranz holds an MA in American Studies from Humboldt University of Berlin and a BA in Ethnic Studies from Brown University. She contributed to the graphic history *Oberbrechen: A German Village Confronts Its Nazi Past* as a student assistant at the Center for Antisemitism Research, Technical University Berlin. She is interested in questions of interdisciplinarity, the ethics of history, and collective memory, with a focus on twentieth-century Germany and the United States. She is currently a History PhD student at the University of Michigan.

ESSAY QUESTIONS

1. The village of Oberbrechen is located in a rural region of Germany where Jewish life and culture flourished for centuries. Choose a scene in the Graphic History narrative that captures some of the most important characteristics of Jewish life in rural areas and discuss how the scene engages with them. In addition, discuss how some of these characteristics shape Jewish–non-Jewish encounters throughout the book. Focus in particular on how the characteristics of rural life shaped interactions between Jews and non-Jews in the postwar years.

2. Nazism opposed Catholicism and oppressed the influence of the church as well as the practice of religious life. At the same time, research has found that many Catholics supported Nazi rule and reconciled their faith with belief in what the Nazis called the Third Reich. Find at least two examples from the Graphic History that show varying forms of behavior in relation to the clash of Catholicism and Nazism in the village. Discuss how Catholics from Oberbrechen acted in the face of the persecution of their Jewish neighbors. Explain why you chose these examples.

3. Gender plays a crucial role in encounters between Jews and non-Jews throughout the Graphic History. Read the medical report on Selma Altman's health, the letter from the Compensation Office in Wiesbaden, and the statement of Gertrud Marx, Selma's former maid (Part II, Documents 16, 17, and 19), and discuss the role of gender in these documents. What do you think the medical report tells us about how perceptions of gender might have shaped decisions about financial compensation in the postwar years?

4. Family ties to German Jews living abroad were crucial for escaping Nazism in the 1930s and early 1940s. Examine the letter from "The Chammer" sent to Herman Stern in 1933 from Venlo, the Netherlands

(Part I, Chapter 2, and Part II, Document 1). How does the unidentified author describe the situation of Jews in Germany in that year? Examine how Herman Stern started rescuing family members in need after receiving this letter. What do the documents presented in Part II tell us about the "wall of bureaucracy" created by the U.S. administration and Herman's strategies for rescuing Jews from Nazi Germany?

5. How can the microhistorical approach of Oberbrechen help us rethink the categories of perpetrator, victim, and bystander? Define the behavior associated with each role and discuss how useful these categories are when researching how Nazism has affected social bonds in the village. Do these categories fit the behavior of the various historical actors in Oberbrechen? Provide reasons to support your view.

6. Research the meaning of the term *transitional justice* and list its objectives. Can the term be applied to processes of denazification as well as Holocaust restitution and compensation instituted in postwar Germany? What did these processes mean for the individuals involved as well as for the official state level? Can past injustices inflicted by Nazi persecution be repaired?

7. Select a scene from the Graphic History that depicts reconnections between Jews and non-Jews after the Holocaust. Describe the encounter from different perspectives: Jewish/non-Jewish; first/second/third generation; and male/female. Can we speak of "friendship" when analyzing these relations?

8. Closely examine Eugen's Diary entry from the year 1944 (Part I, Chapter 3 and Part II, Document 7) and Eugen's analysis of the Nazi dictatorship published in the "Orange Book" in 1975 (Part II, Document 25). Briefly describe the words Eugen uses to testify to the horrific events of the Second World War in both documents. Next, discuss the claims he makes about the agency of individuals during the Nazi years. Show how Eugen saw the choices individuals had and the decisions they made during the Nazi dictatorship. In other words, discuss if and how Eugen's perception of the Nazi dictatorship had changed over the years.

9. Analyze the correspondence between Eugen Caspary and Gustave Stern (Part I, Chapter 5). Based on their letters, why do you think they engaged in a correspondence that developed into in-person visits? What do you think the correspondence suggests about relations

between Jewish and non-Jewish Germans after the Holocaust? What did you learn about these encounters from the primary sources or Part IV: The Making of *Oberbrechen* that the Graphic History did not mention?

10. To write history, we need to assemble the widest possible array of sources and then make sense of their diverse perspectives. Choose different sources that serve as evidence of Oberbrechen's Nazi past, summarize what they say, and reflect on the historian's task to relate them to one another. How do different actors shape different narratives about the past, and how do these narratives diverge from one another? Are there outright contradictions? How can we arrive at a balanced historical account?

11. What role does the personal dimension play in history writing, and should historians openly reflect on their own position, background, and possible biases? Read what the authors have to say in Part IV and reflect on your own motivation to study history. What interests you most in studying the past?

TIMELINE

500

772 — First documentation of Oberbrechen in the historical record.

1000

1148 — Earliest known written source referring to a church building in Oberbrechen.

1700

1711 — First documented mention of Jewish life in Oberbrechen.

1800

1803 — Eight Jews are recorded living in Oberbrechen, among them the couple Samuel and Jettchen Jessel, the grandparents of Samuel Löb Stern and great-grandparents of Isaac Stern.

1850

1866 — Oberbrechen, previously a part of the Duchy of Nassau, comes under Prussian rule and forms part of the Prussian province of Hesse-Nassau.

1869 — The Jews of Oberbrechen and the region receive full civic rights.

1875

1871 — Samuel Löb Stern marries Mina Strauß from Heringen. The couple have eight children: Moses, Adolf, Salli, Julius, Gustav, Dora, Jettchen, and Hermann.

1900

1900 — Rosa Stern, wife of Isaac Stern, gives birth to the twins Max and Selma Stern, whose older siblings are Adolph and Hedwig.

1901 — Gustave Stern is born in Duisburg.

1903 — Hermann Stern emigrates to the United States and settles in Valley City, North Dakota. In 1912, he marries Adeline Roth.

1915 — In the First World War, Adolph Stern, Selma's older brother, is killed in action on the Eastern Front.

263

TIMELINE

1925

1921 — Siegfried Lichtenstein marries Flora Hess. In 1927 they move from Münster to Oberbrechen with their two children Irene and Kurt. The family is joined by Flora's parents Moritz and Lina Hess.

1925 — Josef Kramm and Kurt Lichtenstein are born only eight days apart.

1928 — The first two men from Oberbrechen join the Nazi Party. By January 1933 the Party has seventeen members from both Oberbrechen and Niederbrechen.

1929 — Eugen Caspary is born in Oberbrechen.

1931 — Selma Stern marries Max Altmann. They run an upholstery business. Selma also works as a seamstress and Max trades with textiles. Selma's twin brother manages external trade.

1932 — Alois Kunz is appointed parish priest in Oberbrechen. He will serve in this position until 1961.

1933 — Hugo Trost, a member of the Nazi Party, becomes mayor of Oberbrechen.

Paul, Max and Moritz Stern are ousted from the local sports club.

Max Stern and Moritz Stern flee Nazi persecution to the Netherlands and France, respectively. Gustave Stern and his family escape to Paris.

Oberbrechen's church building, originally from 1737, is consecrated again after renovations.

1935 — Teacher Bruno Semrau is transferred from Berlin to Oberbrechen, where he will stay until 1938.

Kurt Lichtenstein is taken out of the Oberbrechen school and sent to a Jewish school in Frankfurt am Main. His father Siegfried Lichtenstein has to give up his business as a consequence of antisemitic persecution.

1936 — Irene Lichtenstein leaves the Oberbrechen school due to ongoing discrimination.

Kurt Stern escapes Nazi persecution to the United States.

Ida Stern escapes to the United States with her children Cäcilie "Cilly" and Paul Stern to avoid Nazi persecution.

Moses Stern sells the family house in Lange Straße 14 to Albert and Maria Schmidt.

Chaplain Franz Pabst takes up his first position in Oberbrechen and stays there until 1939.

1937 — The Lichtenstein family flees to the Avigdor Colony in Argentina to avoid Nazi persecution.

Father Kunz leads a pilgrimage of some forty young Catholics to Altötting.

1938	Following the November pogrom, Max Altmann and Siegfried Stern are deported to the SS concentration camp of Buchenwald. Selma Altmann, her sister Hedwig, and their cousin are arrested in Limburg.
	Maria and Josef Deisel buy the Lichtenstein family house on Frankfurter Straße 17.
1939	Selma and Max Altmann escape Nazi Germany. They reach the United States and eventually settle in Los Angeles.
1940	Moses Stern is forced to leave Oberbrechen for Frankfurt am Main.
1941	Siegfried and Sophie Stern, together with Siegfried's sister Jette, are forced to leave Oberbrechen for Frankfurt am Main.
	The Oberbrechen Municipality buys the house of Siegfried, Sophie, and Jette Stern in Lange Straße 2.
1942	Gustave Stern and his family immigrate to the United States.
	Siegfried and Sophie Stern are deported from Frankfurt and murdered. Jette Stern is deported and murdered in Maly Trostinec. Moses Stern is deported to the Theresienstadt ghetto, where he dies.
1944	Max Stern, Selma's twin brother, is deported from the Netherlands via the Westerbork transit camp. He is registered in the Auschwitz and Buchenwald concentration camps and is declared dead on May 8, 1945.
	An Allied air raid causes damage to buildings in Oberbrechen. Additional assaults by low-flying aircraft follow.
1945	US Army troops liberate Oberbrechen at the end of March.
	Denazification, restitution, and compensation begins in Oberbrechen, as elsewhere in the American sector of occupied postwar Germany.
1948	Herman Stern strikes a deal with the Schmidt family in the restitution case of the Stern family house in Oberbrechen.
1952	Maurice (formerly Moritz) Stern visits Oberbrechen.
1954	Father Kunz becomes an honorary citizen of Oberbrechen.
1955	A large cross to commemorate the war dead is erected on the Werschauer Höhe overlooking Oberbrechen.
1957	Kurt Lichtenstein and his family leave the Avigdor Colony and settle in Buenos Aires. Siegfried and Flora Lichtenstein will leave in 1958. Their daughter Irene, Kurt's sister, lives in Córdoba.
1965	Selma Altman visits Oberbrechen and stays with Gertrud Marx.
1972	Herman Stern visits Oberbrechen together with his wife Adeline and their grandson Richard "Rick" Stern.
	Josef Kramm is elected mayor of Oberbrechen and remains in office until 1980.

	1973	The Oberbrechen Municipality decides to issue a chronicle to commemorate the 1,200th anniversary of the village and commissions Eugen Caspary to write an article on the Jews of Oberbrechen. Eugen and Josef Kramm reach out to the Jews who had been driven from the village. The anniversary, although taking place in 1972, is celebrated in 1974. The chronicle is published in 1975.
1975	1974	With the administrative-territorial reform, Oberbrechen now forms part of the Municipality of Brechen together with Niederbrechen and Werschau.
	1976	Gustave Stern visits Oberbrechen for the first time after the Holocaust. He is accompanied by his wife Gertrude and gives a public concert, conducting the orchestra of the Oberbrechen musical society.
		Siegfried Lichtenstein dies in Buenos Aires.
	1977	Hugo Trost dies in Brechen.
	1978	Kurt Lichtenstein visits Oberbrechen for the first time after the Holocaust. He is accompanied by his wife Susi, and their friends Anita and Paolo Landau.
	1980	Irene Lenkiewicz, née Lichtenstein, visits Oberbrechen for the first time after the Holocaust. She is accompanied by her husband Arno.
		Herman Stern dies in Valley City.
	1985	Kurt Lichtenstein visits Oberbrechen with his wife, daughter, and son-in-law.
	1986	Kurt Lichtenstein visits Oberbrechen and meets villagers of his age cohort at Josef Kramm's house.
	1989	Gustave Stern visits Oberbrechen with his partner Marcia Smith. He performs in Niederselters and in Niederbrechen.
	1990	Gustave Stern dies in Seattle.
		Franz Pabst dies in Fischbach/Taunus.
		Kurt Lichtenstein visits Oberbrechen with his wife, and Pablo and Anita Landau.
	1994	Selma Altman dies in Los Angeles.
2000	2002	Kurt Lichtenstein dies in Buenos Aires.
	2004	Josef Kramm dies in Limburg an der Lahn.
	2013	Stefanie Fischer and Kim Wünschmann start discussing visits of Holocaust survivors to their former hometowns and reach out to Jewish and non-Jewish families involved.

2015	*Stolperstein* memorials commemorating Siegfried and Sophie Stern, Kurt and Ilse Stern, Jette Stern, as well as Dora and Moses Stern are laid in Oberbrechen.
2019	Eugen Caspary dies.
2022	The fate of Jewish Oberbrecheners is featured in a play staged on the occasion of Brechen's 1,250th anniversary.
2023	A memorial plaque dedicated to the 22 Jews who lived in Oberbrechen in 1933 and were either displaced or murdered is unveiled.
2024	*Oberbrechen: A German Village Confronts its Nazi Past* is published. Exchange and visits continue.

FURTHER READING

Arendt, Hannah. "The Aftermath of Nazi Rule: Report from Germany." *Commentary* (October 1950): 342–353.

Arnsberg, Paul. *Die Jüdischen Gemeinden in Hessen: Anfang, Untergang, Neubeginn*. Frankfurt: Societäts-Verlag, 1971.

Aschheim, Steven E. *Beyond the Border: The German-Jewish Legacy Abroad*. Princeton, NJ: Princeton University Press, 2007.

Aschheim, Steven E., and Vivian Liska (eds.). *The German-Jewish Experience Revisited*. Berlin: De Gruyter, 2015.

Barkai, Avraham. *Branching Out: German-Jewish Immigration to the United States, 1820–1914*. New York: Holmes & Meier, 1994.

Baumann, Ulrich. "The Object's Memory: Remembering Rural Jews in Southern Germany." In *Restitution and Memory: Material Restoration in Europe*, ed. Dan Diner and Gotthard Wunberg. New York: Berghahn Books, 2007, 117–140.

Biess, Frank, Mark Roseman, and Hanna Schissler (eds.). *Conflict, Catastrophe and Continuity: Essays on Modern German History*. New York: Berghahn Books, 2007.

Brenner, Michael (ed.). *A History of Jews in Germany since 1945: Politics, Culture, and Society*. Transl. Kenneth Kronenberg. Bloomington: Indiana University Press, 2018.

Caspary, Eugen. *Jewish Citizens in Oberbrechen 1711–1941*. Transl. Justin J. Mueller. Manchester, VT: no publisher, 1999.

Caspary, Eugen. "Jüdische Mitbürger in Oberbrechen 1711–1941: Eine Bestandsaufnahme." In *Geschichte von Oberbrechen*, ed. on behalf of Brechen Municipality by Hellmuth Gensicke and Egon Eichhorn. Brechen-Oberbrechen: Gemeinde Brechen, 1975, 157–231.

Chute, Hillary L. *Disaster Drawn: Visual Witness, Comics, and Documentary Form*. Cambridge, MA: Belknap Press of Harvard University Press, 2016.

Connor, Ian. *Refugees and Expellees in Post-war Germany*. Manchester, VT: Manchester University Press, 2007.

Dack, Mikkel. *Everyday Denazification in Postwar Germany: The Fragebogen and Political Screening during the Allied Occupation*. Cambridge: Cambridge University Press, 2023.

Dean, Martin, Constantin Goschler, and Philipp Ther (eds.). *Robbery and Restitution: The Conflict over Jewish Property in Europe*. New York: Berghahn Books, 2007.

Fischer, Stefanie. *Jewish Cattle Traders in the German Countryside, 1919–1939: Economic Trust and Antisemitic Violence*. Transl. Jeremiah Riemer. Bloomington: Indiana University Press, 2024.

Fischer, Stefanie. "Jewish Mourning in the Aftermath of the Holocaust: Tending Individual Graves in Occupied Germany, 1945–1949." In *German Jewish Studies: Next Generations*, ed. by Kerry Wallach and Aya Elyada. New York: Berghahn Books, 2023, 213–230.

Fischer, Stefanie, Nathanael Riemer, and Stefanie Schüler-Springorum (eds.). *Juden und Nicht-Juden nach der Shoah: Begegnungen in Deutschland*. Berlin, Boston: De Gruyter, 2019.

Friedländer, Saul. *Nazi Germany and the Jews. Vol. 1: The Years of Persecution, 1933–1939*. London: Weidenfeld & Nicolson, 1997 and *Vol. 2: The Years of Extermination, 1939–1945*. London: Weidenfeld & Nicolson, 2007.

Friedlander, Saul (ed.). *Probing the Limits of Representation: Nazism and the "Final Solution."* Cambridge, MA: Harvard University Press, 1992.

Gassert, Philipp, and Alan E. Steinweis (eds.). *Coping with the Nazi Past: West German Debates on Nazism and Generational Conflict, 1955–1975*. New York: Berghahn Books, 2006.

Geller, Jay Howard. *Jews in Post-Holocaust Germany, 1945–1953*. Cambridge: Cambridge University Press, 2005.

Geller, Jay Howard. *The Scholems: A Story of the German-Jewish Bourgeoisie from Emancipation to Destruction*. Ithaca, NY: Cornell University Press, 2019.

Geller, Jay Howard, and Michael Meng (eds.). *Rebuilding Jewish Life in Germany*. Newark, NJ: Rutgers University Press, 2020.

Grossmann, Atina. *Jews, Germans, and Allies: Close Encounters in Occupied Germany*. Princeton, NJ: Princeton University Press, 2007.

Grossmann, Atina. "Transnational Jewish Refugee Stories: Displacement, Loss, and (Non)Restitution." In *Three-Way Street: Jews, Germans, and the Transnational*, ed. by Jay Howard Geller and Leslie Morris. Ann Arbor: University of Michigan Press, 2016, 239–258.

Henry, Frances. *Victims and Neighbors: A Small Town in Nazi Germany remembered*. South Hadley, MA: Bergin & Garvey, 1984.

Kaplan, Marion A. *The Making of the Jewish Middle Class: Women, Family, and Identity in Imperial Germany*. New York: Oxford University Press, 1991.

Kaplan, Marion A. *Between Dignity and Despair: Jewish Life in Nazi Germany*. Oxford: Oxford University Press, 1998.

Kaplan, Marion A. (ed.). *Jewish Daily Life in Germany, 1618–1945*. Oxford: Oxford University Press, 2005.

Kauders, Anthony D. *Unmögliche Heimat: Eine deutsch-jüdische Geschichte der Bundesrepublik*. München: Deutsche Verlags-Anstalt, 2007.

Kauders, Anthony D. "Weimar Jewry." In *Weimar Germany*, ed. Anthony McElligott. Oxford: Oxford University Press, 2009, 234–259.

Kaufman, Menahem. "The Daily Life of the Village and Country Jews in Hessen from Hitler's Ascent to Power to November 1938." *Yad Vashem Studies* 22 (1992): 147–198.

Kingreen, Monika. *Nach der "Kristallnacht": Jüdisches Leben und antijüdische Politik in Frankfurt am Main 1938–1945*. Frankfurt am Main: Campus, 1999.

Kropat, Wolf-Arno. "Die Emanzipation der Juden in Kurhessen und in Nassau im 19. Jahrhundert." In *Neunhundert Jahre Geschichte der Juden in Hessen: Beiträge zum politischen, wirtschaftlichen und kulturellen Leben*. Wiesbaden: Kommission für die Geschichte der Juden in Hessen, 1983, 325–350.

Leder, Bettina, Christoph Schneider, and Katharina Stengel. *Ausgeplündert und verwaltet: Geschichten vom legalisierten Raub an den Juden in Hessen*. Berlin: Hentrich & Hentrich, 2018.

Leßau, Hanne. *Entnazifizierungsgeschichten: Die Auseinandersetzung mit der eigenen NS-Vergangenheit in der frühen Nachkriegszeit*. Göttingen: Wallstein, 2020.

Lillteicher, Jürgen. "Who Is a Victim of Nazism? West Germany and Its Approach to Private Participation in the Aryanization Policy during the Nazi Era." In *The Post-War Restitution of Property Rights in Europe: Comparative Perspectives*, ed. by Wouter Veraart and Larens Winkel. Amsterdam: RVP Press, 2011, 79–93.

Lowenstein, Steven M. *Frankfurt on the Hudson: The German-Jewish Community of Washington Heights, 1933–1983, Its Structure and Culture*. Detroit: Wayne State University Press, 1989.

Ludi, Regula. *Reparations for Nazi Victims in Postwar Europe*. Cambridge: Cambridge University Press, 2012.

Meng, Michael. *Shattered Spaces: Encountering Jewish Ruins in Postwar Germany and Poland*. Berlin: De Gruyter, 2011.

Neiman, Susan. *Learning from the Germans: Race and the Memory of Evil*. New York: Farrar, Straus & Giroux, 2019.

Richarz, Monika, and Reinhard Rürup (eds.). *Jüdisches Leben auf dem Lande: Studien zur deutsch-jüdischen Geschichte*. Tübingen: Mohr Siebeck, 1997.

Rosmus, Anna Elisabeth. *Widerstand und Verfolgung: Am Beispiel Passaus 1933–1939*. Passau: Andreas-Haller-Verlag, 1983.

Schenderlein, Anne Clara. *Germany on Their Minds: German Jewish Refugees in the United States and Their Relationships with Germany, 1938–1988*. New York: Berghahn Books, 2020.

Sheridan Allen, William. *The Nazi Seizure of Power: The Experience of a Single German Town 1922–1945*. Revised edition. New York: Franklin Watts, 1984 [1965].

Shoptaugh, Terry. *"You Have Been Kind Enough to Assist Me": Herman Stern and the Jewish Refugee Crisis*. Fargo: North Dakota State University, Institute for Religious Studies, 2008.

Sorkin, David. "Emancipation and Assimilation: Two Concepts and Their Application to German-Jewish History." *Leo Baeck Institute Year Book* 35 (1990): 17–33.

Strauss, Herbert A. "Jewish Emigration from Germany: Nazi Policies and Jewish Responses," Parts I and II. *Leo Baeck Institute Year Book* 25 (1980): 313–361, and *Leo Baeck Institute Year Book* 26 (1981): 343–409.

Walker, Lawrence D. *Hitler Youth and Catholic Youth 1933–1936: A Study in Totalitarian Conquest*. Washington, DC: The Catholic University of America Press, 1970.

Walser Smith, Helmut. "It Takes a Village to Create a Nation's Memory: Returning Jews and Local Communities Worked Together to Lead Germany toward Historical Reckoning." In Zócalo (https://www.zocalopublicsquare.org/2021/01/11/post-war-germany-jewish-return-memory-national-reckoning/ideas/essay), January 11. 2021 [March 1, 2021].

Wildt, Michael. *Hitler's* Volksgemeinschaft *and the Dynamics of Racial Exclusion: Violence against Jews in Provincial Germany, 1919–1939*. New York: Berghahn Books, 2011.

Wünschmann, Kim. *Before Auschwitz: Jewish Prisoners in the Prewar Concentration Camps*. Cambridge, MA: Harvard University Press, 2015.

Wünschmann, Kim. "Gezeichnete Erinnerung: Zeitzeugenschaft und Geschichte in Comics und Graphic Novels." In *"Aus der Erinnerung für die Gegenwart leben": Geschichte und Wirkung des Shoah-Überlebenden Ernst Grube*, ed. by Matthias Bahr, Pater Poth, and Mirjam Zadoff. Göttingen: Wallstein, 2022, 190–207.

Wüstenberg, Jenny. *Civil Society and Memory in Postwar Germany*. Cambridge: Cambridge University Press, 2017.

FAMILY TREES

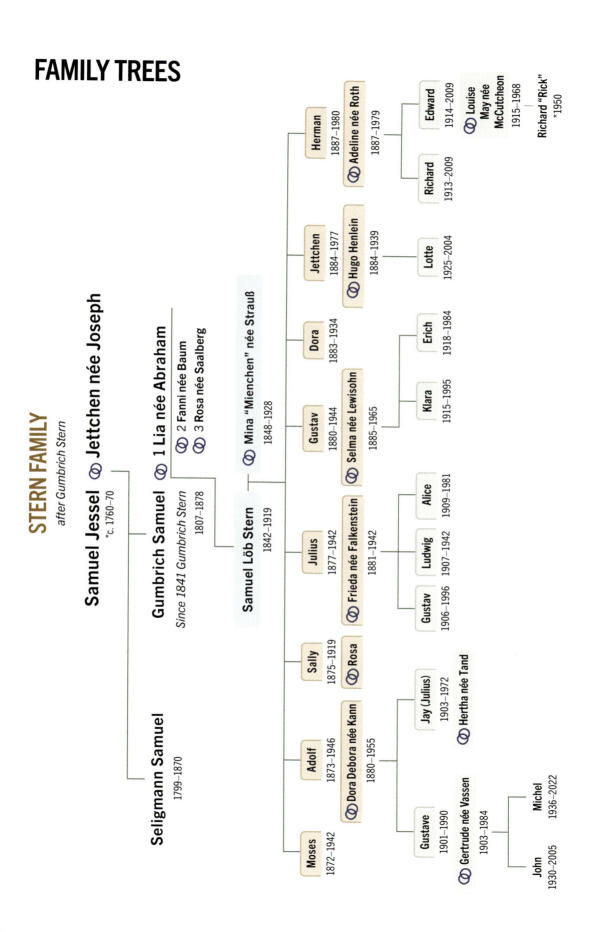

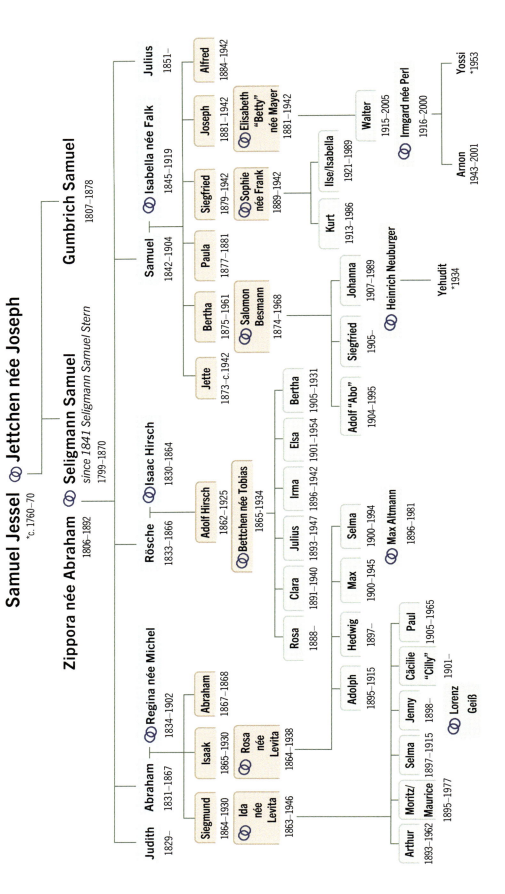

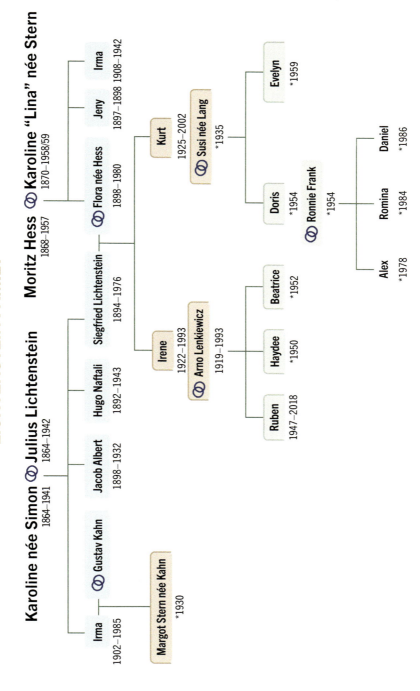

A NOTE ON THE FAMILY TREES

The Lichtenstein and Stern families who once lived in Oberbrechen have by now grown into many branches. The Graphic History focuses on a number of key protagonists from both families, and these family trees illustrate their family relationships. As a result of this focus, the family trees depicted here do not include all family members, especially among the younger generations born after the Holocaust, who, so we hope, will carry their ancestors' history and memory into the future. We are grateful to them for all their vital support.